Best Songs of the Movies

Chicago Public Library

REFERENCE

Form 178 rev. 11-00

Best Songs of the Movies

Academy Award Nominees and Winners, 1934–1958

JOHN FUNNELL
VISUAL & PERFORMING ARTS

McFarland & Company, Inc., Publishers
Jefferson, North Carolina, and London

LIBRARY OF CONGRESS CATALOGUING-IN-PUBLICATION DATA

Funnell, John, 1939–
    Best songs of the movies : Academy Award nominees and win-
ners, 1934–1958 / John Funnell.
        p.   cm.
    Includes bibliographical references and index.

    ISBN 0-7864-2193-2 (softcover : 50# alkaline paper)

    1. Motion picture music — United States— History and
criticism.   2. Academy Awards (Motion pictures)— Songs and
music.   I. Title.
ML2075.F86   2005
782.42'1542'0973 — dc22   2005012764

British Library cataloguing data are available

Cover photograph: Judy Garland as Dorothy Gale sings the Academy
Award-winning song "Over the Rainbow" in the 1939 MGM musical
The Wizard of Oz.

Manufactured in the United States of America

McFarland & Company, Inc., Publishers
  Box 611, Jefferson, North Carolina 28640
  www.mcfarlandpub.com

Acknowledgments

I owe a great deal to a host of people who have contributed in various ways to this book. So grateful thanks to:

Sue and Bernie Millar for giving me access to their wonderful home library of movie books.

Peter Salisbury for enabling me to view many of the movies from his extensive video collection.

Alan Moore for supplying me with song sheets for a number of the more obscure tunes mentioned in this book.

David A. Brown, editor of *Cine-Musical,* in which excellent journal early versions of parts of this book first appeared. David may be contacted at Box 718, GPO Melbourne, Victoria 3001, Australia.

Gene Massimo of Fan*Fare and Jerry Ohlinger of the Movie Material Store for their excellent help with photo research.

Members of the Victorian Bing Crosby Society, Melbourne, Australia, for sparking my enthusiasm for the greatest popular singer of the twentieth century. The society publishes an excellent newsletter—contact the Secretary, Peter de Ryk, 11 Holden Road, Kallista, Victoria 3791.

The many very knowledgeable members of the 20s-to-50sPopMusic chat list, especially Del Owens, Janet Fisher and the list's moderator, Rob Lenhart. Anyone interested in the songs and music of the pre–rock-'n'roll era may find the list at www.yahoogroups.com.

My wife, Rita, who encouraged me greatly in the writing of this book and made many insightful suggestions for improvement.

Contents

Introduction

The first Academy Award for Music (Original Song) was presented in 1935 for the year 1934. Between the years of 1934 and 1958, which are the focus of this book, a total of 160 songs by 114 songwriters received nominations. Some of these songwriters are household names, especially those who wrote highly successful Broadway shows: Irving Berlin, Cole Porter, the Gershwins, and so on. And when these and other Broadway songwriters were induced to write for Hollywood musicals, they were usually given prominent billing. But the songwriters under extended contracts to Hollywood studios rarely received that kind of recognition. Well-known and enduring movie songs such as "Thanks for the Memory," "Pennies from Heaven" and "Boogie Woogie Bugle Boy" are familiar standards, but few of us recall their songwriters: Leo Robin and Ralph Rainger, Arthur Johnston and Johnny Burke, and Hughie Prince and Don Raye respectively. The great talents of these and many other men and women made the most vital contribution to the success of the Hollywood musical.

In the 1930s and 1940s, Hollywood musicals produced hundreds of new songs each year and competition for the Best Song Oscar was fierce. Choosing the best of anything is an almost impossible task, and it is easy to find instances where the Academy slipped up. For example, "Sweet Leilani"—an ordinary song that only Crosby devotees now recall—won the 1937 Oscar and the Gershwins' "They Can't Take That Away from Me" was passed over. Yet many of the 160 nominated songs were the most popular of the day and of such strong appeal that they have gone on to become classics of the great American song book. Winning songs such as "The Way You Look Tonight" (1936), "Thanks for the Memory" (1938) and "It Might As Well Be Spring" (1945) are of the highest quality and thoroughly deserved their Oscars. Two other winning songs of the same era—"Over the Rainbow" (1939) and "White Christmas" (1942)—were identified by a wide-ranging public poll in the year 2001, conducted by the Recording Industry of America and the National Endowment for the Arts, as the most significant "Songs of the Century."

But there were also many more nominated songs of top quality and huge popularity that failed to win: Fred Astaire's "Cheek to Cheek" was the best selling record of 1935 and Bing Crosby's recording of "Pennies from Heaven" was the best seller in 1936, but neither won the Oscar. Other "failures" include "I've Got You Under My Skin," "Chattanooga Choo Choo" and "Blues in the Night." And such was the toughness of the competition that among those not even nominated were such gems as "A Fine Romance," "A Foggy Day" and "Love Is Here to Stay."

While many nominated songs have survived the test of time, others have lapsed into obscurity and the films in which they featured have all but disappeared. For example, how many people now remember "When There's a Breeze on Lake Louise" from *The Mayor of 44th Street*, or "Pennies for Peppino" from *Flying with Music?*

In part it was a desire to track down songs such as these, and to try and discover what led to their nomination, that provided the impetus for this book. Another motivation was the desire to discover how nominations for the Best Song Oscar come about.

The Academy of Motion Picture Arts and Sciences is made up of various associations of the people involved in the filmmaking process, including the producers, the actors, the cinematographers, the writers, the editors—and the songwriters. These associations are known as guilds, and membership is not automatic for everyone engaged in film production. A prospective member must be sponsored by at least two members of the guild he or she wishes to join, and then that person's application is considered by the executive committee of the guild. If the committee gives its approval, the application is then submitted to the Board of Governors of the Academy. If the board gives its approval, an invitation to join is issued.

Members of the songwriters' guild decide on the list of nominations for Best Song, voting in secret. Later, the full membership of the Academy votes to determine the winner from the list of nominees. The criteria for the Best Song Oscar nominations have changed over time, but the award has almost always been given only to a song that, as the Academy rules, must be "specifically created for the eligible feature-length motion picture." This rule means that the songs from film versions of Broadway shows are ineligible. Therefore, when *Roberta* was filmed in 1935, Jerome Kern and Otto Harbach's lovely song "Smoke Gets in Your Eyes" could not be nominated, though "Lovely to Look At," written especially for the film, could be. Songs that became popular and were then included later in a film should always have been ineligible, and the Academy's rules now state that the song must be "recorded for use in the film prior to any other usage including public performance or exploitation through any of the media whatsoever." This rule was not enforced in 1941 when "The Last Time I Saw Paris" won.

There have been a number of changes to the rules over the years. For example, originally there was no limit on the number of songs that could be nominated, but when the list grew to an unwieldy 14 in 1945, the Academy decided to limit nominations to five songs per year. Also in the early years, only one song per film could be nominated, a rule that meant many fine songs were passed over. For instance, Irving Berlin wrote at least three songs for *Top Hat* that have become great standards: "Isn't This a Lovely Day," "Top Hat, White Tie and Tails" and "Cheek to Cheek." The songwriters' guild decided to nominate the latter for the 1935 awards, but even then it lost to "Lullaby of Broadway."

The first years of the Academy Award for Best Song coincided with a time when the popular music of the day appealed to people of all ages. The primary reason was that whole families listened to the radio together, all age groups hearing and enjoying the music of the top artists of the day: for instance, 50 million Americans a week (approximately 40 percent of the population) listened to Bing Crosby's *Kraft Music Hall* in the 1930s, and Benny Goodman's radio show *Let's Dance* also attracted huge audiences. Most listeners would have become very familiar with all of the songs nominated for the Academy Award, and so the Best Song Oscar attracted widespread interest at that time, just as much as the awards for Best Film, Best Actor and Best Actress.

Things are very different today. Far fewer people are aware of the nominations for Best Song. Media speculation in the lead-up to each year's Awards rarely mentions them. Today most people would be sorely pressed to hum, whistle or sing any of the winners of the last few years, let alone be able to name the titles of other nominated songs. Why has this shift occurred? It has taken place slowly over the years and, as with any historical process, it is difficult to pin down an exact cause. But there appear to be three major reasons: the fragmentation of popular music into different styles and genres aimed at different age groups, the decline in production of original screen musicals, and the rise of the title song for non-musical films.

The fragmentation began in the 1950s with the emergence of rock 'n' roll: The new phenomenon of the teenager with money to spend led to the development of a music aimed specifically at this age group. The trend has continued over the years, and today there are many styles and genres, each with its devotees who rarely listen to any other kind of music. Popular music is no longer the unifying force it was in the time of Bing Crosby and Benny Goodman.

In the latter half of the 1950s, teenagers turned on to rock 'n' roll commonly tuned in to the radio stations featuring that music and were exposed much less to the types of songs nominated for the Oscar. Fans of Bill Haley, Elvis Presley or Little Richard generally did not want to listen to songs from a different genre such as Vic Damone singing "Gigi" or Frank Sinatra and his "High Hopes," the winning songs of 1958 and 1959. Thus, a whole generation lost interest in the Best Song Oscar. Exacerbating this lack of interest, the Academy, in turn, ignored the music most popular with this generation: No song from an Elvis Presley film or any other 1950s film containing rock 'n' roll was ever nominated. This trend continued into the 1960s when the songs from the Beatles' movies were passed over, presumably deemed not worthy of nomination. Some attempt has been made in recent years, though, to reflect the music popular with the younger generation, with a nomination, for example, in 2000 for Bjork's "I've Seen It All"; the 2002 Award for Best Song went to Eminem's "Lose Yourself." Even so, today, compared to the early years, the Best Song Oscar attracts very little interest.

The decline in production of original screen musicals is also significant in the shift from high levels of interest and awareness of the nominated and winning songs to the current situation where they are largely ignored. In the first years of sound, film musicals were often screen versions of Broadway shows and were somewhat stagy and static. The ones that were originals were usually little more than variety shows, cumbersome vehicles for as many of its stars as the studio could cram in. Small wonder that the public eventually tired of them and that by 1932 production of musicals had slumped. But the Depression made it hard to raise the money for a Broadway show, and many leading songwriters headed for Hollywood, reviving studio interest in the possibilities of the musical. By 1933 their influence was such that film musicals were developing an original approach and becoming something of an art form. Nineteen thirty-four, the first year of the Best Song Oscar, coincided with the beginning of a golden age for the Hollywood musical.

Between 1934 and 1938, the first five years of the Award, all but four of 27 nominated songs came from musicals. But as the cost of producing musicals increased and public interest in them declined, fewer and fewer original musicals were produced.

The decline in the production of original screen musicals gave rise to a burgeoning use of title songs for non-musical films. In the 1950s, more and more nominated songs came from non-musicals, and many were merely sung over the opening or closing credits. This trend was confirmed in 1952 when *High Noon* won the Best Song Oscar. Actually, this song was not merely a title song sung over the credits but was an integral part of the film's narrative. But its tremendous success helped producers to realize that a hit song could sell tickets for their films. Theme or title songs for otherwise non-musical films therefore proliferated, whether or not they added anything to the story. The commercial drive was for a hit song with instantaneous appeal that would serve to promote the film before its commercial release. And if the composer of the film's music score could write the title song too, then the studio would not have the extra cost of hiring another songwriter. In the five years 1954–58, 17 out of the 25 nominated songs came from non-musicals, and most of these were merely title songs sung over the opening or closing credits.

Today, nominated songs typically have little or no dramatic relevance to the story of the films with which they are associated, and so there is little to say about their function in the film. Some exceptions to this include films from the Disney Studio. In fact, Disney has been very prominent in the Best Song award in recent years, being virtually the only studio making original musicals, albeit mostly animated ones. Through the 1990s, the Disney Studio had six winning songs.

But it is the first 25 years of the Best Song Oscar that are featured in this book. These years, 1934–1958, coincide with the golden age of the Hollywood musical, and so all the great American songwriters are represented. The 25th year, 1958, is the year that *Gigi* collected nine Academy Awards, including Best Song. And "Gigi," a superb song from one of the finest screen musicals of all time, makes an appropriate pinnacle on which to conclude this book.

A note on how the material is presented: A section for each year of songs from 1934 to 1958 includes first a list of nominated songs for that year in alphabetical order. Every song is then discussed in that order except for the winner, which is covered last.

Because many of the 114 highly talented writers of these 160 songs are often overlooked, I have included an appendix that gives biographical information about each.

1934

This year's awards, the first in which music scores and songs were honored, were held at the Los Angeles Biltmore Hotel, with Irvin S. Cobb as the host and presenter of all the awards.

The Nominations

Vincent Youmans, Gus Kahn and Edward Eliscu for "The Carioca" from *Flying Down to Rio* (RKO)

Con Conrad and Herb Magidson for "The Continental" from *The Gay Divorcee* (RKO)

Ralph Rainger and Leo Robin for "Love in Bloom" from *She Loves Me Not* (Paramount)

The Carioca

from *Flying Down to Rio*
Music: Vincent Youmans
Lyrics: Gus Kahn and Edward Eliscu

Fred Astaire was one of the biggest stars of the musical stage in the 1920s but his name meant little to the moguls of Hollywood. He began his movie career inauspiciously in 1933 with a small role in the MGM picture *Dancing Lady*, and his first screen partners there were Joan Crawford and Dolores Del Rio. Though this picture was never going to make him a Hollywood star, it did give him the chance to learn the ropes of filming and he was able to carry that experience to RKO. There he was teamed for the first time with Ginger Rogers, to make *Flying Down to Rio*. It was the only film for which Ginger was billed above Fred—she had made 19 screen appearances before this one.

The new team of Astaire and Rogers had fourth and fifth billing behind

7

Dolores Del Rio, Gene Raymond (in a role originally intended for Joel McCrea) and Raul Roulien. But when filmgoers left the cinema, it was Fred and Ginger they talked about. The dance number that launched them as stars was "The Carioca."

In the movie, Fred and Ginger are Fred Ayres and Honey Hale, members of an American dance band that has just flown to Rio de Janeiro to play at a luxury hotel. On their first night they all visit the Carioca Casino to check out the local musicians. They find the clientele calling out for the resident band to play "The Carioca." A waiter explains to the Americans that, in Rio, the foxtrot is considered too tame and dull.

Now the huge production number begins and there are three distinct parts to it, with three different Brazilian singers, one white, one a mulatto and one black, played respectively by Alice Gentle, Movita Castenada and Etta Moten, who is billed as "The Colored Singer." Their contributions are separated by instrumental interludes that present three distinct Latin-style melodies danced by groups representing various ethnicities; all of this emphasizes the multicultural nature of Brazil.

The band starts to play: At first just a trumpet gives out the sensuous melody, then more and more instruments join in as the Brazilian dancers take to the floor. The dance is like a fast rumba with tango variations. The basic steps call for partners to press their foreheads and pelvises together and stare into each other's eyes. They clasp hands above their heads, then make a complete turn without breaking head contact. This action comes from lines in the song that say that the dance begins with the dancers putting their heads together.

The American observers are taken aback by the eroticism of it all. And one of the ladies asks, "What have those girls got below the Equator that we haven't got?" Ginger is puzzled by the business with the foreheads and Fred tells her that it's mental telepathy. Ginger responds, "I can tell what they're thinking about from here!" Then she pretends to be shocked: "Oh Freddy, is my mind red!" But the pair of them cannot resist joining in and soon they are up and dancing.

They perform at one point atop seven white grand pianos pushed together to form a circle, the locals looking on admiringly. The pair even manages to inject a little humor into the proceedings as they try for the "business with the foreheads" and bang their heads together.

Now Movita Castenada takes over the singing while new dancers dance "The Carioca." After this section of the dance, the rhythm develops a jazzy feel and Etta Moten sings as a troupe of black dancers treat us to some lively jitterbugging. Fred and Ginger leap onto the pianos and join in once more.

The words of the song insist that the Carioca is a completely new dance that will put all the others in the shade—and it will also bring true love. The lyric suits the swaying, sensual melody perfectly—the first lines of each verse have hard consonants, which support the energetic and rhythmic tune at this

Fred Astaire and Ginger Rogers put their heads together to dance the Carioca in *Flying Down to Rio* (RKO, 1933).

point. The next two lines have long vowel sounds, which slow the tempo to a languorous pace.

The entire sequence lasts for nearly 12 minutes and it made the picture such a huge box office smash that RKO looked immediately for a new project to cash in on Fred and Ginger's success. The vehicle chosen was Cole Porter's 1932 Broadway success *The Gay Divorce*, in which Fred had starred with Claire Luce. Ironically, Astaire had to rush off to London to appear in the West End stage production of *The Gay Divorce* and he missed the New York opening of *Flying Down to Rio*. When he returned to America, he found that the movie had launched him and Ginger Rogers into Hollywood stardom.

The lyric of the song describes the Carioca as a new dance that would eliminate every other kind but it was not all that new: It bears a strong resemblance to the Maxixe, sometimes known as the Machichi, which also originated in Brazil and had been introduced to the USA by Vernon Castle 20 years earlier. But it made little impression on the American dancing public, unlike the Carioca that became a dance craze all over the U.S. For their next movie together, the first in which they had top billing, Fred and Ginger were dubbed "The King and Queen of the Carioca."

One of the singers who sang "The Carioca" in *Flying Down to Rio*, Etta Moten, was, at one time, a significant name in the world of entertainment but her name means little to today's audiences. She was one of the first black Americans to appear in Hollywood movies and the first to be cast in a romantic role: She appeared in *Gold Diggers of 1933* as a featured singer of the classic Harry Warren-Al Dubin song "Remember My Forgotten Man," tearfully singing in remembrance of her husband who had been killed in the Great War. She was also the first black woman invited to perform at the White House. On November 5, 2001, she celebrated her hundredth birthday; she died on January 2, 2004, aged 102.

Many of the bands of the day recorded "The Carioca" but the most successful—reaching number one on the charts for two weeks—was an instrumental version by Enric Madriguera.

Love in Bloom

from *She Loves Me Not*
Music: Ralph Rainger
Lyrics: Leo Robin

For many years, comedian Jack Benny mangled "Love in Bloom" on his violin—he used it as his signature tune and the song became closely identified with him. But it was Bing Crosby who introduced it in the movie *She Loves Me Not*, an amusing college farce directed by Elliott Nugent. Harry Revel and Mack Gordon wrote most of the songs but the producers commissioned an extra one from Ralph Rainger and Leo Robin: "Love in Bloom." They had written it originally for a picture called *Kiss and Make Up* but it had not been used. It became the most popular of all the songs from *She Loves Me Not*.

The 33-year-old Crosby plays the part of pipe-smoking Princeton student Paul Lawton, while Miriam Hopkins is Curly Flagg, a showgirl on the run after witnessing a gangland killing. She turns up at Bing's college, peeps in at his window and sees him at the piano—he is apparently writing the melody for "Love in Bloom." She knocks at his door, tells him her sad story and our gallant hero helps her to hide, lending her some clothes and cutting her hair short in an attempt to make her look like a male student.

But Bing's romantic involvement in *She Loves Me Not* is not with Miriam Hopkins but with the lovely Kitty Carlisle, who plays Midge Mercer, the daughter of the college dean. Bing sings "Love in Bloom" to her, demonstrating it as a song he has written for the college revue. His rendition is tender and sensitive and soon Kitty joins in. Their happy duet is clearly the beginning of romance. But as is the way in the movies, there is a series of complications and misunderstandings and it looks as though their love will encounter doom rather than bloom. When Bing telephones Kitty to say goodbye forever, they sing "Love in Bloom" as a poignant finale to their relationship. Of course the misunderstandings are cleared up and love does indeed bloom.

Leo Robin was capable of writing urbane and witty songs such as "Love Is Just Around the Corner" and "Thanks for the Memory" but he often crafted highly poetic lyrics. He was fond of using delicate images and metaphors from nature and did so repeatedly in "Love in Bloom." In the song, the singer wonders at the source of the ecstasy he is feeling—is it the trees, is it the spring, or is it all a dream? No, he decides, it's "Love in Bloom."

The imagery is well-sustained through the song and Robin uses internal rhymes (trees/breeze, spring/bring and so on) with great skill. The song also has a carefully balanced structure, asking a question in the first two lines of each verse, then giving the answer in the last two.

The song's publishers had no faith in its popular appeal; they told composer and lyricist that it was too rangy musically and that the lyrics were too fancy. But public taste proved them wrong and Bing Crosby's recording of the song, backed by Irving Aaronson and His Commanders, reached No. 1 in the U.S. charts and stayed there for six weeks. Bing's former boss Paul Whiteman also had a hit with it.

Though Bing introduced the song, most people in the age group that heard Jack Benny on their radios or saw his TV shows associate "Love in Bloom" with him. Benny's association with the song began when he and his wife were in a supper club where the leader of the band asked him to play the violin. He borrowed an instrument and picked out some sheet music: the song was "Love in Bloom." A gossip columnist wrote up his performance and when Mr. and Mrs. Benny went to another club the following week, the band struck up with "Love in Bloom" as they entered. Benny continues:

The thing just caught on, so I decided to adopt it as my theme song. Let's face it, it's also a pretty easy tune to play on the fiddle. I love it from that aspect, but actually "Love in Bloom" has nothing to do with a comedian. I mean, "Can it be the breeze that fills the trees with rare and magic perfume…" sounds more like it should be the theme song of a dog—not a comic! [quoted in *Jack Benny* by Mary Livingstone Benny and Hilliard Marks, p. 71].

Love in Bloom was the title of a 1935 picture starring Bing Crosby's wife Dixie Lee but the song was not used in it. Its second screen airing occurred in Bing Crosby's 1936 Western musical *Rhythm on the Range*. Here, Martha Raye—in her first movie—becomes rather merry on homemade vodka and bursts into a tipsy chorus of "Love in Bloom." In the 1941 picture *New York Town*, Lynne Overman sings the whole song in a more sober vein; in 1942, Judy Canova sang it in *True to the Army*. The latter was actually a poor remake of *She Loves Me Not*—Paramount intended the picture as a star vehicle for Canova but it flopped, as did Judy's Hollywood career. Betty Grable's last picture *How to Be Very, Very Popular* (1955) was also a remake of *She Loves Me Not* but "Love in Bloom" was not used.

And the Winner Is….

The Continental

from *The Gay Divorcee*
Music: Con Conrad
Lyrics: Herb Magidson

In 1932, *The Gay Divorce* had been Fred Astaire's final Broadway show. Now, in 1934, he was to star with his new dancing partner, Ginger Rogers, in the movie version—but the title was changed to *The Gay Divorcee*. The change came about because the censorious Hays Office objected to the notion of a divorce being called gay, but they allowed the adjective to be applied to a divorcee.

Changes were made to the original story and only "Night and Day" from the Cole Porter score remained in the picture. Among the casualties was a superb song, one of Porter's exquisite love ballads, "After You, Who?" But the film was nominated for five Oscars and won for one of the new songs.

Two different Hollywood songwriting teams—Harry Revel and Mack Gordon, Con Conrad and Herb Magidson—supplied four new numbers. The latter pair contributed two of them: "A Needle in a Haystack" and "The Continental." Choreographer Hermes Pan, who had assisted with the dance sequence for "The Carioca," worked with Fred Astaire on this new picture and their relationship lasted for many years afterwards.

Like "The Carioca," "The Continental" was another new dance sensation performed by Fred and Ginger and a huge chorus of singers and dancers. The entire musical production occupies 17 minutes and is the climax and highlight of the picture. Part of the effectiveness of the sequence comes about because of the superb use of black-and-white, in the dress of the huge chorus of dancers and in the Art Deco set.

When they first hear the dance band playing the music of "The Continental," Fred and Ginger are being held captive in a hotel room by Erik Rhodes. Ginger sings a few lines, telling Fred that it's a daring new dance craze and warns him that, whilst the music is beautiful, the rhythm is dangerous and full of passion, especially because it involves kissing while dancing.

Ginger and Fred now decide to escape from Rhodes and join in. This they do by ingenious means: Fred cuts out a silhouette of himself and Ginger and mounts it on the turntable of a record player. As it turns, it throws a shadow on the wall. Rhodes, who is in the next room, sees it and believes they are dancing together. He too is enjoying the sound of the music and repeats a few lines of the song, accompanying himself on the concertina. And

Fred Astaire and Ginger Rogers dance the Continental in *The Gay Divorcee* (RKO, 1934).

as the shadows on the wall whirl and spin, so do the real dancers downstairs, their movements reflecting the words of the song.

In extra verses, Lillian Miles sings of the cities in Europe where "The Continental" is all the rage. During this sequence, the remarkable music piles on the European variations, including some Spanish tango-like steps, a waltz in Viennese style and even a Russian dance. Fred and Ginger dance them all. And then we hear again the words that have given Fred permission to kiss Ginger, though the kiss is only on the hand—their first full kiss has to wait for another movie.

Because the Carioca had become an enormously popular dance craze across America earlier that year, RKO tried a piece of cross fertilization by advertising Astaire and Rogers in their new picture as "The King and Queen of Carioca." The publicity department also managed to get newspapers to illustrate the dance steps and movements of the Continental; the sheet music (which sold in vast quantities) carried photographs on the back cover, demonstrating the dance. The promotion worked and there was an instant flash of huge popularity, enough to influence the Academy: "The Continental" became the first song to win an Oscar. There were many recordings but the most successful was the one by Leo Reisman and His Orchestra, with Reisman himself supplying the vocal.

1935

Three songs were nominated in 1935. The awards Ceremony was held again at the Biltmore Hotel, Los Angeles, and the host was Academy President Frank Capra. He presented three of the awards, including the one for Best Song.

The Nominations

Irving Berlin for "Cheek to Cheek" from *Top Hat* (RKO)

Jerome Kern and Dorothy Fields for "Lovely to Look At" from *Roberta* (RKO)

Harry Warren and Al Dubin for "Lullaby of Broadway" from *Gold Diggers of 1935* (Warner)

Cheek to Cheek

from *Top Hat*
Music and Lyrics: Irving Berlin

Top Hat was Irving Berlin's first foray into the musical film and he produced one of his finest scores, with such great American standards as "Isn't This a Lovely Day?" and "Top Hat, White Tie and Tails." It also contains "The Piccolino," his clever parody of "The Carioca" and "The Continental," but the Oscar nominated song was the brilliant "Cheek to Cheek."

The song occurs late in *Top Hat* when the action has shifted from London to an opulent Venice nightclub. After a series of misunderstandings, Ginger, as Dale Tremont, is very hostile towards Fred, who plays a character named Jerry Travers, believing him to be heartlessly flirting with her while married to her best friend, Madge Hardwick, played by Helen Broderick. In spite of this, she agrees to dance with him and then is appalled to see that

15

Madge, from her signals, is encouraging the get-together. "Well, if Madge doesn't care, I certainly don't," she says. "Neither do I," answers Fred "All I know is that it's Heaven ... I'm in Heaven...." And, as if he were sighing with pleasure, he slips almost imperceptibly from speech to song.

As they dance together, Fred sings his song of seduction. He courts her with delicate approaches but at first she resists his advances by swirling away. Then, as Fred pulls her close, Ginger looks mistily into his eyes and seems to have given in. As the music swells, the dreamlike dance takes them out of the ballroom, over a bridge and a balcony and soon they are the only dancers to be seen. It seems that Fred and Ginger will become lovers in spite of the fact that Ginger believes Fred to be married. The music of the song builds to a climax then ends in soft satisfaction with Ginger sinking almost exhausted onto a chair, her face glowing. The song, the music and the dance have enchanted her and there is the clear feeling that pleasure and romance have won out over conventional morality. But then she seems to come to her senses, to realize what has happened between them. She slaps his face. Fred is delighted: With his hand to his cheek, he declares, "She loves me!"

Astaire's suavely romantic performance of the song in the film is superb. Perhaps the greatest dancer of the twentieth century, Fred is often underestimated as a singer, yet every one of the finest American composers of popular songs—Gershwin, Kern, Porter, and Rodgers, as well as Irving Berlin—rated him highly. Though his voice doesn't have a wide range, his presentation of lyrics is always true to the songwriter's intentions and his style and timing are as graceful as his dancing.

"Cheek to Cheek" celebrates the superiority of dancing and romance over traditional masculine pastimes such as fishing and mountain climbing, and it is the longest hit song that Irving Berlin ever wrote; it is a masterpiece of original songwriting. "Speak" is the first of six rhymes ("seek," "week," "streak," "peak" and "creek" are the others) that Berlin has to find for "cheek" and it is an indication of his mastery that none of them sound contrived or forced.

The song has subtle changes of rhythm and consists of 64 bars (twice the conventional length) and it has not one but two middle sections. It was Fred's idea to sing the song almost as though he were talking and Berlin, who was on the set every day, thoroughly approved.

"Cheek to Cheek" has another place in film history because of the extravagant gown (covered with ostrich feathers) worn by Ginger Rogers for the number. There are two slightly different versions of what happened. In the one that usually appears in books on the Hollywood musicals, when Fred and Ginger rehearsed their dance routine, the feathers kept coming loose, flying everywhere. Fred couldn't dance for sneezing. After hours of putting up with these interruptions, Fred finally lost his temper and started to shout at Ginger. Ginger promptly burst into tears and Lela, her protective mother who was on the set, sprang to her defence. Fred walked off in exasperation and the situation was only saved when the costume designer offered to sew on each ostrich feather individually.

But Ginger puts a different slant on the story in her autobiography *Ginger: My Story* and plays down the annoyance caused by the fluttering feathers. She writes that Fred disliked the dress even before dancing began. She battled with the director and everyone else to keep it, even threatening to quit the film if she couldn't wear it. Thus rehearsals began with Ginger wearing the dress and Fred feeling peeved. She goes on to write that the song should have been called "Horns to Horns," not "Cheek to Cheek."

None of this conflict shows in the finished film and the sequence is one of the most romantic that Fred and Ginger ever performed.

There was an amusing postscript to the feathers incident: The next day, Fred and dance director Hermes Pan amused themselves by writing some new words to "Cheek to Cheek":

> Feathers, I have feathers,
> And I hate them so that I can hardly speak.
> And I never find the happiness I seek,
> With those chicken feathers, dancing cheek to cheek.

Ginger doesn't mention this in her autobiography *Ginger: My Story* but does say that four days after filming the scene,

> ...a small, plain white box with a tailored white bow was delivered to my permanent dressing room. I pulled off the lid and there was a note, which said simply: "Dear Feathers, I love ya! Fred." Underneath the cotton layer was a gold feather for my charm bracelet.

Top Hat became the highest-grossing film that RKO produced in the 1930s. It was nominated for five Oscars, including Best Film. Hermes Pan was nominated for his direction of the dance sequences for "The Piccolino" and "Top Hat."

Fred Astaire's own recording of "Cheek to Cheek," backed by the Leo Reisman orchestra, topped the American charts and was the biggest-selling record of the year. Another successful recording was by Guy Lombardo and His Royal Canadians, which has a vocal by Guy's brother Carmen Lombardo. Eddy Duchin's band, with Lew Sherwood singing, also performed their own version.

Part of the "Cheek to Cheek" sequence is used to great effect, and as an important part of the plot, in the 1999 film *The Green Mile*.

In her feathery dress, Ginger Rogers dances to "Cheek to Cheek" with Fred Astaire in *Top Hat* (RKO, 1935).

Lovely to Look At

from *Roberta*
Music: Jerome Kern
Lyrics: Dorothy Fields and Jimmy McHugh

"Lovely to Look At" is the first song that Dorothy Fields and Jerome Kern wrote together. Kern had been commissioned to adapt his 1933 Broadway show *Roberta* for Hollywood. His lyricist then was Otto Harbach but for his first movie assignment he asked for help from two well-established film songwriters in Fields and her composer partner Jimmy McHugh. In the end, McHugh's talents were not needed but he is credited as co-writer, and also shares the Oscar nomination—a courtesy extended to him by his regular partner.

Roberta has a very weak plot with Randolph Scott cast as John Kent, an all–American football star who inherits a Parisian fashion house from his aunt; this establishment is known as "Roberta." There, Scott falls in love with the woman who had been his aunt's assistant, a Russian princess named Stephanie, played by Irene Dunne. Despite the silliness of the plot, the film entertains mostly because of the superb songs: "Smoke Gets in Your Eyes" and "Yesterdays" were two retained from the stage show, "Lovely to Look At" and "I Won't Dance" were among the great new numbers.

Writing lyrics for "Lovely to Look At" was no easy task as the music has only 16 bars with no middle section. The film's autocratic producer, Pandro S. Berman, complained about this brevity. Jerome Kern stood up to him and declared, "That is all I have to say," and the song remained short. But Berman certainly had a point when such an attractive melody finishes so frustratingly soon.

Berman had told Dorothy Fields that her lyric was required to perform two functions: To be used in a fashion show and also to be a love song. Fields completed the words overnight and showed them to Berman the next day. He was satisfied and filmed the scene immediately, without getting Jerome Kern's approval. Dorothy knew that this was no way to treat the famous composer and was very apprehensive. But Kern saw the footage, liked what he saw and heard, and so the new songwriting partnership was off to a good start.

Irene Dunne had top billing for the picture and she it is who sings "Lovely to Look At." The setting is an opulent fashion show, with musical entertainment provided by a band led by one Huck Haines, played by Fred Astaire.

The band plays the cascading melody of "Lovely to Look At" as the models parade, then Irene Dunne appears at the top of a staircase. She begins to sing and the camera closes in on her, showing her face framed by a frothy white fur stole. The song begins with a brief verse addressed to the ladies at the show, telling them how important it is to choose carefully the clothes to win a man's heart. Then the refrain assures them that if they make the correct selection, their men will be sure to tell them how delightful, how heavenly, how "lovely to look at" they are. They will be dreams come true and moonlit romance is sure to follow. The gushing femininity of the song captures perfectly the frivolous atmosphere of a fluttery fashion parade of the 1930s.

As Irene Dunne finishes the song, she descends the staircase and exits, pursued by the man who loves her—Randolph Scott. Now the fashion show continues and then Ginger Rogers enters, looking herself as glamorous as the models. Fred sings "Lovely to Look At" with her. Then, as they start to dance, the melody changes to "Smoke Gets in Your Eyes."

There were a number or recordings of "Lovely to Look At": Irene Dunne had a version, as did the Leo Reisman band, which had a vocal by Phil Dewey. Easily the most successful, though, was the one by the Eddy Duchin band and vocalist Lew Sherwood, which topped the American charts. The song was not used in the 1956 biopic *The Eddy Duchin Story*, but when *Roberta* was remade in Technicolor in 1952 as *Lovely to Look At*, Howard Keel sang the title song.

And the Winner Is...

Lullaby of Broadway

from *Gold Diggers of 1935*
Music: Harry Warren
Lyrics: Al Dubin

The Oscar-winning song for 1935 was the brilliant "Lullaby of Broadway." It appears in the film *Gold Diggers of 1935*, choreographed by Busby Berkeley at the top of his form. The sequence he devised for the song is perhaps his finest work and he received his first Oscar nominations for Dance Direction for this and another number from the film, "The Words Are in My Heart."

Berkeley's dance direction represents a new approach to the making of movie musicals, which up to now had mostly been very stagy. The sequence for "Lullaby of Broadway" is a piece of real cinema in which the song is transformed into a montage of arresting images. Not least of its startling ideas was to have Wini Shaw, the main character in this story within a story, fall to her death.

The sequence shows a day in the life of a Manhattan socialite, played by Wini Shaw. It begins with just a small white dot in the middle of blackness. It grows in size and becomes the face of Wini Shaw, filling the screen. Now she begins to sing of the "hip-hooray," the "hi-de-ho and boop-a-doo" of her Broadway nightlife. She continues the song with her face in full-close up, and then her face turns upside down, becoming the Manhattan skyline. A city clock shows the time as 6:37 and, as the New York people bustle off to work, Wini the party girl arrives home after her night on the town. As she enters the apartment block, other residents going off to work wish her goodnight and we see that the milkman is on his way. These workaday people are a telling contrast with Wini and her frivolous life of pleasure. She gives her kitten some milk, then prepares to sleep all day before another night of partying. Now she is back in a nightclub, escorted by Dick Curtis (played by Dick Powell). They seem to be the only patrons and they are entertained by two dancers on a surrealistic set (short flights of steps everywhere, leading to different levels). Then troupes of dancers enter, all dressed in black and white. The women tap rhythmically and the men approach them, their arms beating the air in a gesture that is almost threatening. The music takes on a staccato rhythm and the intricate show of formation tap dancing becomes louder and more and more feverish. (The thunderous sound of the dancers' feet in this sequence had to be recorded separately so as not to drown out the orchestra.) Soon there is a strong feeling of danger in the air. "Everything goes crazy," says the song and the dancers chant to Wini, "Come and dance! Come and dance!" "Come and get me!" she cries—and they do. She is whirled from partner to partner then, as Dick Powell tries to claim her; she rushes up the stairs in a mad game of chase. She goes out onto a high, narrow balcony, shutting the glass doors behind her; the dancers press forward, the doors open and push Wini to her death on the sidewalk far below. Broadway, its frivolities and party life, has finally claimed her. As screams fill the air, the camera whirls and becomes the spinning face of a clock, moving from 2:30 to 6:45.

Now a chorus sings the lullaby quietly and we see Wini's empty apartment, where the kitten mews plaintively for its milk. The Manhattan skyline appears again, turns to become Wini's face once more. She draws on a cigarette and sings of calling it a day, almost defiantly, and her short and superficial existence is over. Her image shrinks back and back until it becomes a white dot in the middle of blackness.

The song is something of a masterpiece in its use of contemporary American slang, and it captures perfectly the driving rhythms of the city at dawn and dusk. The use of short rhyming couplets, clipped, hard-edged words and short vowels ("rattle" and "Manhattan") in the fast-paced sections reflects the vitality and restlessness of the city. The music at this point has an almost feverish quality, enhanced by the excellent use of repeated notes. Then long vowels and softer sounds ("good night, baby," "sleep tight, baby") reflect a slower pace.

Harry Warren wrote the melody before the words were added and he presented lyricist Al Dubin with a difficult task. The melody's construction is unusual in that it is longer than the average film song and has no verse. Warren gave the music to Dubin, who then went away to write the words. In his book *Harry Warren and the Hollywood Musical*, Tony Thomas refers to Warren's own account of what happened next. Apparently he and Al Dubin often argued about the relative merits of New York and Hollywood. Warren hated Hollywood and wanted to return east, whereas life in California suited Dubin. In spite of this, Al wrote a lyric about New York especially for his partner. When they showed it to Busby Berkeley and Jack Warner, the reaction was lukewarm and Warner demanded a rewrite. Warren stood by the song and goes on to say:

> We were at this time also working on *Go Into Your Dance* with Al Jolson. I played it for him, and even before I finished he was hopping around, saying that he had to have it ... Warner shrugged and agreed. Soon after that Berkeley, who hadn't even thought of using the song, heard what Jolson had done, and now he ran to Warner's office and protested that we had written the song for his picture. He put up such a stink that Warner had to let him have it. But it might never have been used as it was if it hadn't been for Jolson's enthusiasm. A lot of negative things can be said about Jolie, but he was an instinctive showman.

"Lullaby of Broadway" was recorded by most of the top singers and bands of the day, the most successful being the version by the Dorsey Brothers, which has a vocal by Bob Crosby. The song has turned up in a number of films: in *The Jolson Story* (1946), where it was part of a montage of songs; in the 1950 film loosely based on Bix Beiderbecke's career, *Young Man With a Horn*; in *Lullaby of Broadway* (1951) where Doris Day is the singer; on the soundtrack of Woody Allen's *Radio Days* (1987), sung by Richard Himber. The song was also the highlight of the 1980 Broadway hit *42nd Street*, performed by Jerry Orbach and the company. The original soundtrack recording of "Lullaby of Broadway" actually made the British pop singles chart in 1976, albeit at number 42.

1936

The number of Best Songs nominations doubled to six for 1936. The venue was the Los Angeles Biltmore Hotel again, with George Jessel as host. Leopold Stokowski presented the awards for Best Song and Best Score.

The Nominations

Walter Donaldson and Harold Adamson for "Did I Remember" from *Suzy* (MGM)

Cole Porter for "I've Got You Under My Skin" from *Born to Dance* (MGM)

Louis Alter and Sidney Mitchell for "A Melody from the Sky" from *The Trail of the Lonesome Pine* (Paramount)

Arthur Johnston and Johnny Burke for "Pennies from Heaven" from *Pennies from Heaven* (Columbia)

Jerome Kern and Dorothy Fields for "The Way You Look Tonight" from *Swing Time* (RKO)

Richard Whiting and Walter Bullock for "When Did You Leave Heaven?" from *Sing, Baby, Sing* (Fox)

Did I Remember

from *Suzy*
Music: Walter Donaldson
Lyrics: Harold Adamson

Suzy starred Jean Harlow, Franchot Tone and Cary Grant. The amusing sequence in which "Did I Remember" appears has Harlow (her voice convincingly dubbed by Virginia Verrill) as "Suzy" Trent, performing the tender love song in a noisy, smoke-filled cafe. It is the early days of the First World War and Harlow, an American chorus girl, is in Paris. Cary Grant is Cpt. Andre Charville, a French air ace, and he and his pals are laughing loudly and making raucous remarks about the singer. Grant is sitting at a table with his back to her and he asks one of his pals to describe her: "Is she blonde or brunette ... fat or thin?" Harlow becomes more and more annoyed and splashes her tormentor's face with his own drink.

The words she is singing are full of tender romance, telling a lover that she lives for him alone, but in all the noisy by-play we scarcely hear them. Harlow's face reflects feelings that are quite opposed to those expressed in her song. She looks daggers at Grant and, as she finishes, she turns on him. He is applauding enthusiastically but she angrily accuses him of not listening. He proves that he has heard every word by singing the song back to her, with a few clever variations of his own, telling her that she has lovely eyes, especially when she glares at him.

Grant performs the song with consummate style and wit, while the looseness of the melody enables him to deliver it as though he is making the words up on the spot. In spite of her initial antagonism, Harlow softens and so

Cary Grant, Jean Harlow and Franchot Tone in *Suzy* (MGM, 1936).

another romantic relationship begins, underscored by the sweet sadness of the song's melody.

But the song has also functioned to warn us that the character played by Grant is a selfish and thoughtless charmer. Later, when they are married and Grant is further revealed as a faithless womanizer, Harlow is waiting sadly for him at home. Close to tears, she sits at the piano and sings "Did I Remember" again. This time we can hear every word and it is clear that she means all that she sings.

The song has an unusual rhyme scheme, with the second and third lines rhyming. And in these rhymes the accent is on the penultimate syllable rather than on the last (*"adore you"/"for you"* and *"without you"/"about you"*). The melody is tuneful and it has distinct echoes of the song "Fancy Our Meeting" which was introduced in 1928 and was still popular at the time of the film.

The song was very popular for a while in the 1930s and the four most successful recordings were by Shep Fields (with Charles Chester's vocal), Billie Holiday, Dick Powell and the Tommy Dorsey band. Billie Holiday in particular gives the song superb treatment.

I've Got You Under My Skin

from *Born to Dance*
Music and Lyrics: Cole Porter

"I've Got You Under My Skin" is a song that says "I love you" in a very original way. When someone gets under your skin, it usually means that you are irritated by them; here, Cole Porter gives the phrase an elegant twist and uses it to express an addiction from which the singer cannot get free. In spite of warning voices, and the knowledge that the affair is unlikely to last, the singer is helplessly hooked, willing to "sacrifice anything." Unable to give up the habit, the only thing she *can* stop is trying to give it up.

Porter wrote the song for Virginia Bruce to sing in *Born to Dance* and it is a minor masterpiece, a superb depiction of an erotic fixation. Everyday phrases are subtly shifted into paradox and the song has a sensuality that is reinforced by the exotic beguine-like rhythm of the music. Porter's use of triple rhymes—"heart of me/part of me," "go so well/know so well," "mentality/reality"—is very neat and gently emphasises the flowing melody line.

It is the melody we hear first. Dining together in a nightclub, Ted Barker (James Stewart) and Lucy James (Virginia Bruce) watch ballroom dancers Georges and Jalna gliding slinkily to the music. Later, on the terrace of her luxury apartment, Bruce sings the song to Stewart as a declaration of her passion for him. Her dramatic and intense performance leaves the audience—and Stewart—in no doubt of her amorous feelings. As she concludes the song, she leans back in her chair and gazes at young James with open invitation over the rim of her champagne glass. But our hero resists her blandishments—he is saving himself for Nora Paige (Eleanor Powell).

"I've Got You Under My Skin" is one of Porter's best songs and might well have won the Oscar in other years. But it did have its critics—one of them was lyricist Al Dubin. He formed a strong antipathy towards Porter and regarded him as a rich dilettante, writing songs only for a hobby. Dubin predicted that "I've Got You Under My Skin" would never be a hit: "When you say someone gets under your skin, it means they irritate you. It's not the right kind of title for a love song." (Quoted by Patricia Dubin McGuire in *Lullaby of Broadway*, her book about her father, page 147.)

"I've Got You Under My Skin" has been recorded by most of the top singers and is one of the great standards of American popular song. Ray Noble and His Orchestra (vocals by Al Bowlly) and the Hal Kemp Orchestra (vocals by Skinnay Ennis) were the first to achieve chart success with the song; Stan Freberg parodied the song in 1951, and in 1966 the Four Seasons' version entered the hit parade. Perhaps the finest version is Frank Sinatra's, on his 1956 *Songs for Swingin' Lovers* album. More than one critic has referred to it as the single greatest recording of Sinatra's career. Sinatra also made one of the least attractive recordings on his ill-advised *Duets* album, where his ungracious partner is Bono from the band U2.

The song was one of many featured in the almost totally fictitious film biography of Cole Porter, *Night and Day* (1946), sung by Ginny Simms. In 1948, Marina Koshetz performed it in the shipboard musical *Luxury Liner* in 1959, Debbie Reynolds and Tony Randall used the song as the basis for a comedy number in *The Mating Game*.

A Melody from the Sky

from *The Trail of the Lonesome Pine*
Music: Louis Alter
Lyrics: Sidney Mitchell

"A Melody from the Sky" is an almost forgotten song, written for a movie that has a place in history as the first in three-strip Technicolor to be shot on location. It was filmed near Cedar Lake, in California's San Bernardino Mountains.

The Trail of the Lonesome Pine stars Sylvia Sidney, Henry Fonda and Fred MacMurray and tells of a murderous feud between the Tollivers and the Falins, two Appalachian families similar to the Hatfields and the McCoys. The conflict has gone on for generations; gunfights erupt like sudden storms. In a rare lull, Fuzzy Knight, playing a character named Tater, sings "A Melody from the Sky," a song which dwells on the joys of nature and the ubiquitousness of love. It draws an ironic contrast between the violence of the feud and the harmony of the natural world. The music of love comes from all creation, from the song of the whippoorwill and the blackbird as well as the whispering of the breeze in the trees.

Knight sings the first two lines of the song early in the film as he sees Sylvia Sidney and Fred MacMurray walking together in the forest, indicating that romance is on the way. Later, Fuzzy sings the whole song in an idyllic scene where he and little Spanky McFarland walk by a mountain lake. When Henry Fonda sees the pair, he can't help but join in, whistling a joyous accompaniment. His joy doesn't last though—Fonda is later shot, a casualty of the feud. Shocking as this is, filmgoers were even more devastated by the death of the character played by Spanky McFarland, one of the more appealing child stars of the *Our Gang* comedies.

The sentiments expressed in the song are hardly novel but Knight's performance is pleasant and unassuming and there is a certain charm in the wistful melody. Hugo Friedhofer, the film's musical director, liked it well enough to make extensive use of it as incidental music, underscoring the developing romance between Sidney and MacMurray.

There were vocal versions of "A Melody from the Sky" from singing cowboys Gene Autry and Tex Ritter but the best-selling records were by Jan Garber and His Orchestra, with Lee Bennett's vocals, followed closely by recordings from the Eddy Duchin and Bunny Berigan bands.

Pennies from Heaven

from *Pennies from Heaven*
Music: Arthur Johnston
Lyrics: Johnny Burke

"Pennies from Heaven" was the first title song to be nominated for the Best Song Oscar, though in this case it is integrated into the movie as well as being played over the credits. As they roll, the tune is heard and we see pennies falling from the rain clouds above, then bouncing on the wet ground below.

The movie was a star vehicle for Bing Crosby, with Madge Evans supplying his love interest. The plot is rather flimsy with Bing playing a character named Larry. Early in the film he is in prison and about to be released. A condemned man (John Gallaudet) hears him singing and asks him to deliver a letter when he gets out. When Bing asks, "Why me?," the reply is, "Anyone who can sing sappy sentimental songs in prison wouldn't double-cross a guy taking his last walk."

The condemned man wants to apologize to the family of the man he murdered and this is the message in the letter Bing is charged with delivering. The only surviving family members are "Gramps" (Donald Meek) and his granddaughter Patsy (Edith Fellows) and it is to little Edith that Bing sings "Pennies from Heaven." She has been woken in the night by a violent

Bing Crosby with Madge Evans in *Pennies from Heaven* (Columbia, 1936).

thunderstorm. Frightened and crying, she is comforted by Bing, who tells in her song that she should keep her hope and optimism even in the darkest storm. And Crosby is just the singer to put across the comforting message of "Pennies from Heaven," one that must have had special meaning in 1936, the depths of the Depression.

"Pennies from Heaven" is an excellent song. It has a memorable melody and the lyric is simple but never banal, using clear and effective symbolism to show that a proper attitude to life's darkest moments will supply the strength to get through them. Raindrops are sent from Heaven not as tears of misery, but the coins of hope that must be collected and used to ensure a future supply of "sunshine and flowers."

Bing Crosby and the film's director, Norman Z. McLeod, thought the song so powerful and convincing that they decided to follow the unusual practice of shooting it live, with the orchestra on the soundstage.

Crosby's "Pennies from Heaven" recording shot to the top of the American charts and dominated sales of records and sheet music for more than 12 weeks. The song proved amazingly popular in other versions, too: Eddy Duchin (with Lew Sherwood singing), Billie Holiday, Hildegarde, the Hal

Kemp orchestra (vocals by Maxine Grey) and the Jimmy Dorsey band (vocals by Bob Eberly) all had hits with it. Dick Haymes in the 1953 film *Cruisin' Down the River* and Bing Crosby in *Pepe* (1960) sing it again. Louis Prima's recording of the song turns up in the 2003 movie *Elf.*

When Did You Leave Heaven?

from *Sing, Baby, Sing*
Music: Richard Whiting
Lyrics: Walter Bullock

> Ladies and gentlemen, Tony Renaldo, a local boy made good. Only this afternoon he was working for an electrical company but tonight he will electrify you with his golden voice!

Thus a radio announcer introduces Tony Martin in *Sing, Baby, Sing*. Nightclub singer Joan Warren, played by Alice Faye, has heard him singing in the street as he worked and offered him a spot on a Kansas City radio broadcast. The song he sings is "When Did You Leave Heaven?" An all-girl band— Miss Ames' School Orchestra—accompanies him and some of the young ladies are clearly bedazzled. This is his only appearance in the film but his confident performance is full of romantic bravura and his song was the one that was put up for the Oscar, rather than any of the ones performed by Faye, the movie's star. The others included the title song and the hit number "You Turned the Tables on Me." Unusually, these two songs and "When Did You Leave Heaven?" were all on the American charts at the same time.

In his song, Martin serenades his lady as though she were an angel and wonders why Heaven let her go. He asks what she has done with her halo and her wings and worries that she might not be allowed back into Paradise. There is a slight tongue-in cheek air to the lyric and this prevents it from becoming too sentimental.

In 1976, Martin published a joint autobiography (*The Two of Us*) with his then-wife Cyd Charisse and he makes some puzzling remarks about the clothes he wore for the scene:

> I was supposed to be dressed in absolutely dreadful clothes. I wore the worst stuff I had, but it still wasn't bad enough. They sent me down to the wardrobe department and dredged up a wild and gruesome outfit—a plaid suit with extra wide shoulders and lapels, awful shirt and tie.

Anyone reading this before viewing the movie might expect to see Martin looking something of a clown but in fact the suit he wears, though plaid as he says, is gray and rather sober with shoulders not excessively wide. The tie has a square design and, though it clashes a little with the suit, it is by no means "awful." The so-called "awful" shirt is plain white.

Martin's "When Did You Leave Heaven?" recording was not particularly popular and a version by Guy Lombardo and His Royal Canadians easily outsold it; Guy's brother Carmen was the singer. Another popular recording was by Bunny Berigan and the Rhythm Makers, which had a vocal by Bernie Mackey. Martin had his first real hit in 1938 with "I Hadn't Anyone Till You," recorded with the Ray Noble orchestra. "When Did You Leave Heaven?" was additionally heard in the 1937 musical Western *Wild and Woolly*. It has also become something of a favorite as a bluesy number with notable recordings by Big Bill Broonzy, Joe Williams and British singer-songwriter Ralph McTell. Bob Dylan recorded it on his 1988 album *Down in the Groove*.

Martin and Alice Faye were married in 1937, the year after the release of *Sing, Baby, Sing*. The marriage did not last and in 1942 Faye married Phil Harris, while Martin married Cyd Charisse in 1949.

And the Winner Is...

The Way You Look Tonight

from *Swing Time*
Music: Jerome Kern
Lyrics: Dorothy Fields

After the presentation of the Academy Awards for 1936, a story circulated that Jerome Kern was disappointed with his Oscar for "The Way You Look Tonight." He felt that "A Fine Romance," another song he and Dorothy Fields had written for *Swing Time*, was a far better song and should have received the nomination. But the 1936 Best Song Oscar certainly went to one of Kern's loveliest melodies and Fields' lyrics are superb.

In *Swing Time*, Fred Astaire plays a character named Lucky Garnett and he sings the song to Ginger Rogers (as Penny Carroll) while she is in the bathroom washing her hair. Their developing romance has run into the obligatory obstacles and misunderstandings; Ginger refuses to see Fred, but even so, her best friend Mabel, played by Helen Broderick, suspects that she loves him is spite of this. While Ginger is shampooing her hair, Helen lets Fred into the apartment and encourages him to believe that Ginger has forgiven him. He sits down at the piano and sings the lovely, if slightly melancholy love ballad "The Way You Look Tonight."

She is so captivated by his declaration of love that she joins him at the piano to listen to the rest of the song. As Fred sings the tender words, telling Ginger to stay looking the way she is just at this moment, he cannot see her standing behind him with her head covered in frothy shampoo. At the end of the song, she touches him on the shoulder and he slowly turns to look at

Fred Astaire and Ginger Rogers in *Swing Time* (RKO, 1936)

her. His amazed expression reminds her of the way she really looks and she rushes back to the bathroom in embarrassment.

Dorothy Fields' lyrics are conversational and deceptively simple and the words bring out all the elegant sensuality of the warm, flowing melody, as does the relaxed grace of Fred's performance. The scene, with its mixture of sophistication and humor, epitomizes the gentle romance and easygoing charm of the Astaire-Rogers partnership.

At the end of the film, when Fred and Ginger are set to marry, Fred serenades her with a snatch of the song she had sung earlier, "A Fine Romance." She counterpoints him with his song, "The Way You Look Tonight." As they both look down at Central Park, the snow is falling but the sun breaks through the clouds as they embrace and the film ends.

In *The Fred Astaire and Ginger Rogers Book*, Arlene Croce reports that the original conception for the "shampoo scene" had Ginger cooking in the kitchen. Her hair becomes a mess and she smudges her face so that she looks thoroughly dishevelled. When she goes into the room and stands behind Fred, he looks up at her on the phrase "the way you look tonight" and sees her grubbily disordered condition. This might have made for a more effective and certainly a more humorous scene but the producers lacked the courage to show Ginger in such a state and opted for the shampoo treatment. But, as Croce points out, the foam is so beautifully sculptured that it could have been a white wig.

In her autobiography, Ginger tells the story behind the use of the shampoo. Director George Stevens had tried various kinds of soap but none of them were satisfactory. He even tried egg whites but the heat from the studio lights started to cook them as they streamed down Ginger's face. She suggested to Stevens that they use cream and this worked.

Astaire's recording of "The Way You Look Tonight" was very popular and topped the charts. There were other successful versions by Billie Holiday with the Teddy Wilson band, and by Peggy Lee with the Benny Goodman outfit. The song remained for 14 weeks on *Your Hit Parade*, topping that radio program's charts for six of them. Pop vocal trio The Lettermen took the song back into the American charts in 1961 and earned themselves a gold record in the process. In 1964, Frank Sinatra recorded an album of Academy Award winners and his lightly swinging rendition of "The Way You Look Tonight" is quite the best track.

1937

Five songs were nominated for the 1937 Best Song Academy Awards and Irving Berlin was selected to make the presentation. The Biltmore Hotel in Los Angeles was again the venue for the Awards Ceremony, hosted by entertainer Bob "Bazooka" Burns, who had appeared as Bing Crosby's sidekick in *Waikiki Wedding*. Irving Berlin presented the Oscar for Best Song.

The Nominations

Harry Warren and Al Dubin for "Remember Me?" from *Mr. Dodd Takes the Air* (Warner)

Harry Owens for "Sweet Leilani" from *Waikiki Wedding* (Paramount)

Sammy Fain and Lew Brown for "That Old Feeling" from *Vogues of 1938* (United Artists)

George and Ira Gershwin for "They Can't Take That Away from Me" from *Shall We Dance* (RKO)

Frederick Hollander and Leo Robin for "Whispers in the Dark" from *Artists and Models* (Paramount)

Remember Me?

from *Mr. Dodd Takes the Air*
Music: Harry Warren
Lyrics: Al Dubin

Kenny Baker was a popular radio singer in the 1930s, notably on Jack Benny's show. Warner Bros. hoped to make a movie star of him but *Mr. Dodd Takes the Air* was a flop in spite of the presence of Jane Wyman in her first leading role.

Baker was noted for his high tenor voice but we first encounter him in the movie as a baritone. He is Claude Dodd, a small-town electrician who sings only for friends and family until he is "discovered" and groomed for a career on New York radio. But illness strikes and the inept doctor who treats him damages his tonsils, turning him from baritone to tenor. The boss of the sponsoring company hates tenors and Baker loses his job. But the public loves his new voice and he becomes popular anyway. The radio station has to rehire him.

Composer Harry Warren enjoyed working with Kenny Baker, finding him very professional. He thought that Baker's enjoyable performance of "Remember Me?" led to its Oscar nomination.

"Remember Me?" pokes gentle fun at the institution of marriage. Baker claims via the long introductory verse to have written the song, and then ruefully chides his wife for taking him for granted. He reminds her that he pays the bills; he is the father of her child and he hurries home to her every day after work. The neat use of internal rhymes (remember/September; recall/small) heightens the whimsical qualities of the song.

Bing Crosby's recording was easily the most successful. Also popular were ones by the Teddy Wilson band with singer Boots Castle, and the Hal Kemp orchestra, which has a breathless vocal by Skinnay Ennis. The latter recorded it again in the 1950s with his own band. On the soundtrack of the 1946 Errol Flynn–Eleanor Parker *Never Say Goodbye* starrer, a studio chorus sings "Remember Me?" Various singers have revived the song since and Shirley MacLaine used it in her 1976 Broadway show. Fred Ebb and Bob Wells modified the lyrics to suit her.

That Old Feeling

from *Vogues of 1938*
Music: Sammy Fain
Lyrics: Lew Brown

Vogues of 1938 is an expensively mounted Technicolor musical set in the world of high-class fashion. Warner Baxter plays George Curson, the proprietor of a New York fashion house who falls for wealthy debutante Wendy Van Klettering (Joan Bennett). Many of America's top models appear in the picture and they show off a stunning array of fashions. The art director of the film, Alexander Toluboff, was nominated for the Interior Decoration Oscar.

Virginia Verrill, playing the small role of a nightclub chanteuse, is given the best song. The sequence in which "That Old Feeling" occurs has Baxter and Bennett touring the New York nightspots. He is drowning his sorrows because his wife has just left him, while Joan is celebrating her freedom after jilting her fiancé on their wedding day. They are drinking champagne at the club where Verrill is singing and the maudlin Baxter declares that it is "my wife's favorite place." "That Old Feeling" turns out to be his wife's "favorite song."

Bedecked in a black dress, black hat and long red gloves, Verrill sings "That Old Feeling" melodramatically, making it an out-and-out torch song. She tells the story of one who is dancing at her "favorite" cabaret when she sees a former lover and realizes that she has never gotten over him—she still has "That Old Feeling."

At the end of the familiar song, the band picks up the tempo and Verrill delivers some new lines in a more swinging fashion, inviting everyone to get up and dance. The paying customers accept her invitation but soon leave the floor to a gentleman in a white tuxedo who performs an energetic tap routine. Warner Baxter tells Joan Bennett that the dancer is "my wife's favorite" and asks Joan to dance the rumba—"my wife's favorite dance." Exasperated, Bennett sighs, "No, let's go home and read your wife's favorite book."

The simple conversational flow of the lyric matches the minor key melody to produce a touchingly understated song that avoids the self-pitying tone of most torch songs. But it does have a rather weak ending, both musically and lyrically; the song seems to merely peter out in the last verse, rather than coming to a strong conclusion.

There is a story that lyricist Lew Brown got the idea for the song from a friend who was trying to get over a torrid love affair with a woman named Julie. One night he walked into a nightclub looking rather dishevelled and red-eyed. Brown saw him and asked what had happened. His friend replied, "I saw Julie last night and got that old feeling."

Virginia Verrill's brief appearance in this picture was as close as she got to a leading role on screen but she frequently provided the singing voice for other stars, notably for Jean Harlow in *Suzy* (1935), singing another Oscar-nominated song, "Did I Remember?," and for Andrea Leeds in *The Goldwyn Follies* (1938).

The most popular American recordings were by the orchestras of Shep Fields (vocals by Bobby Goday) and Jan Garber (vocals by Russell Brown). "That Old Feeling" later became identified with Jane Froman. She sings the song in the 1952 story of her life *With a Song in My Heart*, in which Susan Hayward plays her.

They Can't Take That Away from Me

from *Shall We Dance*
Music: George Gershwin
Lyrics: Ira Gershwin

Easily the finest song of those nominated in 1937 was the Gershwins' "They Can't Take That Away from Me." That it failed to win the Oscar for that year is a great injustice.

The song occurs in *Shall We Dance*, a movie in which Fred Astaire plays the part of "Petrov," a ballet dancer who is pretending to be Russian. Ginger Rogers plays Linda Keene, an American musical comedy star who has just completed a successful season in Paris. The pair meets as they board the liner that is take them back home to the U.S. Romance is soon in the air and the gossip columnists and scuttlebutt journalists have a field day. The newspapers are full of stories that Petrov and Linda are secretly married.

The unhappy pair now decides that they should scotch the gossip by obtaining a very public divorce—but in order to do this, they must be really married. They travel from Manhattan to New Jersey for a secret wedding and are now heading back on the Hoboken ferry. Fred sings "They Can't Take That Away from Me" to express the rather depressed feelings that have overtaken both of them as they sadly anticipate their divorce. The damp, foggy weather adds to the downcast atmosphere.

It is a very wistful ballad of romantic loss, expressing the idea that any real experience of love, however short-lived, is worth having. It has the easy flow of conversation and every phrase sings with truth. What is it that Fred will

Fred Astaire and Ginger Rogers in *Shall We Dance* (RKO, 1937).

remember about Ginger when they part? The apparently minor but endearing details—the way she wears her hat and sips her tea—lend the song real poignancy. Clearly Fred is singing about a woman he has observed closely with loving eyes and is not using the generalized images of conventional romantic ballads. In the concluding verse, Fred mentions the way she holds her knife as she eats, and the way that they danced "till three," and these mundane memories give way to the transcendental importance of the way she changed his life. This enormous lift is in the music too. Though he sings lightly and with a cool veneer, there is no doubting the passion that Fred feels. As he reaches the end, of the song a close-up of Ginger's face shows tears moistening her eyes.

And why did this masterly song fail to win the Oscar? Writing in a letter about *Shall We Dance*, George wrote, "the picture does not take advantage of the songs as well as it should. They literally throw one or two songs away without any kind of plug." George was particularly concerned at the very low-key treatment of "They Can't Take That Away from Me." Certainly, Fred's wistful singing captures the heart of the song but Gershwin clearly expected a big dance number. The one that occurs later in the movie would not have satisfied him; only a snatch of the melody is heard as part of the ballet sequence. Fred's partner this time, though, is not Ginger Rogers but Harriet Hoctor, who seems to be more contortionist than ballerina. Ironically, Fred and Ginger perform a spectacular dance routine to "They Can't Take That Way from Me" in the last picture they made together, the 1949 *The Barkleys of Broadway*.

Ira Gershwin was equally disappointed with the song's treatment but wondered if this song (as well as the others they wrote for the picture) were too good; "all the songs were smart, a little sophisticated. Maybe that was a mistake, to put so many smart songs in one picture."

Also in his book *Lyrics on Several Occasions*, Ira ruefully discusses the three songs of his that were nominated for the Best Song Oscar, the other two being "Long Ago (and Far Away)" and "The Man That Got Away":

> These three songs have two things in common: [1] in the final voting none won; and [2] the title of each contains the word "away."
> So? So—away with "away."

Joan Peyser uses a line from "They Can't Take That Away from Me" as the title of her biography of George Gershwin *The Memory of All That*. In the book, she asserts that Ira Gershwin kept a close eye on his brother's life and often based his lyrics on his observations. George once told Ira that the only woman had loved was Paulette Goddard, the movie actress, and Ira expressed this in "They Can't Take That Away from Me," writing about the way Goddard wore her hat, sipped her tea and sang off-key.

There are at least two other great Gershwin songs in *Shall We Dance*, "They All Laughed" and "Let's Call the Whole Thing Off." But the rules of the Academy at this time indicate that only one song per picture could be nominated.

Over the years this beautiful ballad has established itself as one of the truly great standards and many fine singers have recorded it. In the 1930s, the best-selling record was Fred Astaire's but one by Billie Holiday and another by the Tommy Dorsey Orchestra (vocal by Jack Leonard) were also successful.

Whispers in the Dark

from *Artists and Models*
Music: Frederick Hollander
Lyrics: Leo Robin

Connie Boswell sings "Whispers in the Dark" as a specialty number in *Artists and Models*, a stylish and enjoyable musical comedy that features Jack Benny as the chief of an advertising agency. The flimsy story involves the crowning of a model girl as queen at an advertising industry's ball, and a romance between characters played by Ida Lupino and Richard Arlen. The dialogue is often very witty and some of the musical numbers are brilliantly choreographed, especially "Public Melody Number One," the first Hollywood assignment for Vincente Minnelli. The performers for it are Martha Raye and Louis Armstrong.

Hollander and Robin originally wrote "Whispers in the Dark" for the 1936 picture *Desire*, where it was to have been sung by Marlene Dietrich. But it was cut and the songwriters recycled it for *Artists and Models*.

The song is staged by night at the pool of a luxurious Miami hotel. Moonlight shimmers on the water as Andre Kostalanetz and His Orchestra begin playing the melody. Connie Boswell takes up the song on a shadowy terrace, singing to a man who resolutely keeps his back to the camera. Now the melody accompanies a pair of ladies who treat us to a display of synchronized swimming and the scene is rounded off with another shot of the moon on the water. Ida Lupino and Richard Arlen later dance to the melody and from this point it occurs frequently as their love theme.

Like "Love in Bloom," Oscar-nominated in 1934, Leo Robin's lyric for "Whispers in the Dark" is gently poetic and even has a similar line about the breeze in the trees. It is a delicate little song with a melody that flows pleasantly and gently. The lyric achieves its poetic effects without strain, describing two shadowy lovers whispering and kissing in the dark night, and the scene has a dreamlike intensity. But when the breeze begins to whisper in the trees, a sign that dawn is approaching, this paradise will fade away.

Andre Kostelanetz accompanied Connie Boswell in the picture but the Ben Pollack orchestra did the honors on her recording, which reached the top ten. Bob Crosby's version—with a vocal by Kay Weber—outsold it and was the number one song for four weeks. The orchestras of Benny Goodman (vocal by Martha Tilton) and Dick Jurgens (vocal by Eddy Howard) also recorded the song, as did Hal Kemp, whose version was an instrumental.

And the Winner Is...

Sweet Leilani

from *Waikiki Wedding*
Music and Lyrics: Harry Owens

If "They Can't Take That Away from Me" had been defeated in 1937 by a song of genuine quality, then the injustice of it all might not have been so galling. But the year's winner was "Sweet Leilani," a turgid and dreary song and perhaps one of the worst to gain an Oscar, even including more recent winners.

Bing himself found the song. On holiday in Honolulu with his wife Dixie, he stayed at the Royal Hawaiian Hotel where Harry Owens was the resident bandleader. "Sweet Leilani" was the band's signature tune—Owens had written it in 1934 for his daughter Leilani, his "heavenly flower," when she was one day old.

Bing loved the song—though he pretended to have trouble pronouncing the title—and thought it would be a good number for his forthcoming picture *Waikiki Wedding*, which had a Hawaiian setting. Owens' first impulse was to hang onto the song but eventually he agreed to let Bing take it back to Hollywood.

But even then, Bing had trouble persuading producer Arthur Hornblow to include "Sweet Leilani"—he didn't like it much and, anyway, he had already commissioned the songs for the picture from Ralph Rainger and Leo Robin. But Bing was adamant and headed for the golf course, declaring he would be back at the studio when Hornblow changed his mind. The picture was half-completed at this stage and Hornblow was forced to let Bing have his way.

Perhaps Hornblow's initial judgment was correct—the lyric is full of cliched imagery and is banal to the point of embarrassment. The function of the scene in which the song is sung is to show the romantic Hawaii of the travelogues. Shirley Ross plays "Miss Pineapple Princess," a contest winner taking part in a publicity scheme in Hawaii. Bing, playing Tony Marvin, an advertising executive for the company running the promotion, is pursuing her. Shirley is supposed to be recording her impressions of the islands for the newspapers and with the help of Bing has found the "part of Hawaii I'd always dreamed about."

The scene then changes to illustrate her fancies: palm-fringed sands with a group singing "Sweet Leilani" in Hawaiian. (Jimmy Lowell wrote the Hawaiian lyrics.)

Shirley Ross and Martha Raye (as Myrtle Finch) appear bedecked in flowers and wearing grass skirts "like real Hawaiian girls" and the song continues in the background. Now Bing takes up the song, singing it as a lullaby to a little girl in a hammock—she is Princess Leilani. As he croons, Hawaiian dancing girls sway their hips to the music. The little princess appears to sleep but Bing's magic has failed to work on her—she sits up brightly as soon as the song is finished. But song has had a more soporific effect on comedian Bob Burns, who plays Shad Buckle, Bing's sidekick—he dozes off in a nearby hammock, cuddling his pet razorback pig.

The whole clichéd sequence occupies little more than two minutes of screen time and is very poorly staged. Some reviewers seemed to have enjoyed the squealing of the pet pig more than the song; *Time* reported that the squealer stole the show. But in spite of this low-key presentation the general public agreed with Bing's view of the song and "Sweet Leilani" was a worldwide hit, the very first of Bing's many million-selling records. It was on the sales charts for 28 weeks and was the biggest seller since the onset of the Depression in 1929. But record sales were easily eclipsed by the astonishing sales of the sheet music (reported by *Billboard* as selling more than 54 million copies).

Crosby was backed on the recording by Lani McIntire and His Hawaiians. Record buyers may have been a little disconcerted when they listened to it for the first time: It begins not with Crosby's baritone but Lani McIntyre himself singing a chorus in his high-pitched voice. The song was more successful as a lullaby in 1942 when Bing was appearing in Seattle to help the War Savings Bond drive. During his performance, a baby girl became separated from her mother. Bing picked her up to hold her so that she could be seen. She stopped crying only when he started to sing "Sweet Leilani" to her as he held her in his arms. Her mother then saw her and they were reunited.

Another Rainger—Robin song from *Waikiki Wedding*, "Blue Hawaii" (released as the B side of Crosby's recording of "Sweet Leilani"), became the title song of the 1961 Elvis Presley picture, the plot of which is loosely based on the 1937 musical.

George Gershwin died in July 1937 and by this time "They Can't Take That Away from Me" had become popular. Many of George's friends and colleagues felt sure that the Academy would take the obvious opportunity to honor one of America's greatest composers. There was a great deal of disquiet when Irving Berlin announced that "Sweet Leilani" was the winner of the Best Song award. The actor-pianist-composer Oscar Levant was especially bitter: "I'd like to say something about Harry Owens: His music is dead but he lives on forever."

Some people blamed film extras for the debacle: After years of political infighting between the studios and the various branches of the Academy, President Frank Capra had extended voting rights for some awards to all members of the Actors, Directors and Writers Guilds, whether or not they were members of the Academy. This meant that even extras had the chance to vote for Best Song—and, of the 15,000 people now entitled to vote, 12,000 were extras. Many people felt, rightly or wrongly, that lowly extras were not musically sophisticated enough to appreciate the Gershwins' song. The rules were changed yet again for the 1938 Awards and extras were not allowed to vote.

1938

The number of nominated songs increased to ten for the 1938 award, and this year extras were *not* allowed to vote. The Biltmore Hotel was again the venue for the Awards Ceremony, with Frank Capra as host. Jerome Kern presented the Best Song Oscar.

The Nominations

Edward Ward, Chet Forrest and Bob Wright for "Always and Always" from *Mannequin* (MGM)

Irving Berlin for "Change Partners" from *Carefree* (RKO)

Lionel Newman and Arthur Quenzer for "The Cowboy and the Lady" from *The Cowboy and the Lady* (Samuel Goldwyn)

Johnny Marvin for "Dust" from *Under Western* Stars (Republic)

Harry Warren and Johnny Mercer for "Jeepers Creepers" from *Going Places* (Warner)

Phil Charig and Arthur Quenzer for "Merrily We Live" from *Merrily We Live* (Hal Roach)

Ben Oakland and Oscar Hammerstein II for "A Mist Over the Moon" from *The Lady Objects* (Columbia)

Jimmy McHugh and Harold Adamson for "My Own" from *That Certain Age* (Universal)

Irving Berlin for "Now It Can Be Told" from *Alexander's Ragtime Band* (Fox)

Ralph Rainger and Leo Robin for "Thanks for the Memory" from *The Big Broadcast of 1938* (Paramount)

Always and Always

from *Mannequin*
Music: Edward Ward
Lyrics: Bob Wright and George Forrest

Mannequin is the only movie to team Joan Crawford and Spencer Tracy. It presents a fairly realistic picture of poverty during the Depression, with Crawford playing Jessie Miller, a working-class woman who dreams of romance and a better life. Unfortunately the man she falls for is Eddie Miller, a crooked boxing promoter, played by Alan Curtis. When, inevitably, Crawford sees Curtis for what he is, the marriage falls apart and Joan finds herself back in the slums. But she escapes again, this time into the arms of rich shipping magnate John L. Hennessy played by Spencer Tracy.

The scene in which the song occurs takes place in the neighborhood café where Crawford and Curtis are having their wedding supper with Crawford's family and a few friends. Tracy is there too, going back to his working-class roots. He sees the wedding party and sends over a bottle of champagne. When the newlyweds go to thank him, Curtis sees an opportunity for advancement and pushes the rich man into dancing with his wife. They dance briefly but when the music changes to a new tune, Crawford, hesitates. She explains to Tracy that "this is our song—we always dance to it together" and so she begins to dance with her husband. She melts into his arms and begins to hum the melody. Then, in a pleasant contralto voice, she sings the words.

The scene is a complex one, full of ironic overtones with the audience aware of Curtis' true character and the inevitability of Crawford finding true love with Tracy. But in the meantime, the song "Always and Always" is her promise of undying love for Curtis. The words are the conventional promise of a love that will last for centuries. But while she sings, her husband is tense and distant, not really listening to her.

Composer Edward Ward also wrote the score for the picture and he makes extensive use of the melody of "Always and Always." The song was a sizeable hit in the U.S. for Larry Clinton and his vocalist Bea Wain and there was also a popular version by Benny Goodman and His Orchestra, with a vocal by Martha Tilton. Other versions came from Kay Weber singing with the Bob Crosby band, and Mildred Bailey with the Red Norvo outfit.

Change Partners

from *Carefree*
Music and Lyrics: Irving Berlin

"Change Partners" is a prophetic title because Berlin wrote it for the picture that signalled the end of the Fred Astaire-Ginger Rogers partnership.

At the country club dance in *Carefree* (RKO, 1938), Fred Astaire persuades Ginger Rogers to "Change Partners" and dance with him.

Ginger wanted to get away from musicals and establish herself in straight roles, while Fred had felt for a while that it was time to end the Astaire-Rogers formula before the public tired of it. But the RKO studio was still making good money from their pictures and wanted to keep them together. Although they had both made a few movies separately, *Carefree* became the eighth musical in six years for the dancing couple. It was the first in which they kissed.

Fred also sings one of Irving Berlin's best songs and "Change Partners" suits his suave style perfectly. The song fits so well into the plot of *Carefree* that it is strange to learn that Berlin had actually written it two years earlier. The song occurs after a series of complications: Ginger plays the part of Amanda Cooper, who is engaged to Ralph Bellamy, playing a rather pompous lawyer named Stephen Arden. She is having doubts about the relationship. Fred plays Bellamy's friend Tony Flagg, a psychiatrist, who agrees to psychoanalyze Ginger and remove her doubts. The treatment goes wrong and Ginger falls for Fred but by the time he realizes that he loves her too, he has used hypnotism to implant the idea that she hates him and loves her fiancé.

One evening all the main characters are at a country club dance. Bellamy is dancing with Ginger, Fred with her aunt (Luella Gear). Fred must somehow find a way to dance with Ginger and reverse the hypnotic command so that she will love him. Every time they pass on the dance floor, Fred pleads with Ginger to dance with him. Asking her to "change partners" is no idle flirtation but a dramatic imperative. The lines of the song fit the rhythm of the dance perfectly and nicely suggest Fred's annoyance at Ginger's refusal to dance with him. Next, Fred tells her in song to sit the dance out and he'll get a waiter to tell Bellamy that he's wanted on the telephone. A waiter does indeed carry out the task and Bellamy finds himself tied up with a phoney long distance call. Fred now has Ginger to himself and he dances her out onto the terrace. He puts her into a trance but before he can perform the reversal, Bellamy appears and takes his fiancée away. But rest assured that all ends happily.

"Change Partners" was a chart-topper for Fred, who recorded the song with Ray Noble and His Orchestra; there were other popular recordings by the Jimmy Dorsey band, with Bob Eberly's vocal, and by Ozzie Nelson, singing with his own orchestra. The film also collected Oscar nominations for its score and interior decoration.

The Cowboy and the Lady

from *The Cowboy and the Lady*
Music: Lionel Newman
Lyrics: Arthur Quenzer

The Cowboy and the Lady is a fairly undistinguished and unsuccessful romantic comedy that starred an uncomfortable looking Gary Cooper as Stretch Willoughby, the "Cowboy." He attracts the attentions of Merle Oberon as Mary Smith, the "Lady"—she is the daughter of a presidential candidate.

The Goldwyn studios planned originally to call the movie *The Lady and the Cowboy* but as Gary Cooper's contract guaranteed top billing, the order had to be reversed to make the title *The Cowboy and the Lady*. Unfortunately Paramount had rights to this title and Goldwyn had to pay for permission to use it.

The film won an Oscar for sound recording and was nominated for Alfred Newman's score but why anyone thought the song worthy of Oscar nomination is a mystery. Almost as undistinguished as the picture, its only sung version is barely noticeable. It occurs early: Merle, bored with society life, has gone out for the evening with two of her housemaids. They are on a blind date to meet three cowboys from a rodeo and Merle pretends to be one of the housemaids. Her date is Gary and at the end of the evening the three girls take the cowboys back to Merle's mansion. As they walk up the hill towards the house, they sing together a few lines from "The Cowboy and the Lady." The sequence lasts for barely 30 seconds but this is virtually all we hear of the words, apart from an even briefer snatch when Merle and Gary are caught kissing by the others.

But though the lyrics receive scant treatment, the melody of the song is featured extensively throughout the picture as well as being played over the opening and closing credits. We hear it in many forms: Gary Cooper plays it on a mouth organ as he herds some cattle; a fairground organ plays it at a rodeo; a small string orchestra plays it in waltz time at a society dinner. With all this emphasis, the catchy little tune has some impact, but with such an uninspired lyric, full of banal rhymes, it is clear why the song is not given a full airing.

No one thought the song worth releasing on record and it is now virtually forgotten.

Dust

from *Under Western Stars*
Music and Lyrics: Johnny Marvin

In *Under Western Stars,* "Dust" is warbled by Roy Rogers, accompanied by The Maple Leaf Four. Singing cowboy Gene Autry was originally cast in the film but he was in dispute with the Republic studios over salary and Rogers took over. It launched Rogers' career and he became Republic's number one star. His talented horse, Trigger, became a star too.

Roy Rogers' real name was Leonard Slye. His movie surname was borrowed from Will Rogers; Republic wanted to give him the first name Leroy but the actor preferred the shorter version.

In the picture, Roy Rogers, playing a character named Roy Rogers, journeys to Washington as a new Congressman, his mission to round up federal funding for his home state to combat the erosion caused by dust storms. As Roy prepared to sing the song, a wind machine was readied to blow the required dust. But before the action could begin, a real storm blew up and the scene as filmed portrays the genuine article.

The song has a plaintive tune and the almost monotonous repetition of the word "dust"—used eight times in the first verse alone—expresses something of the cowboy's weariness, as well as the desperation of the scene.

"Dust" was reused in 1948 in another Roy Rogers picture, *Under California Skies.* In an Internet poll conducted in 2000, fans of cowboy songs voted "Dust" third in their list of all-time favorites.

Jeepers Creepers

from *Going Places*
Music: Harry Warren
Lyrics: Johnny Mercer

Johnny Mercer, above all other American songwriters, had remarkable skill in using vernacular language in his lyrics. "Jeepers Creepers" is a prime example: The song is a veritable compendium of slang expressions and idiomatic contractions, all fused together with great wit and style. There is a story that Mercer first heard the expression "jeepers creepers" used by Henry Fonda.

The song was used in *Going Places*, an enjoyable picture that starred Dick Powell and Anita Louise; a suave Ronald Reagan was in there, too. Jeepers Creepers is actually the name of a highly strung racehorse that will only behave itself when its groom, played by Louis Armstrong, sings or plays the song to calm him. Louis and his band have to sing the song as they ride in a wagon alongside the racetrack, to ensure that Jeepers wins the big race. Dick Powell rides the horse and when he loses sight and sound of Louis he has to sing "Jeepers Creepers" into the horse's ear himself.

The song is used as a love song to a horse but the lyrics could be a celebration of a woman's eyes, her "peepers." However dull the weather, the singer will always see sunshine in his beloved's eyes. He wonders where they came from, how they got so big—a line made doubly funny when sung to a horse. The lyric is in perfect harmony with the merry bounce of Harry Warren's simple and unpretentious melody, and Louis Armstrong's performance of the song brings out its best. It is such a prominent song that *Jeepers Creepers* would have made a more marketable title for the film than *Going Places*.

The most successful recording of "Jeepers Creepers" was by Al Donahue's band, with a vocal by Paula Kelly, a version that topped the U.S. charts in 1939. Larry Clinton and His Orchestra (with vocalist Ford Leary) reached number 12 and it was also a big hit for Louis and was as much associated with him by the general public of the day as "What a Wonderful World" has been by a later generation. "Jeepers Creepers" has turned up in a number of other pictures including *Yankee Doodle Dandy* (1942), where the teenage Charles Smith sang it. In the horror movie *Jeepers Creepers* (2001), a version of the song is continually played on a record player. The record used here is the one by Paul Whiteman and His Swing Wing; it has a vocal by the Four Modernaires and Jack Teagarden.

Merrily We Live

from *Merrily We Live*
Music: Phil Charig
Lyrics: Arthur Quenzer

Merrily We Live was the last picture Hal Roach made for MGM before he went over to United Artists. A box once hit and nominated for Oscars in five categories, it is a screwball comedy concerning the Kilbournes, an eccentric and wealthy family who take in a supposed tramp as their chauffeur and eventually find that he is a well-known novelist. Brian Aherne plays Wade Rawlins, the chauffeur, while Constance Bennett is the oldest daughter who falls in love with him. Billie Burke plays the scatterbrained Mrs. Kilbourne, the lady of the house, and she earned an Oscar nomination for Best Supporting Actress. The script is often very witty, due in part to Ed Sullivan, who was hired to write additional dialogue. Sullivan was a well-known newspaper columnist at the time.

The film opens with the ten actors who play the family members and their servants walking together, while the opening titles run. Dressed in character, they link arms and walk through the gates and into the grounds of the mansion in which most of the action takes place. As they stroll along merrily, a studio chorus sings the title song. The words are fairly meaningless but they create a carefree, sunny atmosphere. With the bright and breezy tune, the tone is set for the madcap happenings to come. The lyric refers to showman Barnum and certainly life in the Kilbourne mansion resembles a circus at times. The song is heard once more over the closing credits.

The original presentation of the song, its verve and vitality, gained it the attention that must have led to its Oscar nomination. It has had no life outside of the picture and no one has ever recorded it.

A Mist Over the Moon

from *The Lady Objects*
Music: Ben Oakland
Lyrics: Oscar Hammerstein II

Lanny Ross, who sings "A Mist Over the Moon" in *The Lady Objects,* was a very successful singer in the 1930s; in 1936, he was voted Most Popular Male Vocalist in the U.S.A. He also had a popular radio series and is always associated with "Moonlight and Roses," his signature tune. His popularity led him to Hollywood but he was a better singer than actor and he never became a big star.

The Lady Objects is a melodramatic picture with Ross cast as William Hayward, a college football hero who marries fellow student Ann Adams, played by Gloria Stuart. She makes the big time and big money as a lawyer, overshadowing Ross, who struggles along as a not-too-successful architect. When they separate, Ross sings in a nightclub to earn extra money and is wrongly accused of murder. His estranged wife saves him and a tearful reconciliation follows. Career women were not entirely accepted in the 1930s and a lobby card for the film contained the wife's admission of failure, a message for all married women of the time: "Gentlemen of the Jury! If my husband murdered this other woman … I am to blame! I've been a success as a lawyer … but a failure as a wife!"

We hear the song first early in the film, at a party where Ross is trying to impress a client. He sits at the piano, singing and playing "A Mist Over the Moon," but is frustrated by a series of interruptions. Later, in the nightclub, he gets the chance to sing his party piece all the way through—and this time with full orchestral accompaniment.

The words paint a very poetic picture of two lovers on a boat drifting at night through a misty, silent world where everything is unreal and dreamlike. But their love is the exception, the only clear reality in a darkening world where the stars no longer shine and "A Mist Is Over the Moon."

Oscar Hammerstein's gently poetic words are well supported by the long, flowing phrases of Ben Oakland's atmospheric and haunting melody. It is a subtle song that repays repeated listening but perhaps does not have immediate and popular appeal. Of the day's singers, only Tony Martin thought it worth recording and the song is now so little-known that there is doubt about its title. Most film histories refer to it as "A Mist Is Over the Moon" and Tony Martin recorded it under that title. But the official nomination by the Academy leaves out the verb and calls it "A Mist Over the Moon."

My Own

from *That Certain Age*
Music: Jimmy McHugh
Lyrics: Harold Adamson

Deanna Durbin was just 17 when she made her fourth picture, *That Certain Age*. She is cast as Alice Fullerton, an innocent young thing who develops a crush on an older man, Vincent Bullitt, played by the suave Melvyn Douglas. Jackie Cooper is Kenneth Warren, the more suitable teenage boyfriend temporarily spurned by the lovesick Deanna. The Oscar-nominated song "My Own" is used to heighten the poignancy of the situation.

At a party thrown to celebrate Douglas' birthday, the miserable Cooper tells the older man that Deanna has fallen for him. Douglas stands dumbfounded while the inconsolable Cooper wanders off alone. At this point Deanna sings "My Own," directing all the yearnings in the song at Douglas. We glimpse poor Jackie looking in on the scene through the window.

The song has an attractive melody but the lyric never rises above the conventional, using well-worn phrases of romantic longing. But at least the words, with the long sound on the rhyme points (own, alone, known), are very singable, enabling Durbin to sustain the notes to euphonious effect. Her singing is very appealing and crystallizes the sad sweetness of the moment.

Durbin's recording of "My Own" was quite popular for a while but it was surpassed in sales by a version from the Tommy Dorsey band that had a vocal by Edythe Wright. The Gene Krupa band also recorded it (with vocalist Irene Daye).

Now It Can Be Told

from *Alexander's Ragtime Band*
Music and Lyrics: Irving Berlin

"Now It Can Be Told" is one of six new songs Berlin wrote for *Alexander's Ragtime Band*. The film also incorporated some of his earlier classics such as "Easter Parade," "Blue Skies" and the title song.

The movie traces the story of a band and its leader, played by Tyrone Power, from humble beginnings in a San Francisco dive to a triumphant sell-out concert in Carnegie Hall. Producer Darryl F. Zanuck intended it as Irving Berlin's life story but when Berlin himself became involved he altered the scenario and the finished picture has little in common with the great songwriter's real life. But it does show the important part that Berlin's songs played in American life and in the popular music of the twentieth century.

The film was very successful and received six Oscar nominations, with Alfred Newman winning for his score.

Early in the picture, Alexander (Tyrone Power) and band vocalist Stella Kirby (Alice Faye) dislike each other with intensity, a sure Hollywood sign that they will end up together. In the meantime, it is pianist Charlie Dwyer, played by Don Ameche, who makes a run for Faye's affections.

In the scene that introduces "Now It Can Be Told," the band is about to open at a swank San Francisco hotel: Alice finds Don at the piano playing the melody. When she asks him what it is, he tells her that it's "just a little hit tune I've been working on." He sings it for her (without the verse), then asks her if she likes it. "Why, it's great!" she says. "It's got everything. Imagine you having that in you. Why, it'll make you famous!" Don's hesitant response is to tell her that he wrote it just for her: "If it's any good, that's why." But before he can say more, she rushes off to show the song to Tyrone Power. That evening, Alice sings the new ballad, complete with introductory verse.

At first Don proudly watches her from the piano but then he becomes more and more crestfallen as he realizes that she is directing the song's message to Power. Power receives it loud and clear but, from his expression, he is somewhat nonplussed, clearly unaware of her feelings for him. But at the end of the song, when Alice rushes off in confusion, Power follows her. As the band continues to play the melody, they embrace and kiss on a balcony that overlooks a moonlit ocean. The song that Don wrote as his declaration of love has been the means to bring them together.

"Now It Can Be Told" has a rich and beautiful melody, one of Berlin's best, though the short lyric does not match it, relying on conventional rhymes and sentiment to describe the singer's assertion that this love story is the greatest ever told, out-romancing all the famous accounts of other lovers.

But it remains an attractive song, perhaps better suited to Don Ameche's intimate and low-key approach when we first hear it, rather then the rather opulent, showy interpretation that Alice Faye gives it.

There were a number of contemporary recordings but easily the most popular was the one by the Tommy Dorsey band, with Jack Leonard's vocals. It outsold not only Tony Martin's version (singing with the Ray Noble Orchestra) but also Bing Crosby's. After its brief popularity in the late 1930s, the song largely disappeared from most singers' repertoires until Ella Fitzgerald revived it on her *Irving Berlin Songbook* album in 1958. Tony Bennett recorded another superb version on his 1987 album *Bennett/Berlin*.

And the Winner Is…

Thanks for the Memory

from *The Big Broadcast of 1938*
Music: Ralph Rainger
Lyrics: Leo Robin

Leo Robin was set a very difficult task in writing the lyric for "Thanks for the Memory": Mitchell Leisen, the director of *The Big Broadcast of 1938*, demanded a song that would be sung by a formerly married couple who meet again by chance on a cruise liner. They find that they are still in love but dare not say so in case the other does not reciprocate. In this way, the song has to imply the love they feel without actually stating it. A team of studio scriptwriters had failed to come up with a way of presenting the situation satisfactorily in dialogue but Leo Robin's lyric solves the problem perfectly. Unusually, he wrote the words first, at Rainger's suggestion, and the composer was able to give the music a similar poignancy.

The fact that this sophisticated, delicate song has to be sung in the picture by funny man Bob Hope, playing the role of Buzz Fielding (with Shirley Ross as Cleo, his ex-wife), was an added difficulty because the director also wanted the song to get a few laughs. But the words Robin wrote succeed completely, cleverly verging on saying what must not be said, then casually deflating the emotional build-up with levity. Most of the verses combine momentous memories with the trivial: "burning lips" with "burning toast," "gardens in Versailles" with "beef and kidney pie." The bitter sweetness of the lyric stands comparison with the songs of Noël Coward; in fact, the situation that Hope and Ross find themselves in is very reminiscent of the famous opening scene of Coward's play *Private Lives*.

The setting for the song is the bar of a transatlantic liner. The picture until now has been sheer nonsense but this sequence brings a touching reality to the proceedings. Bob and Shirley are studying their drinks, unsure of what to say to each other, so they recall the highlights of their marriage in song. They remember only the good things, not the bad, and as they sing alternate lines they seem determined to sustain a mood of fond nostalgia, not allowing their illusions to fade. Shirley weeps as the song ends and is unable to complete the last line. The scene fades with Bob comforting her; clearly they will get back together before the end of the picture. The song tells more about their feelings for each other than pages of dialogue could.

Songwriters Rainger and Robin originally intended the tempo for "Thanks for the Memory" to be quick—it was director Mitchell Leisen who thought it should be slower, and certainly it has more feeling that way. Leisen also heightened the emotional impact of the song by recording it directly

Bob Hope and Shirley Ross in *The Big Broadcast of 1938* **(Paramount, 1938).**

instead of following the usual practice of prerecording and having the actors synchronize their lip movements to the playback. He moved the entire Paramount studio orchestra onto the set for the occasion.

Robin and Rainger were delighted with the way their song was treated and film folklore has it that they—and most of the people on set—joined in with Shirley Ross' tears when the recording ended.

Leo Robin had a brush with the Hollywood censors over some of the lines from "Thanks for the Memory." The censor objected especially to the line about "that weekend in Niagara" which originally continued "when we never saw the Falls." The censor thought that the word "never" made the line suggestive and described it as "dirty." He insisted on changing the line to "That weekend in Niagara when we hardly saw the Falls." Robin felt that the change was more suggestive.

Bob Hope was a big star on Broadway but was an unknown in Hollywood. He made his feature film debut in this picture and made a huge impact with "Thanks for the Memory." Ironically, Hope was at first a little disappointed with the song, but only because he was to sing it as a duet with Shirley Ross, not perform it as a solo. But in the final analysis it was his performance of "Thanks for the Memory" that convinced Paramount to persist with him, thereby setting him on the road to screen stardom. The song did very little for Shirley Ross' career.

The success of the song and the picture led to a sequel called *Thanks for the Memory* that portrays Hope and Ross more or less as the couple in the song. The studio was hoping to duplicate the success of the earlier picture and its hit song but saw fit not to employ Rainger and Robin. Instead, Frank Loesser and Hoagy Carmichael got the job of writing another poignant duet for Hope and Ross, and the song they produced together stands comparison with "Thanks for the Memory." The song was "Two Sleepy People" and it is very surprising that it was not nominated for a 1939 Oscar.

Damon Runyon wrote an entire newspaper column on "Thanks for the Memory," describing it as the best thing he had seen on screen in years. Hope's agent made sure that William LeBaron, head of production at Paramount, saw a copy of the column and shortly afterwards the studio picked up Bob's option for another picture.

Later, Hope was booked for a radio program sponsored by Pepsodent Toothpaste. The theme song for the show was to have been "Hope Is Here for Pepsodent" sung to the tune of "Wintergreen for President," a song the Gershwins wrote for *Of Thee I Sing*. The copyright owners wanted $250 for each use of the song so Hope suggested a much cheaper—and much better—option. It was, of course, "Thanks for the Memory."

When Ralph Rainger died suddenly in 1942, Hope talked about him on his radio show, stating that for as long as he was on the air he would always use "Thanks for the Memory" as his signature tune. Often he would have special lyrics written to suit different occasions and audiences, a process that began when Hope and Ross first recorded the song. This version varies greatly from what they sang in the picture. And although their recording was popular, the biggest seller was by Shep Fields and his "rippling rhythm" orchestra. Bob Goday was the vocalist.

1939

Bob Hope hosted the 1939 Academy Awards for the first of many times. The venue was changed to the Cocoanut Grove at the Ambassador Hotel, Los Angeles, and Gene Buck presented the music awards, including Best Song.

The Nominations

Ralph Rainger and Leo Robin for "Faithful Forever" from *Gulliver's Travels* (Paramount)

Irving Berlin for "I Poured My Heart Into a Song" from *Second Fiddle* (Fox)

Harold Arlen and E.Y. Harburg for "Over the Rainbow" from *The Wizard of Oz* (MGM)

Buddy DeSylva for "Wishing" from *Love Affair* (RKO)

Faithful Forever

from *Gulliver's Travels*
Music: Ralph Rainger
Lyrics: Leo Robin

The first full-length animated film to receive Oscar nominations was not a Walt Disney production but Dave and Max Fleischer's 1939 version of *Gulliver's Travels*. At this time the Fleischer Studios represented a real challenge to the supremacy of Disney, with popular characters such as Popeye and Betty Boop. Disney had released the first feature-length cartoon, *Snow White and the Seven Dwarfs*, in 1937, but it was not honored by the Academy. *Gulliver's Travels*, nominations were Victor Young for Best Original Score and Ralph Rainger and Leo Robin for Best Song.

54

In the Fleischer version of Swift's story, Princess Glory of Lilliput falls in love with Prince David from the neighbouring kingdom of Blefuscu. A civil war breaks out over which national song will be sung at their wedding, Lilliput's "Faithful" or Blefuscu's "Forever." Gulliver achieves peace by having the Prince and Princess sing them together as one song entitled "Faithful Forever." In this way, the song is not a random love ballad but a successful integration of music and plot resolution.

The voices heard on the soundtrack are those of Jessica Dragonette and Lanny Ross, who also supplied the speaking voice for Gulliver. Jessica Dragonette was a major radio star with a career that spanned 22 years. She sang arias and ballads, bringing semi-classical music to Americans in the early days of radio. In 1935, listeners voted her their most popular entertainer.

In spite of its importance in terms of the film's plot, the song is not a great example of the art of songwriting. Leo Robin's lyric is astonishingly banal, using every cliche in the songwriters' manual. The use of rhyme is unusually poor also, with the internal rhymes on the words "fated," "created" and "separated" in the introductory verse having too much emphasis. The rhyme scheme is inconsistent in the two parts of the chorus: in the first, lines one and three rhyme, as do lines two and four; in the second, only lines three and four rhyme.

Rainger's music is just as unmemorable and the song has had little life outside the film, in spite of recordings by the Lanny Ross himself, Glenn Miller band, Kenny Baker, Arthur Tracey, Phil Harris, Mildred Bailey and Ginny Simms.

The film's producers anticipated that "Faithful Forever" would become the song of choice for weddings but brides and grooms showed better judgment.

I Poured My Heart Into a Song

from *Second Fiddle*
Music and Lyrics: Irving Berlin

The story of *Second Fiddle* was loosely based on the search for an actress to play Scarlett O'Hara in *Gone with the Wind*, a search that had received enormous publicity. And though the first part of the film is a fairly amusing satire on the movie business, it soon becomes a routine romance. Trudi Hovland (Sonja Henie), a Minnesota skating teacher, is successful as candidate # 436 for a role in a forthcoming Hollywood epic. Tyrone Power is Jimmy Sutton, the film studio's publicity agent, and he has to play "second fiddle" to singer Roger Maxwell (Rudy Vallee). He has concocted a romance between Vallee and Sonja Henie in order to get publicity for his new star, but—of course—he is secretly in love with her himself.

Power is the first to sing "I Poured My Heart Into a Song," apparently

Tyrone Power and Sonja Henie in *Second Fiddle* (Fox, 1939).

writing the song at the piano. According to the manuscript in front of him, the title is "I Poured My Love into a Song" but we see the creative process at work as he changes "Love" to "Heart." Completing his composition, he sings it over, then the scene fades to a nightclub where the band is playing the tune and Rudy Vallee is dancing with Sonja Henie. Power has written the song as part of the phony romance he has invented, and Vallee's character is named as its composer. The bandleader asks Vallee to step up and sing "this beautiful song which is sweeping the country." The melody is heard in full once more near the end of the film when Henie ice-dances to it.

The ballad expresses the philosophy that genuine feeling rather than witty contrivance should be the basis for writing a good love song. Perhaps this is the perfect reflection of Berlin's own attitude to song writing.

Second Fiddle marked the end of Berlin's association with 20th Century–Fox. He was well below form and none of the other songs he wrote for the film are heard much today. The Artie Shaw band, with vocalist Helen Forrest, reached the Top Ten with "I Poured My Heart Into a Song"; Jimmy Dorsey and Rudy Vallee himself also made recordings of it.

Wishing

from *Love Affair*
Music and Lyrics: Buddy DeSylva

Love Affair is fondly remembered as one of the finest Hollywood romantic dramas of the 1930s. Written and directed by Leo McCarey, it has plenty of witty lines along with the tears and sentiment, all stylishly played by Charles Boyer and Irene Dunne. The movie received six Academy Award nominations, including Buddy DeSylva's for Best Song.

Boyer and Dunne play Michel Marnet and Terry McKay, who meet on an ocean liner. They begin a mild flirtation, avoiding anything serious as both already have partners waiting for them in New York. But as the voyage continues, their involvement with each other deepens and they resolve to test their feelings by meeting again in six months' time at the top of the Empire State Building. On the appointed day, Boyer arrives and believes that Dunne has changed her mind when she fails to turn up. But on the way to the rendezvous, she has been seriously injured in a road accident and is unable to walk. Some time later, the couple meets again; Dunne determines to learn to walk, and they look forward to happiness ever after.

Irene Dunne and Charles Boyer in *Love Affair* **(RKO, 1939).**

Three small girls, accompanied on the ukulele by Dunne, perform "Wishing" in *Love Affair*, their voices dubbed by members of the Robert Mitchell Boy Choir. The song plays a significant role in the plot as lines from it echo a conversation Boyer and Dunne had during their shipboard romance. She seems to be daydreaming and he asks her what she is dreaming about. She answers that she is "not dreaming but wishing." Boyer comments that "wishes are the dreams we dream when we're awake," and that "if you wish very hard with your mind and if you wish very strongly in your heart and if you keep on wishing long enough and strong enough, you will get want you want for Christmas." Buddy DeSylva uses this conversation as the basis for the song. His lyric is ordinary but the melody is very appealing.

The song is used as a dramatic device to underscore the poignancy of the situation and to tug at the heartstrings of the audience. A choir from the orphanage reprises it—Irene Dunne has become a teacher there and is rehearsing them for a Christmas concert. Having the children sing the song could have been horribly sickly but the scene has enough humor to prevent the film from becoming too melodramatic.

At the Christmas concert we hear the melody of "Wishing" as Boyer and Dunne are reunited, receiving the Christmas present they wished for aboard the ship early in the film.

Leo McCarey remade the film in 1957 with Cary Grant and Deborah Kerr, under the title *An Affair to Remember*. This version begins well but does suffer towards the end from the melodrama that *Love Affair* avoided. The title song from the 1957 version was also nominated for an Oscar.

"Wishing" was one of the most popular songs in the summer of 1939. A recording by the Glenn Miller band, with vocalist Ray Eberle, topped the charts for four weeks. Three other recordings—by the bands of Russ Morgan (vocal by Mert Curtis), Skinnay Ennis and Orrin Tucker (who both did their own vocals)—also made the top 20. Ethel Smith performs the song on the organ in *George White's Scandals of 1945*.

And the Winner Is...

Over the Rainbow

from *The Wizard of Oz*
Music: Harold Arlen
Lyrics: E.Y. (Yip) Harburg

The Wizard of Oz was nominated for Oscars in six categories, winning for Herbert Stothart's score and for Best Song. "Over the Rainbow" is one of the most famous songs to win an Oscar and is perhaps the one most closely associated with Judy Garland.

All of the other songs in *The Wizard of Oz* are upbeat and lighthearted but composer Harold Arlen was convinced that something with a slower tempo—a melodious ballad—was needed as balance. The tune came to him quite easily but he was nonplussed to find that Yip Harburg didn't share his enthusiasm for it. Harburg thought the melody rather grandiose and more suited to a male singer like Nelson Eddy than to the young Dorothy. Arlen asked Ira Gershwin for his opinion and he agreed that it did sound a little operatic and suggested that Arlen play it in a more popular, rhythmic style. Harburg also pressed Arlen to come up with a bridge with a more childlike feel; Arlen obliged and Harburg used it for the lines beginning "Someday I'll wish upon a star." Everything else was fine except that Harburg couldn't think of a strong finish and here Ira Gershwin helped again by suggesting the last line about the "happy little bluebirds." With characteristic modesty, Ira refused any credit.

The associate producer on the film, Arthur Freed, loved the song but he and Arlen had to fight hard to secure its place. It was actually cut three times. One objection was that it was too difficult to sing with its operatic octave leap on the word "some—where"; another was that it sounded too simple, especially the middle section ("Someday I'll wish upon a star...") that was likened to a child's piano exercise.

Yip Harburg described how he developed the lyric:

> This little girl thinks: *My life is messed up. Where do I run?* The song has to be full of childish pleasures. Of lemon drops. The book had said Kansas was an arid place where not even flowers grew. The only colorful thing Dorothy saw, occasionally, would be the rainbow. [Quoted in *Who Put the Rainbow in the Wizard of Oz?* by Harold Meyerson and Ernie Harburg]

To ensure that "Over the Rainbow," like all the other songs in the movie, would be fully integrated into the story and fully reflect Dorothy's feelings, Harburg then wrote the dialogue leading into the song: Aunt Em tells Dorothy to stop imagining things, to find her a place where she won't "get into trouble." Dorothy picks up this phrase and wonders if there *is* such a place. If there is, she says to herself, it must be far away..." somewhere over the rainbow."

The sequence is full of movement as Judy walks through the farmyard, stopping only occasionally to rest pensively against a haystack or a tractor. Her restless movements and the words of the song reflect her yearning, the unhappy child longing to escape from her farmyard home when it seems that her beloved pet dog must be destroyed. But it also has a wider resonance and over the years many listeners have heard it as a heartbreaking elegy for Judy Garland's own tragic life; the song has become hers rather than Dorothy's. In his autobiography *I Remember It Well*, Judy Garland's first husband Vincente Minnelli writes:

Toto looks on as Judy Garland sings "Over the Rainbow" in *The Wizard of Oz* (MGM, 1939).

> Audiences would be moved to tears whenever she sang "Over the Rainbow." They may have been crying over their lost innocence, but they also realized that—whatever her personal tragedies— Judy's essential purity remained. Her whole being was suffused with emotion, and we her public were fortunate that she generously shared it with us.

And this resonance has worked for other singers too: Eva Cassidy died of cancer in comparative obscurity in 1996 but when a British deejay began playing her version of "Over the Rainbow" she achieved enormous posthumous success. The song became a metaphor for the unfulfilled promise of her life; there was a huge emotional appeal in the fact that the singer, who had died so young and so little-known, seemed to be yearning for a better life beyond the everyday.

At the time of the release of *The Wizard of Oz* Garland's own recording of "Over the Rainbow" was easily beaten into the 1939 American charts by the bands of Glenn Miller (with vocals by Ray Eberle) and Bob Crosby (vocals by Teddy Grace). There was another popular recording by the Larry Clinton band, with Bea Wain's vocals, and another by the Freddy Martin orchestra with the singer Stuart Wade.

At the Academy Awards for 1939, Mickey Rooney presented 17-year-old Judy with a miniature Oscar for an Outstanding Juvenile Performance in *The Wizard of Oz*. She marked the occasion by singing "Over the Rainbow."

MGM used the song again a year later when James Stewart, over the rainbow in a dreamland of drunken euphoria, sings it to Katharine Hepburn in *The Philadelphia Story*. Stewart was associated with "Over the Rainbow" again when, as Glenn Miller, he led his band playing part of it in *The Glenn Miller Story* (1954). Eileen Farrell (dubbing for Eleanor Parker) sang it in *Interrupted Melody* (1955), and Elizabeth Hartman hummed it in *A Patch of Blue* (1965). This song is used to great comic effect in *The Abominable Dr. Phibes* (1971), where it swells on the soundtrack as Vincent Price climbs into his grave.

1940

Walter Wanger succeeded Frank Capra as Academy President and acted as host for the Awards Ceremony, which returned this year to the Biltmore Hotel, Los Angeles. Songwriter Buddy DeSylva, whose song "Wishing" had lost to "Over the Rainbow" in 1939, presented the Best Song Oscars.

The Nominations

Harry Warren and Mack Gordon for "Down Argentina Way" from *Down Argentine Way* (Fox)

Jimmy McHugh and Johnny Mercer for "I'd Know You Anywhere" from *You'll Find Out* (RKO)

Chet Forrest and Bob Wright for "It's a Blue World" from *Music in My Heart* (Columbia)

Artie Shaw and Johnny Mercer for "Love of My Life" from *Second Chorus* (Paramount)

James Monaco and Johnny Burke for "Only Forever" from *Rhythm on the River* (Paramount)

Roger Edens and Arthur Freed for "Our Love Affair" from *Strike Up the Band* (MGM)

Robert Stolz and Gus Kahn for "Waltzing in the Clouds" from *Spring Parade* (Universal)

Leigh Harline and Ned Washington for "When You Wish Upon a Star" from *Pinocchio* (Walt Disney)

Jule Styne and Walter Bullock for "Who Am I?" from *Hit Parade of 1941* (Republic)

Down Argentina Way

from *Down Argentine Way*
Music: Harry Warren
Lyrics: Mack Gordon

"Down Argentina Way" misses being the title song for the musical *Down Argentine Way* by just one letter. The movie title has the adjectival form of the country's name, while the song title uses the noun.

It was the first of many 20th Century–Fox musicals with an exotic Latin American setting and it was made partly in an attempt to pull in more business from South America, as World War II had greatly reduced Hollywood's market in continental Europe. The film is good to look at and gathered Oscar nominations for its cinematography and interior decoration. It was only the second Fox movie for which Harry Warren wrote the songs, following his prolific years at Warner Bros. It was also the movie that launched Betty Grable to stardom and marked the screen debut of Carmen Miranda.

Miranda was the spearhead of the North American foray south of the border. She already had some fame in the United States with her appearance in the Broadway revue *The Streets of Paris*. *Down Argentine Way* was her first U.S. film and she does in it what she does in most of the others—she wiggles her hips, flashes her eyes and curls her fingers while wearing tutti frutti hats—a parody of Latin American culture. Because of her Broadway commitment, her scenes were shot in New York.

Part of "Down Argentina Way" is first heard sung by the studio chorus over the opening credits, and extensive use is made of the melody on the soundtrack. But its most significant use comes when Don Ameche and Betty Grable sing it early in the film. Betty plays Glenda Crawford, an American girl on holiday in the Argentine who falls for Ricardo Quintana, a wealthy racehorse owner played by Ameche. They are in a smart club and Ameche sings the song in Spanish as he plays the piano, all the while gazing soulfully into Betty's eyes. The voice we hear dubbing for Ameche belongs to Carlos Albert, who also supplied the Spanish lyric.

Now Betty sings the English version to him, leaning on the piano. When the chorus begins, with its rhythmic rumba tempo, Betty swivels her hips like Carmen Miranda and dances as she sings. The song is an enthusiastic tribute to the joys to be found in Argentina, a land of gaiety and romance, where rumbas and tangos will "tickle your spine." Once there, you will always want to stay "Down Argentina Way."

The studio chorus takes up the singing as Betty and Don begin to dance the rumba. Then the happy couple sing alternate lines of the song together, he in Spanish and she in English. At the end of the song they dance out onto the terrace where he declares his love.

It's an enjoyable, lively song, and Harry Warren's exuberant music has genuine Latin American flavor. Mack Gordon's clever use of rhyme accentuates the rhythm and it was this film—and perhaps her performance of this song—that set Grable on her way to stardom. She landed the role only because first choice Alice Faye had appendicitis.

The Nicholas Brothers also sing "Down Argentina Way" in Spanish and dance to it with another of their displays of athleticism. At the end of the film, some of Betty Grable's co-stars (Charlotte Greenwood, Leonid Kinskey and Henry Stephenson) dance to the melody of the song and sing a few lines. The Nicholas Brothers join in the dance and J. Carrol Naish, playing an Argentinean stable hand, sings new words to the melody of the song, lauding his favorite horse, Furioso, which has just won an important race.

The film was a success and the song was very popular, with many of the top bands of the day recording it. Bob Crosby and His Orchestra (vocal by Bonnie King) had the most successful version, reaching number two in the charts, but also selling well were records by the bands of Eddy Duchin (vocal by the Three Earbenders), Shep Fields (vocal by Sonny Washburn), Leo Reisman (vocal by Sara Horn) and Gene Krupa (vocal by Irene Daye). A version by Dinah Shore failed to chart. The song was revived by Desi Arnaz some years later in an episode of the *I Love Lucy* TV series.

I'd Know You Anywhere

from *You'll Find Out*
Music: Jimmy McHugh
Lyrics: Johnny Mercer

The charming ballad "I'd Know You Anywhere" features extensively in *You'll Find Out*, an enjoyable send-up of horror movies. The setting is a formal twenty first birthday party in a ghostly mansion and the villains are played by the wonderful trio of Boris Karloff, Bela Lugosi and Peter Lorre. Their mission is to murder Helen Parrish, who plays Janis Bellacrest, the birthday girl, and make off with the money she is about to inherit.

Kay Kyser has star billing and his band provides the entertainment for the party. And it's the zany bandleader who gives us the first taste of "I'd Know You Anywhere," whistling the tune as he dresses for dinner. Later, Ginny Simms gives us the major presentation of the song, accompanied by the band. She sings that she has already met the love of her life in her dreams.

"I'd Know You Anywhere" is a delightfully unpretentious ballad with charming words complemented by a very attractive melody. And just to remind us that Karloff, Lugosi and Lorre are villains at heart, we see the trio staring menacingly at Ginny as she sings. Lugosi, a musical snob, enjoys her singing but hates the song. He tells her: "You have a real nice voice, my dear. It's a pity to waste it on such trash!"

Lugosi is Prince Saliano, a fake medium; when he conducts a seance he

uses an electrical device to fake spirit voices. While he puts on a performance to summon up the dead, the band plays a suitably spooky version of "I'd
Know You Anywhere."

When the villains are finally confounded, Kay Kyser borrows Lugosi's
gadget to use with his band (the machine will make it seem that the musical
instruments are vocalizing). Kyser introduces it as "a new miracle of electric-
ity—Sonovox!" He explains that vocalist Harry Babbitt will use it to give
"diction to the tunes of the instruments as they play. Harry forms the words
but the instruments sing 'em!" And the song chosen to demonstrate this
miraculous invention first is "I'd Know You Anywhere."

Ginny Simms performs "I'd Know You Anywhere" very prettily and Bela
Lugosi was right to praise her singing. But though she recorded it with Kay
Kyser, it was Bing Crosby's excellent recording of the song that became the
big hit. Glenn Miller and His Orchestra (with Ray Eberle's vocals) also had
a minor hit with it, as did Frank Sinatra, singing with the Tommy Dorsey
band. It was a much-recorded song in 1940—other versions came from Johnny
Mercer, Bonnie King and the Bob Crosby band, Irene Daye with the Gene
Krupa band, Buddy Clark and Dick Haymes.

It's a Blue World

from *Music in My Heart*
Music: Chet Forrest
Lyrics: Bob Wright

This forgettable song comes from a film that at 69 minutes long was little more than a second feature. It stars Rita Hayworth and the romantic tenor
Tony Martin, who sings "It's a Blue World." Martin plays Robert Gregory,
a character who is about to be deported as an alien. On the way to his ship,
he encounters Patricia O'Malley (Rita Hayworth) and they fall in love. A
series of twists and complications keep them apart until he contrives to take
part in a radio broadcast with Andre Kostelanetz and His Music. His singing
of "It's a Blue World" is the catalyst that reconciles the lovers.

Chet Forrest's melody is very appealing and gives the song the little life
it has. The contrived order of some phrases give the lyric a clumsiness, as does
the sometimes awkward choice of words—such as "through" in the second
chorus, used adjectivally just to give an internal rhyme with "blue." But there
are some neat touches, such as all the long "i" sounds, especially in the first
and third lines of the verse. These make the song very singable and Martin
makes the most of it.

Martin's recording was a sizable hit and Glenn Miller and His Orchestra (vocal by Ray Eberle) also had a successful version.

The song turns up again in the 1946 musical *Sing While You Dance*, sung
by Ellen Drew. Frankie Laine sings it in *Make Believe Ballroom* (1949); in the

same year the musical *Jolson Sings Again* uses "It's a Blue World" as an instrumental.

For a while, Tony Martin was considered a star of the future. In the 1930s he was married to 20th Century-Fox's leading lady Alice Faye, and the studio promoted him heavily. But talented and handsome as he was, he never managed the kind of recognition that many thought his due. He did become a leading nightclub attraction after the War, and for some years presented a double act with his second wife, Cyd Charisse.

Love of My Life

from *Second Chorus*
Music: Artie Shaw
Lyrics: Johnny Mercer

Lyricist Johnny Mercer received a total of 18 Oscar nominations between 1938 and 1971, two of them in 1940—for "Love of My Life" and "I'd Know You Anywhere." There is some disagreement about the song's title—in the movie credits it appears as "Would You Like to Be the Love of My Life" but it is usually known by the shorter form.

It is strongly featured in *Second Chorus*, a film that Fred Astaire often claimed to be the worst he ever made. This is a rather harsh judgment, probably made because Fred was still in search of a dancing partner to replace Ginger Rogers. He has one dance number with Paulette Goddard in the film and she was certainly no rival for Ginger. Though Goddard had been both a Ziegfield and a Goldwyn girl, she was more of an actress than a dancer and had experienced great success opposite her husband-to-be Charlie Chaplin in *Modern Times* (1936).

A glaring absurdity of *Second Chorus* is that the 41-year-old Astaire was cast as a college student. The script's explanation for this is that he keeps failing his exams deliberately so that he can stay playing trumpet in the college dance band. (Bobby Hackett dubs his playing.)

But allowing for Goddard's average dancing and Astaire's age, the film is mildly enjoyable and has some genuinely funny moments. Artie Shaw and his band play a prominent part and Shaw himself wrote the music for the Oscar-nominated song. He was an accomplished composer but rarely wrote songs, most of his compositions being instrumentals for his band. He also scored *Second Chorus* and received another Oscar nomination for his efforts.

Astaire's Danny O'Neill is in hot pursuit of Ellen Miller (Paulette Goddard) as well as a place as a trumpet player in Shaw's band. The song is his self-deprecating proposal to her. He sings of all his "blunders," refers to himself as "a dope" and warns her that life with him will be a "merry-go-round." Johnny Mercer uses some clever rhymes ("horoscope"/"for a dope") and the song is very amusing.

The first rendition of the song is fairly brief and the band's playing of the melody fades into the background. Its really memorable performance occurs when Fred has somehow become a bearded and woolly-hatted trumpet player in a Cossack balalaika band. Goddard arrives at the restaurant where the band is playing and Fred, after demonstrating his abilities as a Cossack dancer, treats Paulette to an hilarious mock–Russian version of the song. It gets another brief reprise in the back of a taxi cab at the film's end and this time we know that Fred's proposal in song will be accepted.

Astaire had a minor hit with the song and Artie Shaw also recorded it, with a vocal supplied by Anita Boyer.

Only Forever

from *Rhythm on the River*
Music: James Monaco
Lyrics: Johnny Burke

Rhythm on the River is an attractive musical, wittily scripted, with a strong cast headed by Bing Crosby, Mary Martin, Basil Rathbone and Oscar Levant.

Mary Martin had become a star on Broadway almost entirely on the strength of her sensational rendition of "My Heart Belongs to Daddy" in Cole Porter's *Leave It to Me.* Paramount signed her and *Rhythm on the River* was her third film for the studio. She never quite achieved Hollywood stardom but she went on to great success on the stage, creating a number of notable roles in Broadway shows, including *South Pacific* and *The Sound of Music.*

In *Rhythm on the River,* Basil Rathbone plays Oliver Courtney, a successful songwriter who has run out of inspiration; he hires Bob Sommers (Bing Crosby) to write the music and Cherry Lane (Mary Martin) to write the lyrics for him. Bing and Mary are unaware of the other's involvement and Rathbone is passing the songs off as his own.

We first hear "Only Forever" as Bing is in the act of composing the melody in his "office," which is on an old ferryboat. Mary overhears him and starts to come up with some words to go with his tune. She joins Bing, gives him what she has written and he sings it at the piano. They are both so pleased with it that they vow not to give it to Rathbone but to keep it as "their song."

The song consists of three choruses, each with the same pattern: In each chorus, the singer asks a question—a variation on "how long will my love for you last?"—in the first two lines. He then answers himself in the third with "Only Forever," the title of the song. The bridge varies the pattern and has the neat rhyme of "beckoned" with "second," a feature that Bing's character says he likes too.

The melody is very appealing and Bing gives the song his usual relaxed, almost conversational treatment, lending the unassuming lyric real warmth and charm.

At the end of the movie, when the song is a big hit and Bing and Mary are revealed as the true songwriters, they sing "Only Forever" again, as a duet. The scene is a sparkling New York nightclub where Mary is appearing with John Scott Trotter and His Orchestra. Their performance is broadcast to the whole country via the radio, rounding off the film with a triumphant conclusion.

Bing's recording of "Only Forever" topped the American hit parade for nine weeks. The Tommy Dorsey band, with a vocal by Alan Starr, also put out a successful version.

Our Love Affair

from *Strike Up the Band*
Music: Roger Edens
Lyrics: Georgie Stoll

Just who wrote the lyrics for "Our Love Affair" is a mystery. The Academy of Motion Picture Arts and Sciences cites Georgie Stoll, the musical director of *Strike Up the Band*, as lyricist, but almost all other sources credit Arthur Freed, the picture's producer. Freed was a well-known songwriter and Stoll has no other credits as a lyricist. At ASCAP (The American Society of Authors, Composers and Publishers), Stoll is listed as a composer only.

Babes in Arms had been a smash hit for Judy Garland and Mickey Rooney and MGM wanted another vehicle for their successful team. The studio chose *Strike Up the Band*. This brilliant stage musical, with songs by George and Ira Gershwin, had failed in 1927 without even reaching Broadway. It was a bitterly satirical attack on war profiteering and perhaps ahead of its time. The show was more successful in 1930 in a version where the satire was toned down; it was also sweetened by the addition of two superb romantic ballads, "I've Got a Crush On You" and "Soon."

The rousing, Sousa-like march "Strike Up the Band" was retained from the original show. Ira Gershwin intended to mock jingoistic attitudes with his lyric but the satire escaped Louis B. Mayer, head of MGM, and rumor has it that he bought the movie rights solely because he loved what he felt was the all–American patriotism of the number. In the film, this song is all that remains of the stage production. Mayer threw out the original script and *Strike Up the Band* became a musical about a group of high-spirited kids putting on a show, the formula that Hollywood repeated ad nauseam.

The new songs for the MGM version of *Strike Up the Band* had music by Roger Edens, while most had lyrics by Arthur Freed. But it was "Our Love Affair" that received an Oscar nomination for Best Song.

When Jimmy Connors (Mickey Rooney) starts to talk of "Our Love Affair," Mary Holden (Judy Garland) thinks that he has at long last noticed how she feels about him. But she is disappointed when she finds he is talking of "a dynamite love song, just made to order for you." He sits down at the piano and explains to her how he will orchestrate it for the band. She then joins him and sings the words. The scene is full of piquancy as Judy is using the song to express her feelings for Mickey, but the would-be showman is oblivious to all but his musical ideas.

The verse of the song, rarely heard outside of the film, describes the beginning of an adolescent romance. Then the chorus begins, and though the melody is very attractive, the lyric is rather ordinary, with utterly predictable lines, though there is a witty reference to other famous lovers, including Scarlett O'Hara and Rhett Butler from *Gone with the Wind*—the film had been released the year before *Strike Up the Band*.

It was undoubtedly the brilliant staging of the number by director Busby Berkeley that resulted in the Oscar nomination. The idea for it was suggested to him by Vincente Minnelli, who had joined MGM earlier in the year but as yet had been given nothing to do. Arthur Freed told him one day at lunch that Berkeley was having trouble thinking of a way of presenting "Our Love Affair." Minnelli came up with a brilliant idea when he caught sight of a bowl of fruit and he suggested it as the basis for the scene. After Judy has finished the song, Mickey starts to speculate and imagines he is conducting the band at Carnegie Hall.

He uses fruit and other items of food to represent the sections of the orchestra—a bunch of grapes becomes the conductor, a pear is a violinist, grapefruits are the timpani, two slices of chocolate cake are grand pianos, and so on.

As he speaks, the music plays and each piece of fruit is animated, coming to life as a musician and his instrument. The very clever animation for the sequence is by George Pal and it took 17 takes to get it right.

When the sequence is finished, Mickey leaves Judy's house; as he rushes off, the still frustrated Judy repeats the last line of the song in a voice heavy with irony. Then a part of the song is heard again in the grand finale to the film: Mickey and Judy are sitting under a blossom-laden apple tree, now very much in love and duetting on the song to the accompaniment of harps and sweetly singing girls.

The song has become something of a standard in an abbreviated form, missing all reference to the youth of the two participants in "our love affair." After the film's release, the bands of both Tommy Dorsey (vocal by Frank Sinatra) and Glenn Miller (vocal by Ray Eberle) made successful recordings of the song but the most popular was the one by Dick Jurgens and His Orchestra, with vocalist Harry Cool.

Waltzing in the Clouds

from *Spring Parade*
Music: Robert Stolz
Lyrics: Gus Kahn

Spring Parade was a throwback to the style of frothy Viennese operettas that Broadway had outgrown years before. In the movie, Deanna Durbin plays Ilonka Tolnay, an Austrian peasant girl who travels to Vienna on a hay wagon and there falls in love with Harry Marten, a dashing young army corporal, played by Robert Cummings. He has aspirations to become a great composer and she inspires him to write waltzes in the Viennese style.

"Waltzing in the Clouds" is one; Deanna sings the schmaltzy song as an expression of her delirium at winning his attentions. The scene is an outdoors cafe in Vienna where the military band is playing. Cummings and his fellow army musicians strike up the tune and Deanna begins to sing. When everyone is waltzing and whirling away, the handsome couple joins in.

The song has a lilting Viennese melody but the lyric is fairly predictable and describes the lovers up in the clouds, in a private world of their own.

A more enjoyable and less pretentious song in *Spring Parade* was the amusing "It's Foolish But It's Fun," perhaps more deserving of an Oscar nomination for Robert Stolz and Gus Kahn. The film also collected Oscar nominations for its score, the cinematography and sound recording.

Who Am I?

from *Hit Parade of 1941*
Music: Jule Styne
Lyrics: Walter Bullock

Hit Parade of 1941, an ordinary musical with a radio station for a setting, stars Frances Langford, Ann Miller and Kenny Baker. It collected two Oscar nominations, one for the song and the other for Cy Feuer's score.

The owner of the station has ambitions to get in on the ground floor of the new medium of television and one of his sponsors persuades him to let his daughter Annabelle (Ann Miller) sing and dance on the first broadcast. Unfortunately her singing voice is little better than a painful screech and Pat Abbott (Frances Langford) the station owner's girlfriend, has to dub for her. Pat begins to sing "Who Am I?" but there is a technical hitch and Annabelle's voice goes to air.

The scene is very funny as we switch from the dulcet tones of Frances Langford to the discordant shrieks of Ann Miller. Perhaps the humor does a disservice to what is a very pleasant song. It has a gentle, wistful melody and the lyric is a neatly constructed series of unanswered questions, simply but effectively expressed. Only one word in the entire song has more than one syllable. Full of self-doubt, the singer asks if she is worthy of the object of her affections.

Walter Bullock seems to favor the device of constructing a lyric from a series of questions—he employed it in his other Oscar nominated song "When Did You Leave Heaven?"

Bullock and Styne's other songs for *Hit Parade of 1941* include one entitled "In the Cool of the Evening," not to be confused with the Hoagy Carmichael-Johnny Mercer number from *Here Comes the Groom*.

Frances Langford recorded "Who Am I?" as did the Count Basie band, vocal by Helen Hume. There have been few recordings since 1940 but jazz singer–pianist Shirley Horn revived the song in beautiful style on her 1963 album *Loads of Love*.

And the Winner Is...

When You Wish Upon a Star

from *Pinocchio*
Music: Leigh Harline
Lyrics: Ned Washington

The rather banal words concerning dreams coming true in "When You Wish Upon a Star" are accompanied by a sugary melody over the opening credits of *Pinocchio*. Cliff Edwards' high-pitched, rather plaintive delivery of the song is disarming, in spite of the accompaniment of the Disney studio's celestial choir.

Edwards is the voice of Jiminy Cricket, one of Disney's most inspired creations. Animator Ward Kimball drew him but it was Walt Disney's idea to develop him and make Jiminy the co-star of the film. His presence and down-to-earth narration prevent the film from becoming unduly sentimental.

As the opening credits and the song end, we see Jiminy Cricket sitting on a bookshelf near a book entitled *Pinocchio*. He speaks directly to the audience and refers to the song's message, that a wish upon a star can come true. He admits that this is a difficult claim to swallow but he is going to tell us of the startling experience that caused him to alter his opinion. He opens the book and begins the story of *Pinocchio*.

The song's melody is used at various key points in the story, most notably when Pinocchio's wish has come true and he becomes a real boy. The two songwriters, with Paul Smith, also won the Oscar for their scoring of Pinocchio.

Cliff Edwards was known as "Ukulele Ike" and he appeared in more than a hundred films as well as on Broadway and in vaudeville. He is chiefly remem-

Pinocchio with Jiminy Cricket in a scene from *Pinocchio* (Disney, 1941).

bered now for his role as Jiminy Cricket and for introducing the song "Sin-gin' in the Rain" in *Hollywood Revue of 1929*. He was also the voice of Jim Crow in Disney's *Dumbo*.

Edwards' "When You Wish Upon a Star" recording was popular but it was eclipsed in the charts of 1940 by Glenn Miller's, which had a vocal by Ray Eberle. Kate Smith's version was also popular in the early 1940s. There have been many other recordings since, including one by vocal group Dion and the Belmonts, who revived the song in 1960. In 1977, composer John Williams incorporated "When You Wish Upon a Star" into his soundtrack score for *Close Encounters of the Third Kind*. Ringo Starr sang it on his 1988 album *Stay Awake*.

1941

After the bombing of Pearl Harbor and America's entry into the war, the Academy thought it politic to hold a less ostentatious awards ceremony, with a modest dinner rather than the usual banquet. The female guests were encouraged to dress conservatively and to make donations to the Red Cross with the money saved. The dinner was held once again at the Los Angeles Biltmore Hotel and Bob Hope was the emcee for the evening. Buddy DeSylva again presented the Oscar for Best Song. Those in the know considered that only "Blues in the Night" or "Chattanooga Choo Choo" could possibly win. As in 1937, film extras were able to vote for Best Song and they were once again blamed when the "wrong" song won.

The Nominations

Frank Churchill and Ned Washington for "Baby Mine" from *Dumbo* (Walt Disney)

Gene Autry and Fred Rose for "Be Honest with Me" from *Ridin' on a Rainbow* (Republic)

Harold Arlen and Johnny Mercer for "Blues in the Night" from *Blues in the Night* (Warner)

Hugh Prince and Don Raye for "Boogie Woogie Bugle Boy" from *Buck Privates* (Universal)

Harry Warren and Mack Gordon for "Chattanooga Choo Choo" from *Sun Valley Serenade* (Fox)

Louis Alter and Frank Loesser for "Dolores" from *Las Vegas Nights* (Paramount)

Jerome Kern and Oscar Hammerstein II for "The Last Time I Saw Paris" from *Lady Be Good* (MGM)

Lloyd B. Norlin for "Out of the Silence" from *All-American Co-ed* (Hal Roach)

Cole Porter for "Since I Kissed My Baby Goodbye" from *You'll Never Get Rich* (Columbia)

Baby Mine

from *Dumbo*
Music: Frank Churchill
Lyrics: Ned Washington

Ned Washington, with composer Leigh Harline, won the 1940 Best Song Oscar for the plaintive "When You Wish Upon a Star"; he was nominated for another song from a Disney animated feature in 1941. The picture was *Dumbo* and the song was "Baby Mine."

A clever feature of *Dumbo* is that most of the story is told visually. Dumbo himself never speaks and the only words his mother, Mrs. Jumbo, addresses to him are in "Baby Mine." Betty Noyce dubs her voice for this.

Mrs. Jumbo prepares to give baby Dumbo a bath in *Dumbo* (Disney, 1941).

"Baby Mine" is a gentle, comforting cradlesong and it follows a scene that could disturb a child audience: When baby Dumbo is jeered at and taunted by a crowd of cruel people because of his large ears, Mrs. Jumbo rushes to his rescue; the circus boss thinks she has gone berserk and she is dragged away in chains and leg irons to be locked up. Timothy Mouse takes a tear-stained Dumbo to see his mother that night and she puts her trunk through the grill in her prison door, caresses her baby and sings "Baby Mine." The simple, unpretentious words are the kind that any mother would use to comfort a young child and the melody has a gently rocking rhythm. Dumbo is comforted—and so are the children viewing the film.

As Mrs. Jumbo sings, we see the other animal mothers of the circus nursing their own babies, including Mother Hippo and her baby, sleeping underwater and sending bubbles to the surface as they gently snore.

Frank Churchill received his second and last Oscar nomination in 1942 for "Love Is a Song" from *Bambi*, written with Larry Morey. He was also nominated for his score, along with Oliver Wallace. He died shortly after working on *Bambi*, at the age of 40.

"Baby Mine" was not an outstanding success away from its film context but recordings by the Les Brown band (vocal by Betty Bonney) and Jane Froman achieved some popularity.

Steven Spielberg used "Baby Mine" in his 1979 movie *1941* where Robert Stack plays a macho general crying buckets as he watches the scene in *Dumbo*.

Be Honest with Me

from *Ridin' on a Rainbow*
Music and Lyrics: Gene Autry and Fred Rose

Gene Autry's only claim to fame as far as the Oscars are concerned is "Be Honest with Me," the song he wrote with Fred Rose for his 1941 picture *Ridin' on a Rainbow*. But Autry was the first actor to appear in singing Westerns and his popularity was such that he was three times voted Top Western Star, and he is the only cowboy actor to make the overall box office top ten. Riding his famous horse Champion, he churned out more than a hundred westerns, mostly for the Republic studios. He was already a singing star before he broke into films and "That Silver-Haired Daddy of Mine" was the first of his million-selling recordings. His biggest hit was his 1949 version of "Rudolf the Red-Nosed Reindeer," which remains the second most popular Christmas song of all time, after "White Christmas."

In spite of this success, most of his films are forgotten, except by those with nostalgic memories of Saturday matinees for children. In *Ridin' on a Rainbow*, Gene has lost all his money in a bank robbery. He tries to track down the thieves and along the way meets Patsy Evans, a teenage singer from a showboat, played by Mary Lee. Mary's father, a clown on the showboat, was involved in the robbery.

The title song is the best in the film but it was "Be Honest with Me" that was nominated for the Oscar. Gene sings it on the stage of the showboat. The song is the plea of a separated lover, asking his sweetheart to be true to him until he returns home. The melody is simplistic and it would be hard to find a flatter, more cliché-ridden lyric.

Autry used his award-nominated song in two more of his films, and it was also sung by Tex Ritter in *Flaming Bullets* and by Jimmy Wakely in *Strictly in the Groove* (1942). Wakely recorded the song but the best-selling recording of it was by Bing Crosby. Autry's own sold well, too, as did a version by Freddy Martin and His Orchestra (vocal by Clyde Rogers and Eddie Stone).

Blues in the Night

from *Blues in the Night*
Music: Harold Arlen
Lyrics: Johnny Mercer

A great injustice was done when the Gershwins' "They Can't Take That Away from Me" was passed over for the 1937 Best Song Oscar. One of equal magnitude occurred when "Blues in the Night," one of the greatest examples of American songwriting, did not receive the 1941 award.

The producers of Warner Bros.' *Hot Nocturne* wanted a song for a specific spot in their new picture, in which a group of jazz musicians in a St. Louis jail hear a fellow prisoner singing the blues. The African-American actor and singer William Gillespie, who had a magnificent baritone voice, would play this lonely prisoner. The script revealed the weight that would be put on the song: The jail is a segregated one and the white musicians, arrested after a brawl in a bar, are in one cell, opposite a group of black prisoners in another. The jazzmen discuss the kind of music they would like to play and Richard Whorf, as Jigger Pine, the pianist and leader of the group, talks of "the blues, real blues—the kind that comes out of people, real people, their hopes, their dreams, what they've got, what they want—the whole U.S.A. in one chorus." In the other cell, a black prisoner also talks about the blues: "Comes night you start to thinkin,' then the miseries get ya." The song has to express all of this.

Harold Arlen was asked to write the music and Johnny Mercer the lyric, their first collaboration, and the project looked promising. The two men shared a common interest in jazz and the blues and the studio told them that the movie would be a gritty depiction of the itinerant lives of jazz musicians. The scene in which Gillespie was to sing particularly intrigued them.

For this spot, Arlen wrote one of his strongest pieces of music, an authentic folk blues full of sad loneliness and "the miseries" mentioned in the script. Now Johnny Mercer began work on the lyric. Born in Savannah, Georgia, he had absorbed all the rhythms of Southern speech and its colorful idioms. He listened to Arlen's music and heard the evocative sound of a train in it—that "lonesome whistle."

The earthy flavor of the South is evident in the opening lines, with its use of the phrase "done tol' me" and the reference to "knee pants." Yet this superb opening was not Mercer's original one: At first he began with the phrase "I'm heavy in my heart." Arlen felt that this was rather sentimental and not adequate to carry the emotional force of his melody. But he loved the line with which the song now begins and suggested the change—and Mercer accepted it readily.

The singer is recalling the sound of his mother's voice, warning him about the dangers of sweet-talking women, and the heavy fall on to the word "son" brings the stern sound of it to the listener's mind also. The evocative sounds of the night—the rain, a train in the distance—are there too, echoing the singer's "blues in the night." That sad old mockingbird and the place names—Natchez, Mobile, Memphis—place the song firmly in the South. The lyric says that the mockingbird knows things are wrong and the dissonant near-rhyme of "whistle" with "trestle" adds to the unease of the singer's situation.

Throughout "Blues in the Night," Mercer's words fit perfectly with Arlen's music. This masterpiece impressed everyone connected with *Hot Nocturne* so greatly that the title of the film was immediately changed to *Blues in the Night* and they made sure that the song was used a number of times in the film to give it maximum exposure. It is played with a dramatic flourish over the opening credits and, as well as being sung early in the picture by Gillespie in his prison cell, a number of instrumental versions crop up throughout the movie, particularly at moments of dramatic tension. Unfortunately the finished picture does not live up to its early promise and, after the powerful scene in which "Blues in the Night" first occurs, it disintegrates into weak melodrama and cliché.

In spite of its power, "Blues in the Night" is not sung in full but it was an immediate hit. Jimmy Lunceford appeared in the film with his band and he must have been deeply impressed by "Blues in the Night"—his recording, a double-sided version with a vocal by Willie Smith, was the first to be released. It sold well but it was overtaken by Dinah Shore's version; the first of her million-sellers, it reached number four in the U.S. hit parade. (Mercer adapted his lyric so that a female could sing "when I was in pigtails..." instead of "knee-pants.") Woody Herman's recording did even better than Dinah Shore's and it topped the American charts in 1942; the vocal was by Woody himself. In 1943, John Garfield presented a dramatic version of "Blues in the Night" in *Thank Your Lucky Stars*.

In his book *American Popular Song*, songwriter and music critic Alec

Wilder calls "Blues in the Night" a "landmark in the evolution of American popular music, lyrically as well as musically." The song has become one of the great standards but in spite of its brilliance it failed to win the Best Song Oscar.

Boogie Woogie Bugle Boy

from *Buck Privates*
Music: Hugh Prince
Lyrics: Don Raye

Buck Privates was not Abbott and Costello's first picture but it was the one that launched them to stardom. Universal billed the pair below Alan Curtis and Lee Bowman but it was the two comedians whom moviegoers flocked to see. *Buck Privates* was the studio's top money earner in 1941, grossing almost five million dollars, a huge amount for the time. Bud and Lou rocketed to number three in America's popularity ratings, beaten only by Mickey Rooney and Clark Gable.

The Andrews Sisters (left to right: Patty, LaVerne and Maxene) with Lou Costello and Bud Abbott in *Buck Privates* (Universal, 1941).

In *Buck Privates,* Abbott and Costello play Slicker Smith and Herbie Brown, a couple of bumblers who enlist in the Army by mistake when they are trying to elude the police. But once in uniform they have a whale of a time, making life in the Army look very rosy (the picture was excellent for recruiting purposes). The Andrews Sisters—playing themselves—get into uniform and do their bit by singing four songs, including "Boogie Woogie Bugle Boy" and "Apple Blossom Time." Their career was also boosted by the great success of the film and ensured regular work for them at Universal. Charles Previn, the father of Andre, was nominated for an Oscar for his scoring of *Buck Privates.*

"Boogie Woogie Bugle Boy" is also excellent recruiting propaganda, showing how caring and understanding Army officers can be. It tells the story of a famous trumpeter from Chicago who is enlisted into "Company B" so that he can play the bugle for Uncle Sam. He is cast down because he can no longer improvise on his instrument, but his sympathetic captain provides him with a backing band so that he can blow "Reveille" in boogie rhythm. The tune has the sound of a bugle call in it and the long lines of the lyric, full of short and sharp words, fit it effectively.

The Andrews Sisters give the song a wonderfully energetic yet vocally precise performance, complete with one of their trademark dance routines. They were one of the first vocal groups to introduce choreography into their act. Patty Andrews' wild and exuberant solo is especially memorable. An excerpt of their performance was featured in the 1943 film *Swingtime Johnny* and as part of a medley of their hits in *Follow the Boys* (1944). Walter Lantz, the creator of Woody Woodpecker, used the song for one of his popular *Cartune Specials* in 1941.

Bette Midler paid the Sisters a tribute by reviving "Boogie Woogie Bugle Boy" in 1972; the song became a high spot of her stage act for a while. Because of her revival of the song, the Andrews Sisters' version apperared on the U.S. charts for the second time, more than 30 years after its first run. During one of Bette Midler's concerts, Maxene Andrews showed the Sisters' gratitude by presenting her with a bugle on stage.

Chattanooga Choo Choo

from *Sun Valley Serenade*
Music: Harry Warren
Lyrics: Mack Gordon

Though the first million-selling record was Enrico Caruso's "Vesti La Giubba" ("On with the Motley"), made in 1903, the first actual gold disc ever awarded for sales of a million went to Glenn Miller and His Orchestra for "Chattanooga Choo Choo." Chattanooga is a city along the Tennessee River and the people there were so delighted with the publicity that they made the songwriters honorary citizens.

The novelty song was written for *Sun Valley Serenade* in which the Glenn Miller band appeared with Sonja Henie, the famous Norwegian ice-skating gold medalist. John Payne—who was 20th Century-Fox's leading musical star in the 1940s, even though his voice was unremarkable—is Sonja Henie's leading man in the film. He plays Ted Scott, the band's pianist.

The film was successful at the box office and collected Oscar nominations for Emil Newman's score and Edward Cronjager's cinematography.

The Oscar-nominated song is performed first by the band, with vocals by Tex Beneke, Paula Kelly and The Modernaires. The song describes the whole course of the train journey: Our passenger leaves Pennsylvania station around a quarter to four, has dinner aboard while passing through Baltimore, and breakfast in Carolina ("nothing could be finer"), before arriving in Chattanooga, Tennessee, where he is met at the station by that "certain party."

Harry Warren's tune has superb rhythmic drive, suggesting the train's motion; Mack Gordon's clever lyric is full of neatly alliterative phrases and words that echo the chugging sounds of the locomotive.

After the Glenn Miller band and singers have rehearsed "Chattanooga Choo Choo," a big production number follows. The staging is by Hermes Pan, best known as Fred Astaire's dance director. The famous choo choo appears on

The Nicholas Brothers in *Sun Valley Serenade* (Fox, 1941).

the set, and then Dorothy Dandridge sings and dances with the Nicholas Brothers—a brilliant singing and tap-dancing climax, though perhaps it appears a little Uncle Tom-ish by today's standards. This aspect is reflected in the second line of the song where the singer is clearly addressing a black shoeshine "boy."

In a 1998 interview for the *Lindy Week Review*, Fayard Nicholas makes some interesting comments on *Sun Valley Serenade's* "Chattanooga Choo Choo" sequence. He reflects that the work of African-American artists was often removed when films were shown in the Southern states, their routines often quite separate from the films in which they are set so that they could be taken out easily. For instance, in *Sun Valley Serenade*, all the main characters are involved in the band rehearsal for "Chattanooga Choo Choo" at the ski resort. All of them are dressed informally in ski clothes. The band plays the number and the Nicholas Brothers' routine begins. The setting is quite different for the Brothers, and they are dressed in formal summer outfits: blazers, straw boaters, bow ties and white spats. They perform their dance, then the action returns to the ski resort—with no explanation. The full version of this interview can be found on the Internet at www.jitterbuzz.com/nicho.html.

Another incident Fayard Nicholas recalled from the *Sun Valley Serenade* set was when Glenn Miller called the Brothers over to hear a new tune. Chummy MacGregor played it on the piano and Fayard asked Glenn Miller what he thought of it. Miller replied, "It stinks!" The tune was "Chattanooga Choo Choo."

Miller's recording of it was No. 1 in the American charts for nine weeks and on the bestseller list for 23 weeks. It was so inescapable for a time that Woody Herman felt moved to put the famous train into reverse by recording a parody entitled "Ooch Ooch A Goon Attach (The Backward Song)." In 1963, Nashville country pianist Floyd Cramer cut a version that reached No 36 in the American charts—it was his last hit. In 1978, a group rejoicing in the Millerish name of Tuxedo Junction recorded it disco-style.

"Chattanooga Choo Choo" turns up again briefly at the beginning of Glenn Miller's next film *Orchestra Wives,* and also in the 1942 film *Springtime in the Rockies*, where it is sung in Brazilian Portuguese by Carmen Miranda. In 1949, Dan Dailey sang it in *You're My Everything*, and of course it is given a great performance by Frances Langford and The Modernaires in *The Glenn Miller Story* (1954).

Dolores

from *Las Vegas Nights*
Music: Louis Alter
Lyrics: Frank Loesser

Actor-comedian Bert Wheeler was part of one of America's most successful comic teams, Wheeler and Woolsey: Robert Woolsey played the fast-talking wisecracker, while Wheeler was the sad-faced straight man. They appeared together first in the 1927 Broadway production of *Rio Rita* and repeated their roles in the 1929 film version where their famous slapping routine was a showstopper. (The 1942 remake had Abbott and Costello in the Wheeler and Woolsey parts.)

After the success of *Rio Rita* they made nearly 20 more films together until Robert Woolsey died in 1938. Wheeler continued to work on his own and in 1941 appeared in the film *Las Vegas Nights*, where he sang "Dolores." He was accompanied with a Latin American rhythm by the Tommy Dorsey band.

Wheeler plays Stu Grant, a vaudevillian who lands in Las Vegas with three girl singers. It is here that Wheeler sings "Dolores" in a nightclub. He sings about a trip he has made to a Mexican border town where all the local men are besotted with a lady named Dolores. He too falls for her, and dreams of making her his own.

It's a catchy song and the neat use of internal rhymes makes it very appealing. Unfortunately for Wheeler, *Las Vegas Nights* does little to demonstrate his solo talents, and his performance of the song does not do it justice.

The film was really a showcase for Tommy Dorsey and His Orchestra, attempting to emulate Glenn Miller's success in *Sun Valley Serenade*. The only memorable feature of the film is that Frank Sinatra made his first feature film appearance, albeit in a non-speaking role. At the time it was made, he was a singer with the Tommy Dorsey band and he sang "I'll Never Smile Again." Released in 1940, this was Sinatra's first major hit, number one on the *Billboard* charts for twelve consecutive weeks. Sinatra and Dorsey must have seen the merits of "Dolores" in spite of Wheeler's weak rendition of it as they recorded the song with the Pied Pipers soon after the film was completed. It was quite popular for a while but Bing Crosby's version outsold it.

"Dolores" gave Frank Loesser his first Oscar nomination. In *A Most Remarkable Fella*, her biography of her father, Susan Loesser reveals that after he failed to win the gold statuette, he sent the certificate of nomination back home to his wife in New York, adding a note: "Always a bridesmaid."

"Dolores" turns up again in the Macdonald Carey film *Dr. Broadway* (1942) and in *Saigon* (1948), which starred Alan Ladd and Veronica Lake.

Out of the Silence

from *All-American Co-ed*
Music and Lyrics: Lloyd B. Norlin

College movies were a popular genre for a while, and one of them, *All American Co-ed*, won two Oscar nominations: Edward Ward for Scoring of a Musical Film and Lloyd B. Norlin for Best Song, "Out of the Silence." This was one of the four songs featured in the film; Charles Newman and Walter G. Samuels wrote the other three.

The film runs for less than 50 minutes and the plot has Bob Sheppard— played by Johnny Downs, remembered as one of the original "Our Gang" kids—dressing up as a girl and trying to gain entrance to a ladies' horticultural college, known as "Quinceton." The ladies are referred to as the "Marr Brynn" girls. The film is relentlessly cheerful and its only reflective moments occur when Frances Langford and a group of her fellow students sing "Out of the Silence."

It is dusk on a balmy summer's evening and the ladies are all posed artificially and rather uncomfortably on the college lawns. Enter Johnny Downs. Having fallen in love with Virginia, Frances Langford's character, he has given up his girl's attire and is about to make his escape from the college when he sees Frances and the Marr Brynn girls on the lawn. He hides in a bell tower so that he can observe without being seen. He overbalances, grabs the bell rope to steady himself, then realizes that if he lets go the bell will ring and he will be found out. He is forced to hang onto the rope until the song ends and any seriousness in it is dissipated by the shots of Downs' predicament.

Langford is dressed in slinky silk while the rest of the girls are artistically posed in long, flowing gowns. They all begin the song, then Langford takes it up alone. She sings to a lover, beseeching him to come "out of the silence" and clasp her in his arms; just the sound of his voice will transport her to Heaven. As she sings, she gazes rapturously into the middle distance.

The song is addressed to no one in particular and the words are rather awkward, verging on the pretentious; the melody is no more distinguished. It is difficult to understand why the song received an Oscar nomination— certainly no one thought it worth recording, not even Frances Langford herself.

Since I Kissed My Baby Goodbye

from *You'll Never Get Rich*
Music and Lyrics: Cole Porter

Cole Porter was disparaging about his own songs for *You'll Never Get Rich* but he felt that the film was even worse. Nevertheless, it was a box office success, receiving reasonable reviews, and "Since I Kissed My Baby Goodbye" was nominated for Best Song. Morris Stoloff was also nominated for his scoring of the picture.

Fred Astaire and Rita Hayworth were the main players; Fred thought Rita a great dancer and the film established her star status with Columbia. Fred plays Robert Curtis, a Broadway choreographer and dancer who is drafted into the Army. The song is sung in the film by the Delta Rhythm

Boys, all of whom happen to be together in the guardhouse at the same time as Fred.

Rita, as showgirl Sheila Winthrop, arrives at the Army base, hears the song emanating from the guardhouse and walks towards that building. Fred is lying on his bunk and he starts to clap in time to the music being played by the Delta Rhythm Boys. He leaps to his feet and begins to dance, the sound of his tapping shoes on the wooden floor almost drowning out the song. Rita arrives and as she talks with Fred, the Delta Rhythm Boys continue to play.

"Since I Kissed My Baby Goodbye" has no relationship to the plot, but it is a gentle, wistful piece expressing the loneliness of parted lovers and nostalgia for the sights and sounds of the South.

But Fred's dazzling and staccato dance steps on the wooden floor of the guardhouse overwhelm the quiet, poetic qualities of the song, and even when his dancing ends, his dialogue with Rita relegates the song to the background again. This offhand treatment suggests that the filmmakers had a low opinion of the song and therefore it is difficult to see why it was nominated.

Astaire, with the Delta Rhythm Boys, recorded "Since I Kissed My Baby Goodbye" as the B-side of another song from the film, "So Near and Yet So Far." Neither song nor any of the other numbers in the film became hits, though they didn't get much promotion via the radio, as there was a contract dispute at that time between ASCAP and the broadcasters. In those days, radio exposure was the most important means by which a song could be popularized.

Between 1941 and 1956, the Delta Rhythm Boys appeared in 15 films, more than any other vocal group of the time. But with the exception of *You'll Never Get Rich,* these movies were mostly obscure, low-budget affairs. The group is nevertheless remembered as pioneers of rhythm and blues and were very popular as a radio act and in live performances.

And the Winner Is…

The Last Time I Saw Paris

from *Lady Be Good*
Music: Jerome Kern
Lyrics: Oscar Hammerstein II

"Much publicity has attended this new Jerome Kern–Oscar Hammerstein song, the first number these two noted writers have ever penned that was not written for a musical comedy or picture score"—so said *Billboard*'s "The Record Buying Guide" for the week ending December 28, 1940. It had always been accepted in practice that the Best Song Oscar was for songs specially written for the screen and not for ones that had been introduced elsewhere. Therefore, *Billboard*'s statement would seem to indicate that "The Last

Time I Saw Paris" was ineligible for the Best Song Oscar. When the 1941 Academy Award went to the song, Jerome Kern said in public that he and Hammerstein had no entitlement to the Oscar. Hammerstein agreed and he and Kern singled out "Blues in the Night" as that year's best song—they felt that Johnny Mercer and Harold Arlen had been robbed.

But no statement actually appeared in the Academy's rulebook concerning the ineligibility of songs not expressly written for a film; therefore Jerome Kern, who was a member of the Academy with full voting rights, saw to it that the rules were changed. From then on, no song has been entitled to win an Academy Award unless specifically written for the film in which it appears.

Oscar Hammerstein wrote the lyrics as a poem on hearing that, on June 14, 1940, the Germans had captured France and marched into Paris. He felt, along with many others, that the beautiful city might be ruined forever now that it had fallen into barbaric hands. But Hammerstein expressed his remembrance of Paris past in rather trite and sentimental verse. The words are self-consciously poetic and the "I" of the song intrudes too much, as though the subject of the song is not Paris but the writer.

Hitherto, Kern had always insisted on writing the music first and then giving it to the lyricist to work on; this time he was prepared to change the rule when Hammerstein contacted him. He came up with a lovely, flowing melody, full of nostalgic sadness. His scoring included the use of car horns (a typically Parisian sound) to accompany the lines about taxi cabs. He borrowed the idea, according to Ira Gershwin, from brother George's "An American in Paris."

The sentimentality of the lyric and the bittersweet music of "The Last Time I Saw Paris" captured the mood of the times perfectly. People must have found the last lines of the song especially poignant, that determination to remember Paris as it was, no matter what the occupying forces might do to the city.

A sentimental song has an amazing power to crystallize feelings and express the emotion of a particular time and place. "The Last Time I Saw Paris" is a perfect example of this phenomenon and it had a staggering reception. It was first performed and recorded by Kate Smith, the large lady who had also brought Irving Berlin's "God Bless America" to public notice. Sophie Tucker and Hildegarde both had tremendous success with it, Jerome Kern himself supervising the latter's recording. Singers on both sides of the Atlantic queued up to make recordings; Tony Martin in America and Noël Coward in Britain did well with theirs. Sheet music sales were enormous.

MGM bought the film rights to the already highly successful song and looked around for a film to include it in. The studio had the rights to the Gershwin stage show *Lady, Be Good*, a success on Broadway in 1924. It had starred Fred Astaire and his sister Adele and now MGM considered reviving the Fred Astaire-Ginger Rogers partnership for the film version. That proved to be impossible and instead Eleanor Powell, Robert Young and Ann Sothern got the starring roles.

The film was typical of Hollywood's cavalier treatment of the Broadway shows it swallowed up: Only a small part of the original score remained, and the story was totally rewritten. Even the title was changed—it lost its comma and became *Lady Be Good.*

Here was the vehicle to cash in on the success of "The Last Time I Saw Paris" and into the film the song went. MGM saw immediately that an Academy Award nomination for it would be great publicity, and if it won, huge ticket sales were guaranteed.

In the film, Robert Young and Ann Sothern play Eddie Crane and Dixie Donegan, songwriters who have a very stormy marriage. They decide to part but not before they write their greatest hit together: "The Last Time I Saw Paris." The song is such a smash that their peers hold a testimonial dinner for them. In a tribute speech specially written for the film by Oscar Hammerstein, the song's publisher Max Milton (Reginald Owen) sums up the appeal of "The Last Time I Saw Paris":

> It isn't just the work of two songwriters. It's as if they had a hundred million collaborators—the Americans who feel in their hearts what Eddie and Dixie have written so beautifully in their song.

At the end of the speech, Ann sings the song with Young at the piano. As she sings, a montage of Parisian scenes—the street cafes, the avenues of trees—appear on a screen behind her.

The song was used again, sung by Dinah Shore in the 1946 homage to Jerome Kern *Till the Clouds Roll By.* The 1954 film *The Last Time I Saw Paris,* starring Elizabeth Taylor and Van Johnson, is not a musical but the Oscar-winning song is sung in French in a Parisian café and the melody is used extensively on the soundtrack. Bob Hope sings the song in *Paris Holiday* (1958).

1942

The number of nominated songs increased to ten for the 1942 Oscar. The awards ceremony took place during a banquet at the Ambassador Hotel, Los Angeles, hosted again by Bob Hope. An orchestra played all the nominated songs during the dinner and Bob had a ready-made joke about the guests eating the meat course while they listened to "Pig Foot Pete." Irving Berlin presented the Best Song Oscar and remarked, "I'm glad to present this award. I've known the fellow for a long time."

The Nominations

Ernesto Lecuona and Kim Gannon for "Always in My Heart" from *Always in My Heart* (Warner)

Jerome Kern and Johnny Mercer for "Dearly Beloved" from *You Were Never Lovelier* (Columbia)

Burton Lane and Ralph Freed for "How About You?" from *Babes on Broadway* (MGM)

Harry Warren and Mack Gordon for "I've Got a Gal in Kalamazoo" from *Orchestra Wives* (Fox)

Jule Styne and Sammy Cahn for "I've Heard That Song Before" from *Youth on Parade* (Republic)

Frank Churchill and Larry Morey for "Love Is a Song" from *Bambi* (Walt Disney)

Edward Ward, Chet Forrest and Bob Wright for "Pennies for Peppino" from *Flying With Music* (Hal Roach)

Gene de Paul and Don Raye for "Pig Foot Pete" from *Keep 'Em Flying* (Universal)

Harry Revel and Mort Greene for "When There's a Breeze on Lake Louise" from *The Mayor of 44th Street* (RKO)

Irving Berlin for "White Christmas" from *Holiday Inn* (Paramount)

Always in My Heart

from *Always in My Heart*
Music: Ernesto Lecuona
Lyrics: Kim Gannon

The music of "Always in My Heart" is rather florid but it was the sentiment in the lyric that captured the hearts of wartime audiences. By this time, the U.S. had entered the war and more and more servicemen were separated from their loved ones. Kim Gannon's lyric spoke for them as the singer declares that her love will reach out to her lover no matter where he is in the world. Every night they are together in her dreams.

The sentimental film in which it features has some excellent acting from Walter Huston as Mackenzie Scott, a freed convict returning home to find that his wife Marjorie (Kay Francis) has another man. And in case any servicemen were worried that Huston's predicament might mirror their own, the film has a suitably happy ending.

Huston's daughter Victoria is played by Gloria Warren and it is she who sings "Always in My Heart," to her screen father's piano accompaniment. The song is performed on a number of other occasions in the film, including a strange rendition by a group of mouth organists known as Borrah Minevitch and His Rascals.

Warner Bros. hoped to make a star of Gloria in competition with Deanna Durbin but the attempt failed; perhaps filmgoers had no need for yet another sweet young thing with an operatic voice. Kenny Baker made a very romantic recording of the song but the best seller was by Ray Eberle, singing with the Glenn Miller orchestra. His older brother Bob (who spelled the family surname Eberly) recorded it with the Jimmy Dorsey band.

Dearly Beloved

from *You Were Never Lovelier*
Music: Jerome Kern
Lyrics: Johnny Mercer

The lovely melody written by Jerome Kern for "Dearly Beloved" is played frequently on the soundtrack, and the title phrase is a central to the plot of *You Were Never Lovelier*. With such strong attention in the picture, it became one of the biggest hits of the year and an inevitable nomination for the Best Song Award. The film received two other Oscar nominations: Leigh Harline for his score and John Livadary for his sound recording.

The musical teamed Fred Astaire with one of his best dancing partners, Rita Hayworth. It was made to extend the success the pair had achieved in *You'll Never Get Rich*, but the slight similarities in the titles and the fact that

Rita Hayworth and Fred Astaire in *You Were Never Lovelier* (Columbia, 1942).

Astaire plays a character called Robert in both are the only link. Fred, as Robert Davis, is in Argentina to play the horses and when he loses his money he has to look for a dancing job.

The song's melody is played at various romantic points throughout the picture but it is first sung by Fred, accompanied by Xavier Cugat and his band, as a wedding song for Maria Acuna's (Rita Hayworth) older sister and her groom. Appropriately, the phrase "Dearly Beloved" is borrowed from the opening of the marriage service. For some years after the film, many couples asked for "Dearly Beloved" to be played at their wedding.

Rita later sings the song as she dreams of the anonymous suitor who daily sends her orchids and romantic verses addressed to his "dearly beloved" (Nan Wynn dubs her singing voice.) Johnny Mercer's lyric is suitably lush and full of celestial imagery of Heaven and angels. The context in which the song is used calls for a flowery, sentimental ballad and the lyric and music manage the task well. The rhyme of "clearly" and "dearly" in the first line of the verse, and "merely" with "dearly" at the end is effective and contrives a pleasing shape to the song.

Early in the movie, the father of the bride is keen for his other daughter, Maria, to marry but knows that she hasn't fallen in love since she was 15. Even then, the object of her starry-eyed passion was Lochinvar, the romantic hero of a song in Sir Walter Scott's *Marmion* who carries off the fair Ellen. Her father refers to him as a "silly knight on a white charger."

Adolphe Menjou—as father Eduardo Acuna—decides to thaw his daughter's coolness to her real suitors by anonymously sending her daily flowers and love notes, as though they are from a secret admirer. The ruse works and she is swept off her feet by the anonymous courtship; the otherworldly romanticism of the song "Dearly Beloved," with its heavenly images and references to angels, echoes this. Rita has always dreamed that Lochinvar will carry her off on his white steed, as he did the fair Ellen; she comes to believe that it is Fred Astaire is sending her the notes, that he is her Lochinvar.

After the obligatory complications, Fred decides that he can win Rita's hand only by doing what the young knight did: "put on his best suit of Sunday armor, ride up to her father's castle," sweep her off her feet and ride off with her. Unfortunately Fred isn't horseman enough and this "silly knight on a white charger" falls off with a great clattering of armour. Rita is still won over and laughs, "Lochinvar? Never heard of him!" She and Fred dance off together and the film ends.

"Dearly Beloved" actually aroused serious controversy: Music critics noticed a strong similarity between Kern's melody and the Love Duet from Puccini's *Madama Butterfly*. Puccini's compositions were still in copyright and a suit for plagiarism was theoretically possible. Kern was unruffled by the accusations and acknowledged that the melodies were similar—but only by sheer accident. He said that if he had intended to steal from Puccini, it would have been easy to disguise the theft and make it less noticeable.

Johnny Mercer recycled one idea in the lyric for "Dearly Beloved": The line "I'll be yours come shower or shine" is clearly the starting point for "Come Rain or Come Shine," a song he wrote with Harold Arlen in 1946 for the stage show *St. Louis Woman*.

The exposure the song had in *You Were Never Lovelier*, and perhaps the Kern plagiarism controversy, caused "Dearly Beloved" to overshadow a better song, one that has been more enduring: "I'm Old Fashioned." The dance sequence by Astaire and Hayworth that accompanies this song is very appealing. But at the time of the movie's release, "Dearly Beloved" was the bigger hit and it remained on *Your Hit Parade* for 17 weeks. The most popular recording was the one by Skip Nelson singing with the Glenn Miller orchestra, though Dinah Shore's version ran a close second.

How About You?

from *Babes on Broadway*
Music: Burton Lane
Lyrics: Ralph Freed

Babes on Broadway was yet another kids-putting-on-a-show vehicle for the team of Judy Garland and Mickey Rooney. Not quite as effective as its immediate predecessor *Babes in Arms*, it did have some very good songs including "How About You?," which has become a standard in the repertoire of many singers.

Judy Garland and Mickey Rooney sing "How About You?" in *Babes on Broadway* (MGM, 1941).

The setting for the song is the plain and ordinary apartment of Penny Morris (Judy Garland); she and Tommy Williams (Mickey Rooney) have only just met and when he asks her to sing for him, she sits at the piano and begins the rarely sung verse of "How About You?" This verse explains exactly what the song is about, that a relationship between a girl and a boy depends on having common interests. Then in the chorus Judy lists a few of her favorite things. The excellent lyric is simple and unpretentious and there are some appealing lines. The choice of words—the clipped rhyme of "chips" and "trips" and staccato consonants combine with the upbeat, swinging melody to produce a very pleasing, happy-go-lucky song.

The reference to Franklin Roosevelt later in the song has often been altered; some singers substituted Jimmy Durante's name, and then Frank Sinatra started to get a mention. In fact, Sinatra made one of the earliest and most popular recordings of the song, as band singer with Tommy Dorsey, and he revived it as the closing number on his classic album *Songs for Swingin' Lovers.*

In the film, "How About You?" has two parts that have rarely been recorded: in these, Judy and Mickey sing alternate lines concerning his liking for Jack Benny's jokes, while she mentions window shopping on Fifth Avenue, as well as banana splits and dining late at the Ritz. Then the last verse reflects the ambition Judy and Mickey have to make the big time on Broadway, their dreams of fame. These words are very relevant to the plot but are now usually omitted.

Director Busby Berkeley's staging of the song is highly inventive. Usually associated with huge production numbers on a large stage, here he is confined to a small, far from luxurious apartment. But he makes very resourceful use of the limited space and everyday objects as Judy and Mickey conclude the number by dancing all around and over the furniture.

I've Got a Gal in Kalamazoo

from *Orchestra Wives*
Music: Harry Warren
Lyrics: Mack Gordon

"I've Got a Gal in Kalamazoo" is another punchy, rhythmic number in the vein of "Chattanooga Choo Choo." Such was the success of *Sun Valley Serenade* that 20th Century–Fox wanted a follow-up: *Orchestra Wives* was that film. And to make a bridge between the two films, *Orchestra Wives* opens with the Glenn Miller band playing a short burst of "Chattanooga Choo Choo."

The plot involves Connie Ward (Ann Rutherford), a star-struck fan of Bill Abbot (George Montgomery) the trumpeter with the Miller band. All of her dreams come true when she marries him and joins the band's tour, but here she learns something of the trials and tribulations of life on the road as an orchestra wife. Also involved are Cesar Romero, playing the band's pianist, and Jackie Gleason as the bassist.

Both songs celebrate exotic-sounding destinations and have similar themes, about a young man catching the train home to meet his childhood sweetheart. "Kalamazoo" was almost as big a hit as "Chattanooga," in the U.S. charts for 18 weeks and number one for seven of those. It was the eighth of Glenn Miller's million-selling recordings.

Harry Warren said that he wrote the tune as a kind of exercise in rhythm with no thought of it ever becoming a full-fledged song. But Mack Gordon heard him playing it on the piano, started to chant the letters of the alphabet in time to the rhythm and the complete song soon evolved. The simple, spare words fit the tune perfectly and captured the imagination of audiences everywhere. The neat internal rhymes such as "gal" and the first syllable of "Kalamazoo," along with "boast" and "toast," lightly enhance the humorous sounds of it all.

The song provides a triumphant ending to the film. The band is playing the ballroom of the Glen Island Casino. After a short instrumental sec-

The Nicholas Brothers begin their dance routine to "I've Got a Gal in Kalamazoo" in *Orchestra Wives* (Fox, 1942).

tion, the vocalists for the number begin the song with a verse, the first two lines of which come from Marion Hutton and the Modernaires as they ask Tex Beneke about the progress of his new romance. Tex replies with enthusiasm, then launches into the familiar chorus, telling of his plans to return to his hometown to propose to that "real piperoo," the "sweetest gal in Kalamazoo." Next the Nicholas Brothers appear and they sing the song too, before going into an athletic and highly inventive dance routine.

The Michigan city of Kalamazoo was an inspired choice for the gal's residence: Even in America many people thought the songwriters had invented the exotic name. The name is derived from a Potawatomi Native American expression, "Kikalamazoo," meaning "the rapids at the river crossing," or "boiling water."

As a result of the popularity of the tune, one of the residents of the Michigan city, Sara Woolley, was selected to represent the "gal in Kalamazoo." Her picture and story were published in newspapers and she quickly became a celebrity. She received mail from her fans, including admiring servicemen, and made many public appearances to sell war bonds and to promote her city.

I've Heard That Song Before

from *Youth on Parade*
Music: Jule Styne
Lyrics: Sammy Cahn

Jule Styne and Sammy Cahn formed a most successful partnership and 15 of their songs reached the top of the U.S. charts. "I've Heard That Song Before" was the first they wrote together. It comes from a now obscure film entitled *Youth on Parade*, where Martha O'Driscoll (as Sally Carlyle) performs it with the Bob Crosby band; Margaret Whiting dubs her voice. The star is Ruth Terry, who plays a Broadway actress hired by some college students to deceive their psychology professor by posing as a model pupil.

At first, Styne was reluctant to work with Cahn, thinking that their songwriting styles were not suited. But Cy Feuer of Republic Pictures, the studio that had Styne under contract, insisted. Cahn, at that time out of work, was all for the new partnership. He wrote in his autobiography: *I Should Care: the Sammy Cahn Story*

> Would I do a picture with Jule Styne? The way I felt right then, I would do a picture with Hitler.... As a result I went out to Republic Pictures and met Jule Styne officially.... He went to the piano and played a complete melody. I listened and said: "Would you play it again, just a bit slower?" He played and I listened. I said again: "One more time, just a little bit slower." I then said, "I've heard that song before"—to which he said, bristling, "What the

hell are you, a tune detective?" No, I said, that wasn't a criticism, it was a title: "I've Heard That Song Before."

Cahn then completed a lyric, typical of his style—conversational, with no flowery imagery but the feel of real speech. The song describes the feelings of the singer as she hears a tune that brings back memories of a lost love affair, one she has tried to forget.

Though Cahn and Styne were eventually to form a successful partnership, immediately after writing the songs for *Youth on Parade* Styne went off to work with other lyricists. Cahn was hurt and, when talking of "I've Heard That Song Before" to fellow songwriter Kim Gannon, he said that he thought it was one of the best lyrics he had ever written. Gannon was quick to point out that Styne had told him that it was the worst he had ever heard.

But then Harry James recorded "I've Heard That Song Before" with vocalist Helen Forrest and it was a hit, one of the biggest of the year. Soon Jule was on the phone to Sammy suggesting that they ought to write some more songs together. Their highly successful partnership continued into the 1950s, picking up six more Best Song nominations and winning the Oscar once, with "Three Coins in the Fountain" in 1954.

Love Is a Song

from *Bambi*
Music: Frank Churchill
Lyrics: Larry Morey

Frank Churchill, the composer of "Baby Mine" from *Dumbo*, scored an Oscar nomination for another song from a Disney cartoon feature, *Bambi*. This time the lyric was by Larry Morey, the first of his two nominations. "Love Is a Song" is heard over the opening credits of the film, sung by an uncredited tenor and accompanied by one of Disney's heavenly choirs. They tell us that love is a never-ending song; life may be short but the music of love will last forever.

Then, as the credits end, the song continues as we see dawn in the misty forest; the scene is painted superbly in shades of grey. An owl is coming home after a night's hunting and the other animals awaken. They all gather around a mother deer who has just given birth to her fawn, Bambi. The animals pay their tribute to the new baby prince and, as the voices of the choir swell, we see the Great Prince of the Forest, Bambi's father, standing proudly on a rock.

Like much of Disney's work, the scene as well as the song tread a line between touching charm and sugary sentimentality. But there is no doubt about the effectiveness of the forest fire sequence, a scene that is full of thrills and edge-of-the-seat excitement.

Soon afterwards, a scene similar to the opening one occurs but this time the mother deer is Bambi's mate, Faline, giving birth to two fawns, the children of Prince Bambi. That heavenly choir is heard again and as their singing swells, the film closes with the Old Stag standing on the rock, this time accompanied by his son, the young Prince Bambi, the proud new father.

The song has an attractive melody and the lyric is unusual in that it avoids rhyme, though this is compensated with a strong rhythmic feeling to the words. *Bambi* also collected an Oscar nomination for the score by Frank Churchill and Edward Plumb, and for Sam Slyfield's sound recording.

Pennies for Peppino

from *Flying with Music*
Music: Edward Ward
Lyrics: Chet Forrest and Bob Wright

Flying with Music is a short (59 minutes) film that has little going for it. The stars, George Givot and Marjorie Woodworth, are barely remembered and the songs have all but disappeared from memory too. Givot sings "Pennies for Peppino" in the course of playing a man on the run from the law. He ends up in Florida where he becomes involved with a group of lovely ladies.

There have been no recordings of "Pennies for Peppino" or any of the other four songs Ward and Forrest wrote for the film: "If It's Love," "Rotana," "Caribbean Magic" and "Song of the Lagoon." The songs and the movie have disappeared almost without trace, despite its two Oscar nominations (the other was for Edward Ward's score). There is one 35mm preservation print of *Flying with Music* loaned to the Library of Congress by the Hal Roach Studios but it is not available to the public for viewing.

George Givot was born in Omaha but he built a career in vaudeville with his portrayal of a Greek migrant speaking broken English. His catchphrase "How ja like that?" became the title of one of his first short films. In 1949 he revived his Greek character for the TV series *Versatile Varieties*. His last screen role was as the voice of the Italian restaurateur in the Disney film *Lady and the Tramp*.

Pig Foot Pete

from *Keep 'Em Flying*
Music: Gene de Paul
Lyrics: Don Raye

The database maintained by the Academy of Motion Picture Arts and Science has this observation about "Pig Foot Pete":

This nomination is a mystery. Both the nominations list and the program from the Awards dinner list the song as being from *Hel-*

lzapoppin', a 1942 release for Awards purposes. The song does not appear in that film, but did appear in *Keep 'Em Flying*, a 1941 release from the same production company and studio, and was therefore ineligible for a 1942 nomination.

The conclusion drawn from this is that studio in question pulled a fast one on the Academy in its nomination of "Pig Foot Pete."

Gene de Paul and Don Raye wrote the songs for five of Abbott and Costello's 36 feature films and box office–wise *Keep 'Em Flying* was one of the comedians' most successful efforts. They had saluted the Army with *Buck Privates*, the Navy with *In the Navy* and now it was the turn of the U.S. Army Air Corps.

Bud and Lou play Blackie Benson and Heathcliff, the usual pair of incompetents, and they are involved with identical twins, Gloria and Barbara Phelps, both played by Martha Raye. It is she who performs the up-tempo, jazzy number "Pig Foot Pete," assisted by a virile chorus of men in uniform.

Just as "Boogie Woogie Bugle Boy" celebrated a musician, that famous trumpet man from Chicago, "Pig Foot Pete" concerns another musician, a celebrated pianist who hails from Kansas City. Pete plays boogie woogie, too, and his style is explosive, with "a cannon in his left hand and a rifle in his right." And he demands no money for his services—he's willing to plays all night for "pigs' feet and beer."

Martha Raye recorded the song, though Dolly Dawn's version fared a little better on the U.S. charts. There was also a record by Ella Mae Morse, singing with the Freddy Slack orchestra.

When There's a Breeze on Lake Louise

from *The Mayor of 44th Street*
Music: Harry Revel
Lyrics: Mort Greene

Harry Revel worked with Mort Greene on four 1942 films, one of them being *The Mayor of 44th Street* in which their Oscar-nominated song "When There's a Breeze on Lake Louise" features. The film stars George Murphy and Anne Shirley, and the music is supplied by Freddy Martin and His Orchestra. The melodramatic plot revolves around a gang of delinquents who demand protection money from nightclub musicians. Joan Merrill, as Vicky Lane, a vocalist with Freddy Martin and His Orchestra, sings the song and it has no relevance to the plot, being just a dance band number.

"When There's a Breeze on Lake Louise" is reminiscent of Maurice Chevalier's signature song "Louise," which also makes great play with the words "breeze" and "Louise." The song as heard in the film has only eight lines and two of them, the first and last, repeat the title. "Lake Louise" is mentioned four times, an intensive promotion for the popular resort in the

Canadian Rocky Mountains that was also the setting for the Betty Grable musical *Springtime in the Rockies* (1942).

The song describes a couple drifting alone on the lake in the moonlight, kissing and then doing "as we please." The melody is pleasant but the lyric is undistinguished and even includes the hackneyed rhyme of "June" and "moon."

Freddy Martin and His Orchestra had three records that sold a million: "Tonight We Love," adapted from the opening theme of Tchaikovsky's Piano Concerto No 1, "I've Got a Lovely Bunch of Coconuts" and a version of "White Christmas," the 1942 Oscar-winning song. Sales of his recording of "When There's a Breeze on Lake Louise," with Joan Merrill's vocals, came nowhere near any of these. The only other recording of the song was by Ray Herbeck and His Modern Music with Romance, which had a vocal by Hal Munbar.

And the Winner Is...

White Christmas

from *Holiday Inn*
Music and Lyrics: Irving Berlin

Christmas songs are so much a part of the festive season today that it is surprising to discover that before "White Christmas" they barely existed. Bing Crosby did record two religious songs for Christmas in 1935—"Adeste Fidelis" and "Silent Night"—and the record sold more than a quarter of a million copies. For the next few years, as the holiday approached, Bing would always sing these and other Christmas hymns on his weekly radio show and the listening public began to think of him as the voice of Christmas. But still there were very few secular Christmas songs in popular music to speak of, until Irving Berlin wrote "White Christmas"—and the great songwriter wanted no one else but Crosby to sing it in *Holiday Inn*.

Holiday Inn is a musical about Jim Hardy (Bing), an unambitious singer who gives up show business to run a country lodge in New England that he intends to open only at holiday times. The plot would give Berlin the opportunity to write a series of songs in celebration of all the American holidays and the film was intended as a morale-boosting celebration of the American way of life at a time when the machinations of Herr Hitler were casting such a long shadow.

The most important holiday being Christmas, Berlin knew that the song he wrote for it had to be very special. He recalled the feelings he had in spending the season in sunny California, nostalgic for the snow-covered Christmases of his childhood in New York. The original lyric has an introductory verse expressing this feeling: The singer is Beverly Hills, amidst the orange groves and palm trees and yearns to be "up north."

Berlin was delighted with his song, believing it to be the best he ever wrote. Bing liked it too and gives a charming performance of it in the film. In the scene he is seated at the piano teaching the song to Linda Mason (Marjorie Reynolds), who is to perform it at the Inn's show. This occurs early in their relationship but, in the warm glow from the open fire and the Christmas tree lights, romance is clearly in the offing.

When Bing reaches the lines about the sleigh bells he taps his pipe to ring the bells on the Christmas tree. Marjorie joins in the song with Bing though the dubbed voice of Martha Mears is the one heard.

The cozy scene is repeated with variation at the end of the picture. By this time, the romance between Bing and Marjorie has not followed the expected course—she has gone to Hollywood with Ted Hanover (Fred Astaire) to make a movie about the Holiday Inn and soon Bing learns the dancing partners are engaged to be married. Bing rushes to California and the film studio, in time to see Marjorie (on a set which has recreated the Holiday Inn) shooting the "White Christmas" scene. As she sings the song, its nostalgic yearning is clearly taking her back to the original warm and cozy fireside that she had shared with Bing. Bing now reveals himself and he and Marjorie are soon on their way back to the real Holiday Inn.

The introductory verse about sunny Beverly Hills and its orange groves was not included in the film as the setting was snowy New England but it was in the original sheet music copies of the song—until Berlin realized that the song's appeal would be enhanced without it.

Film critics at the time of *Holiday Inn*'s release praised Crosby's rendition of "White Christmas" but the general feeling was that "Be Careful, It's My Heart" would be the bigger hit. It was the reaction to "White Christmas" by American servicemen abroad that triggered the song's huge success. It expressed perfectly their longing for home as well as their wish for peace, and the Armed Forces Radio Services received thousands of requests for the song. When Bing entertained the troops, he often hesitated to sing "White Christmas" because it always seemed to produce a nostalgic yearning that made the men sad. But if he tried to leave it out of his program, the soldiers always called for him to sing it.

This nostalgic sadness is there in the melody and it speaks to everyone—to those who are away from home at Christmas, and to everyone who sometimes dreams of a Christmas just like the ones known in childhood.

Bing introduced "White Christmas" to the American public on *Kraft Music Hall*, his NBC radio program, on December 25, 1941. His first recording of it, with the John Scott Trotter Orchestra and the Ken Darby Singers, was on May 29, 1942. *Holiday Inn* was released in August of that year. An interesting piece of trivia about Bing's recording is that Spike Jones was the drummer with John Scott Trotter's orchestra at that time.

The original master recording was used so frequently that it suffered damage and on March 19, 1947, Bing went back to the studio to re-record the song with the same orchestra and singers. It is not identical to the original version—the arrangement and the harmonies are noticeably different. This is the version that is most often heard today, though the original recording with all its scratches and noise is on a double CD entitled *Bing Crosby—The Voice of Christmas*, released by MCA in 1998.

By October 1942, Bing's "White Christmas" reached the U.S. charts and by the end of that month rose to Number One where it stayed for 11 weeks. During its initial run it remained in the charts for a total of 72 weeks. In the following years it was in the U.S. top 30 hits another 16 times, topping the charts again in 1945 and 1947. It has sold more than 30 million copies and was the best-selling single of all time until Elton John's "Candle in the Wind," his 1998 tribute to Princess Diana. But Bing's record has continued to sell and has regained first place. It has also sold millions of copies as part of various albums, from his album *Merry Christmas* in 1949 to the 1998 MCA double CD.

Freddy Martin and His Orchestra's 1942 recording, with Clyde Rogers' vocals, also sold over a million copies; the third to do so was Frank Sinatra's in 1944. Bing sang "White Christmas" again in *Blue Skies* (1946) and sales of the song received another big boost with a 1954 remake of *Holiday Inn*, which was naturally entitled *White Christmas*. This time, though, the song is over-produced, sung by all four stars and some over-cute kids as a big finish. The poignant simplicity of the song, so well presented in the earlier film, is overwhelmed.

1943

The Academy invited 200 servicemen to attend the 1943 Award ceremony, held in Grauman's Chinese Theatre in Hollywood itself. A radio broadcast of the occasion was sent to the Armed Forces overseas. With Bob Hope ill, Jack Benny acted as host and Dinah Shore presented the Best Song Oscar. Harold Arlen composed three of the ten nominated songs.

The Nominations

Jule Styne and Harold Adamson for "Change of Heart" from *Hit Parade of 1943* (Republic)

Harold Arlen and E.Y. Harburg for "Happiness Is a Thing Called Joe" from *Cabin in the Sky* (MGM)

Harold Arlen and Johnny Mercer for "My Shining Hour" from *The Sky's the Limit* (RKO)

Charles Wolcott and Ned Washington for "Saludos Amigos" from *Saludos Amigos* (Walt Disney)

Jimmy McHugh and Herb Magidson for "Say a Pray'r for the Boys Over There" from *Hers to Hold* (Universal)

Harold Arlen and Johnny Mercer for "That Old Black Magic" from *Star Spangled Rhythm* (Paramount)

Arthur Schwartz and Frank Loesser for "They're Either Too Young or Too Old" from *Thank Your Lucky Stars* (Warner)

James Monaco and Al Dubin for "We Mustn't Say Goodbye" from *Stage Door Canteen* (United Artists)

Cole Porter for "You'd Be So Nice to Come Home To" from *Something to Shout About* (Columbia)

Harry Warren and Mack Gordon for "You'll Never Know" from *Hello, Frisco, Hello* (Fox)

Change of Heart

from *Hit Parade of 1943*
Music: Jule Styne
Lyrics: Harold Adamson

Hit Parade of 1943 is considered by most critics to be the best of the *Hit Parade* series of films made by Republic between 1937 and 1947. Walter Scharf's scoring of the picture was nominated for an Oscar, as was the main song, "Change of Heart." In later years, all of the films had a change of title, usually taking a new one from a featured song. This is the case with *Hit Parade of 1943*, reissued as *Change of Heart* in 1949.

It stars John Carroll as a songwriter named Rick Farrell who, like Basil Rathbone in *Rhythm on the River,* passes off songs he has written with collaborators as his own work entirely. Jill Wright, played by Susan Hayward, is one of his victims: She has composed a melody, Carroll adds the lyrics to it and "Change of Heart" is born. He sings the song to her at the piano and her heart melts: "Every word has a special meaning!" she declares. He seems to have written the words just for her; they say that she has changed his world by changing autumn to spring. Surely now, with romance in the air, he will change his ways and share credit for the song with her. But old habits die hard and when it is published his name alone appears on the sheet music. The romance seems to be doomed.

"Change of Heart" is a huge hit but Carroll is sad and lonely, having apparently lost Hayward for good because of his duplicity. To try and win her back, he takes part in a War Bonds drive on the radio, pledging $10,000 on condition that he is allowed to sing "Change of Heart" on air and to make an announcement. He fully intends to make a clean breast of things and give Susan Hayward her proper credit.

Accompanied by Freddy Martin and His Orchestra and chorus, he steps up to the microphone to sing. Of course he is totally unaware that Susan Hayward has received news of his intentions and is speeding towards the studio for reconciliation. Full of woe, Carroll sings and changes the meaning of the song. Now, by leaving him, she has changed spring back to autumn.

In the middle of the song, Susan rushes into the studio and at first sits at the piano, playing along. Then she joins Carroll at the microphone and they sing happily together some words not heard before: He has changed his ways, now she can change her mind about him. But the chorus has to complete the last few words for them—they are too busy kissing. The End.

The song is very effective in terms of the job it has to do in the film, depicting the situation between Carroll and Hayward and the changes in their relationship. The imagery of the trees and the seasons reflecting the emotions of the lover is not original but it is used here fairly strikingly by lyricist Harold Adamson.

Happiness Is a Thing Called Joe

from *Cabin in the Sky*
Music: Harold Arlen
Lyrics: E.Y. (Yip) Harburg

Cabin in the Sky is the movie version of a show that had been a successful on the Broadway stage in 1940. It had an all-black cast and starred Ethel

Ethel Waters in *Cabin in the Sky* (MGM, 1943). She is seen here with "Bubbles" (John W. Sublett).

Waters, who brought the house down nightly with her performance of the big hit from the show, "Taking a Chance on Love." Vernon Duke composed this and the other songs, John LaTouche and Ted Fetter writing the lyrics. When MGM bought the rights, the studio wanted some new songs, but with Duke and LaTouche in the armed forces the studio turned to their successful team from *The Wizard of Oz*, Harold Arlen and Yip Harburg. And like *The Wizard of Oz*, the movie version of *Cabin in the Sky* uses a dream sequence as its main narrative device, and has a tornado sequence which uses the same footage as the earlier film.

Among the songs that Arlen and Harburg supplied was "Happiness Is a Thing Called Joe," sung in the film by Ethel Waters, repeating her stage role as Petunia. Her performance of the Oscar-nominated song from *Cabin in the Sky* is one of its highlights. She believes her husband, Little Joe (played by Eddie "Rochester" Anderson), to be dead but when he is miraculously revived, she joyfully sings "Happiness Is a Thing Called Joe," a song of gratitude and love. Her wonderfully expressive face and smile light up the screen and the simple words she sings are touching, expressing something of the reality of Southern black poverty.

Composer Harold Arlen had had the tune for this song for a long time. As Yip Harburg tells it, Arlen was not keen on it and he was going to throw it away but Harburg begged him to use it for *Cabin in the Sky*. It was only when Harburg came up with the title that Arlen began to like the tune and decided that it could be used in the film.

Of course, it is no ordinary tune—though quiet, it is full of subtlety, just as the lyrics are. The words appear to be simple but the song is built carefully around subtle internal rhymes as in "happiness/jes,' smile/lilac" and "kiss/Christmas." These rhymes occur on stressed notes and give the song a lilting quality, as simple as a nursery rhyme.

Susan Hayward also sang "Happiness Is a Thing Called Joe" in her 1955 film about the life of Lillian Roth, *I'll Cry Tomorrow*.

My Shining Hour

from *The Sky's the Limit*
Music: Harold Arlen
Lyrics: Johnny Mercer

After the success of *Holiday Inn* with Fred Astaire and Bing Crosby, Astaire's original film employers, RKO, offered him the lead in *The Sky's the Limit*. The role was more demanding in acting terms than anything he had done previously, his normally elegant and suave character replaced by a rather scratchy, acid-tongued persona. But Fred is excellent, especially with his realistic and touching performance as a slightly dishevelled, self-pitying drunk for the classic song "One for My Baby." But this song was passed over for

Oscar nomination in favor of "My Shining Hour," a song that was immediately popular though "One for My Baby" has proved more enduring.

"My Shining Hour" is emphasized all through the film: The hymn-like melody is played as the overture to the film over the opening credits and it is integrated into the entire score. Leigh Harline received an Oscar nomination for this score.

Fred plays an Air Force pilot named Fred on leave in New York. He falls for Joan Manion (Joan Leslie), a magazine photographer he meets while she is snapping celebrities in a nightclub. She performs "My Shining Hour" with the Freddie Slack orchestra, their instruments outlined in neon (Sally Sweetland dubs her voice). At this point, the song has no particular dramatic significance; it is, however, a sweet-sounding song of leave taking, even though Johnny Mercer's lyric is full of cliched images and over-poetic sentimentality.

The strained poetic effects and use of quaintly archaic phrases such as "o'er me" seem to indicate that the usually brilliant wordsmith is deliberately writing a conventional song of wartime separation. This becomes more apparent later, when Fred is walking Joan home. He tells her that he quite liked

Fred Astaire and Joan Leslie in *The Sky's the Limit* (RKO, 1943).

her song but "it's like you—it takes itself a little too seriously." He then proceeds to sing his own much lighter and sillier version, apparently making up
the words as he goes along.

From this point Arlen's lovely tune underscores every conversation the
pair has; later, Fred and Joan dance to the melody of the song, played by
Freddy Slack and his Orchestra. They are on a terrace of the penthouse apartment—Joan Leslie has just declared her feelings for Fred and the dance
expresses the romanticism of the occasion.

At the end of the film, the melody of "My Shining Hour" plays for the
last time and now the song comes into its own as a sentimental song of
wartime separation. As the music swells, Fred flies off to war and Joan watches
him go, her eyes shining with tears.

The song became very popular and there were a number of recordings.
The best selling version, one that reached the U.S. top ten, was by Glen Gray
and the Casa Loma Orchestra and vocalist Eugenie Baird. "My Shining
Hour" was used again in the 1945 film *Radio Stars on Parade*, where Frances
Langford sang it.

Age 18, Joan Leslie was Fred Astaire's youngest screen dancing partner
and by no means the worst. She had made her screen debut six years earlier
playing one of Robert Taylor's sisters in the Greta Garbo film *Camille*. She
was billed then as Joan Brodel, her real name. Her most significant roles were
as the disabled teenage girl befriended by Humphrey Bogart in *High Sierra*
and opposite Gary Cooper in *Sergeant York*. She was an appealing actress but
as a devout Roman Catholic chose only roles she regarded as wholesome, and
her career on screen was limited.

Saludos Amigos

from *Saludos Amigos*
Music: Charles Wolcott
Lyrics: Ned Washington

"Greetings, Friends" is the literal translation of "Saludos Amigos," the
title song from a Disney film that was a part of Roosevelt's Good Neighbor
Policy during World War II. U.S. relations with South America were crucial
to the war effort; it was essential that these officially neutral countries
remained good neighbors. Accordingly, the U.S. State Department paid for
a number of prominent Americans to go to South America on goodwill tours
as a counter to any pro—Axis tendencies that might exist there. The Disney
studios had already supported the war effort by producing training and information films for the armed services as well as homefront propaganda such as
Victory Through Airpower and *Der Fuehrer's Face*. Now Walt Disney was
approached to go to South America and he agreed on condition he could use
any material he gathered as the basis for films, the cost underwritten by the

Department. It was also politic for Disney to be away at this time for other reasons: There was a strike at his studios and workers distrusted his role in the negotiations.

The first film Disney made as a result of his trip was *Saludos Amigos* and it is scarcely a feature film, being a collection of four shorts and running only 43 minutes. After the credits there is a dedication, signed by Disney, to "our many friends in South America." The film then opens with live action footage of Disney and his team setting off by plane on "an unusual expedition" to find material for cartoon films. From then on, there is a mix of animation and stock travelogue footage as we follow the Americans on their travels to Peru, Chile, Argentina and Brazil, a story told in each.

The film trots out the usual Latin American clichés but there is one excellent sequence in which a Brazilian parrot by the name of Jose Carioca teaches Donald Duck the samba. The parrot was such a success that Disney built up his character for a second South American extravaganza, *The Three Caballeros*. In spite of the stereotypes, *Saludos Amigos* was well-received in South America where it broke all box office records.

The song, sung by the Disney studio chorus, accompanies the title sequence; it has only two short verses, the first of which salutes the people of Latin America. The second verse is almost meaningless, just a hearty helping of general-purpose optimism.

It is difficult to understand why such an insignificant song should have received an Oscar nomination. It does have a fairly catchy tune but the lyric is ordinary and the song has had no life at all outside of the film. Ignored for nomination was the much better "Brazil" by Ary Barroso, a song that has been used in at least five other musicals, usually with Bob Russell's English lyrics.

Composer Charles Wolcott was also nominated for his musical scoring of the film, along with colleagues Edward Plumb and Paul Smith. C.O. Slyfield was nominated for Sound.

Say a Pray'r for the Boys Over There

from *Hers to Hold*
Music: Jimmy McHugh
Lyrics: Herb Magidson

Deanna Durbin sings "Say a Pray'r for the Boys Over There" in *Hers to Hold*. The film was originally called *Three Girls Join Up* and it was a sequel to two earlier Deanna Durbin films, *Three Smart Girls* and *Three Smart Girls Grow Up*.

Durbin was classically trained and had remarkable control of her appealing soprano voice. She made a series of wholesome family films, a number of which were designed to bring light classical music to a mass audience. The trend continued in *Hers to Hold*, where she sings a lively version of the Seguidilla from Bizet's *Carmen*.

In the film, Deanna, as Penny Craig, does her bit for the war effort by donating blood to the Red Cross, working as a riveter in an aircraft factory and becoming romantically involved with pilot Bill Morley, played by Joseph Cotten. When he is posted overseas, everyone in the audience was able to identify with her situation and take some solace from her singing of "Say a Pray'r for the Boys Over There."

From today's perspective, Herb Magidson's lyric may seem excessively patriotic and rather sentimental, but in 1943 it must have spoken eloquently to Americans who had loved ones serving abroad. The song has echoes of George M. Cohan's jingoistic "Over There" from the First World War, which also has the line "say a prayer" in its chorus.

In the film, the character played by Deanna has just learned that the man she loves is to be sent abroad. She listens to the anxieties of other women at the factory whose men have already gone, some never to return, and when she sings "Say a Pray'r for the Boys Over There" at a lunchtime concert in the canteen, she is singing for them as well as for herself. As she sings we see shots of the other women's expressive faces and share their feelings.

The scene could have been mawkishly sentimental but it is handled with understated taste. Jimmy McHugh's music has a hymn-like quality and is a good vehicle for Durbin's voice. She is often effusive in her singing but here she sings simply, with sincerity and dignity, and the effect is quite moving. In 1943, audiences would have been moved to tears by the scene.

At the end of the film, Deanna reprises the song, again for the workers in the factory canteen. As she reaches the last lines, we see Joseph Cotten's squadron flying off into the clouds.

The song was adapted for use in a number of other countries, including Australia, with its reference to "The Star Spangled Banner" adjusted to the relevant national songs.

Jimmy McHugh also did his bit for the war effort by turning over his royalties for "Say a Pray'r for the Boys Over There" to wartime charities. He and Adamson wrote other patriotic songs such as "Coming In on a Wing and a Prayer" and also encouraged Americans to buy war bonds.

That Old Black Magic

from *Star Spangled Rhythm*
Music: Harold Arlen
Lyrics: Johnny Mercer

Standing out in all the frenetic frivolity of *Star Spangled Rhythm* is a brilliant production number built around a song that has become one of the great American standards: "That Old Black Magic."

Paramount did its bit for the war effort with this all-star musical, parading most of the studio's talent. The film is basically a variety show with many patriotic numbers, including Bing Crosby singing "Old Glory" against a studio backdrop of the Great Old Flag and the U.S. presidents' heads on Mount Rushmore. There are also comic portrayals of Mussolini and Hirohito, and these two gentlemen, along with Adolf himself, join Paulette Goddard, Dorothy Lamour and Veronica Lake (her voice dubbed by Martha Mears) for a chorus of "A Sweater, a Sarong and a Peek-a-Boo Bang." Robert Dolan was nominated for his scoring of the picture.

For "That Old Black Magic," Johnny Johnston is a soldier lying on his bed in a tent far from home. Beside him is a photograph of a scantily clad girl apparently dancing in a snow-covered garden. As Johnny dreams, he begins to sing the song and the photograph comes to life. The words of the song express the feverish intensity of a love-starved man and the dance the girl performs is correspondingly erotic. She dances dreamily in gently falling snow, and as the dance ends she leaves the photograph and appears as a tiny figure on the bed next to Johnny Johnston. The girl of Johnny's dreams is ballet star Vera Zorina; her real-life husband, George Balanchine, choreographed the number.

Harold Arlen's unusual melody has a haunting quality, matched by a lyric that is full of telling, memorable phrases. Its witchcraft theme has some similarity with Cole Porter's "You Do Something to Me" which has the line, "Do do that voodoo that you do so well." Johnny Mercer admitted that this was the lyric that inspired him and, like Porter, he also makes effective use of internal rhymes in such lines as, "The mate that fate had me created for."

Some critics have lighted on the apparent paradox of the line concerning a kiss putting out the fire of love, pointing out that a kiss is more likely to start a fire than to put one out. But the song is full of such paradoxes—the humdrum "same old" is used to describe the strangeness of "witchcraft"; the "icy fingers" cause a "burning desire." This contrariness is quite deliberate, helping to create the feverish confusion that the singer is experiencing.

"That Old Black Magic" has become a popular standard and most of the great singers have recorded it. In 1943, the best-selling version, reaching the top of the charts, was by Glenn Miller, with vocals by Skip Nelson and The Modernaires. It was back in the U.S. charts in 1955 in a version by Sammy Davis, Jr. That clean-cut American boy Bobby Rydell had a minor hit with it in 1961.

"That Old Black Magic" has turned up in many films: Bing Crosby sang it in the 1944 *Here Come the Waves,* accompanied by screaming hordes of bobbysoxers—a satiric comment on the Sinatra craze. The next to sing it on film was Frances Langford in *Radio Stars on Parade* (1945); then in 1950, Billy Daniels sang it in *When You're Smiling* and it became strongly associated with him. He even recorded a disco version in 1978. Sinatra himself sang "That Old Black Magic" in *Meet Danny Wilson* (1952) and recorded the definitive version of the song on his *Come Swing with Me* album. In 1956, Marilyn Monroe sang it in *Bus Stop*; Louis Prima and Keely Smith did it as a duet in *Senior Prom* (1958) and had an enormous hit with their recording of it in the same year, winning one of the first Grammies (for "Best Vocal Performance, Group") in the process. Jerry Lewis had a go at the song in 1963 in *The Nutty Professor* and Ann-Margret performed it in *The Swinger* (1966). In 1997, Kevin Spacey sang "That Old Black Magic" in Clint Eastwood's *Midnight in the Garden of Good and Evil*.

They're Either Too Young or Too Old

from *Thank Your Lucky Stars*
Music: Arthur Schwartz
Lyrics: Frank Loesser

Thank Your Lucky Stars is a patriotic all-star variety show parading most of Warner Bros.' stars, including Eddie Cantor, Humphrey Bogart and Olivia de Havilland; Joan Leslie, fresh from her starring role with Fred Astaire in *The Sky's the Limit*, was there too. The high spot of the film is Bette Davis' performance of "They're Either Too Young or Too Old," the first time she sang on screen.

It is a very witty song about separation in wartime, the wry lament of a woman looking around at the men left behind by the war. Bette Davis is assuring her man that she has no chance of being unfaithful because all the best "pickin's" have been called up. Any man she meets at home is either "too gray" or "green" and she either has "to hold him off" or "hold him up." She sings the song in a smart nightclub where all the males are just as the song says: either staid old gentlemen or brash youths.

Loesser is adept at using carefully contrived triple rhymes to very comic effect, including some hilariously excruciating ones such as "fail ya"/"Australia" and "India"/"bin t'ya." Davis' performance of the song is superb, bringing out the humor of every line. The simple melody enables her to more or less speak most of the lines, as Rex Harrison does the songs he performs in *My Fair Lady*, and she uses all her trademark mannerisms, including the popping eyes, the fluttering hands and clipped inflection.

And as well as singing, Davis was called on to take part in a very acrobatic dance routine to round off the sequence. The dance is basically a jitterbug and she was very apprehensive when she found out what she was expected to do. Her dancing partner was to be the young and very athletic Conrad Wiedell, known as Hollywood's "King of the Jitterbugs." The choreography called for him to throw Bette all around and he was apprehensive too, feeling that this was an almost sacrilegious way to handle the great lady.

Bette arrived on the soundstage to film the sequence dressed in a full-length brocaded gown topped with a matching jacket that really needed Technicolor to bring out its full glory. It was shocking pink and she had set it off with long evening gloves in a very vivid shade of green. She smoked three cigarettes one after the other, and declared her readiness.

Shooting began and, after she had lip-synched the song, the dancing begins. She dances first with a doddery old man, then the brash young Wiedell lunges at her and he is soon swinging her everywhere, up, down and sideways; and when he finally puts her down, she can barely stand. In the finished sequence, we see her stagger out of the club to finish the song in the street and her dishevelled appearance did not have to be contrived. Director David Butler now had the gall to ask for another take but Bette understandably refused and walked off to her dressing room.

A good, humorous song is very hard to write but "They're Either Too Young or Too Old" is a brilliant example of the genre. The skill that goes into creating effective humor is often underestimated and many an excellent example has been passed over for honors. This applies to other categories as well as Best Song: Few comedies have won the Best Film award, and an actor in a comedy rarely wins an Oscar.

The best-selling record of the song was by Kitty Kallen, singing with Jimmy Dorsey's band. It is also sung by Jane Froman, dubbing for Susan Hayward, in the movie *With a Song in My Heart* (1952).

Shortly after writing "They're Either Too Young or Too Old," Frank Loesser was drafted into the Army. He spent the rest of the war in a Special Services unit, writing morale-boosting songs for service shows.

We Mustn't Say Goodbye

from *Stage Door Canteen*
Music: James Monaco
Lyrics: Al Dubin

Like *Thank Your Lucky Stars* and *Star Spangled Rhythm*, *Stage Door Canteen* was a multi-star musical designed to entertain the troops and boost morale. There were cameo appearances by personalities from many branches of entertainment: Yehudi Menuhin, Harpo Marx, Johnny Weissmuller, Gracie Fields, Count Basie, Katharine Hepburn, Gypsy Rose Lee and many others. It was billed as "48 stars and a great love story." The film was nominated for two Oscars, the other being for its scoring by Frederic Rich.

The "great love story" in *Stage Door Canteen* involves William Terry as Dakota Smith, a soldier who falls for Eileen Burke, played by Cheryl Walker. Their romance flowers as Lanny Ross appears at the Canteen to sing "We Mustn't Say Goodbye." The melody is also played at key points in the development of the romance as well as over the opening and closing credits. It is yet another song of wartime separation and the singer attempts to reassure his sweetheart with the words, telling her that they will always be together in their dreams.

Monaco's melody is attractive but Al Dubin, nearing the end of his song-writing career, is below form here. His lyric rarely rises above the conventional, though the image of the singer's heart being in the envelope containing his love letter is rather startling.

You'd Be So Nice to Come Home to

from *Something to Shout About*
Music and Lyrics: Cole Porter

The only memorable composition in the musical *Something to Shout About* is "You'd Be So Nice to Come Home to." The title of the film derives from the phrase used continually in the film by William Gaxton. Playing the part of William Samson, a Broadway producer, he keeps yelling, "I want the kind of a show that there'll be something to shout about!" Cole Porter duly obliged with an optimistic song with the same title but this and four others from the film are almost forgotten.

The film is also notable as the screen debut of Cyd Charisse in a small role as a dancer.

The refrain of "You'd Be So Nice to Come Home to," with its simple and poignant evocation of loving companionship, had strong appeal to most Americans parted by the war. But the opening and closing verses, which are always omitted by recording artists, give the song a very different slant. Don Ameche plays Ken Douglas, the producer's press agent, who has a reputation of being a ladies' man. He sings the first verse and the refrain as a rather original song of seduction; his target is Janet Blair, playing Jeanie Maxwell, the potential star of Gaxton's show. He tells her that he knows of other girls who are just as good-looking and pleasing, but hints that with her he envisages a life of domestic bliss—she stands out from the crowd because she'd "be so nice to come to home to."

Janet's response is to call him a "Lothario" who chases every new girl in town. She'd be delighted to pair up with him one day but only if he grows up and slows down. So, despite the apparent tender romanticism of the refrain, the witty, rather sardonic verses that surround it strike a note of knowing cynicism.

The best-selling record of "You'd Be So Nice to Come Home To," without the cynical verses, was by Dinah Shore with the Paul Weston orchestra. The song remained for 18 weeks on *Your Hit Parade*.

Cole Porter's melody is very attractive and appealing but some music critics accused the great songwriter of borrowing its main theme from Sarasate's piece for the violin *Zigeunerweisen*. Nothing came of this, but Porter had a lawsuit brought against him by a certain Ira Arnstein, a composer who made a habit of suing successful songwriters, claiming that they borrowed his work. He asserted that Cole Porter had based "You'd be So Nice to Come to" on his composition "Sadness O'erwhelms My Soul." The judge found in favor of Porter, and there was a suggestion that Arnstein was suffering from persecution mania.

And the Winner Is...

You'll Never Know

from *Hello, Frisco, Hello*
Music: Harry Warren
Lyrics: Mack Gordon

Hello Frisco, Hello is set in turn-of-the-century San Francisco and most of its songs were revivals from that period. But the producers wanted one new song and asked Harry Warren and Mack Gordon to oblige. The songwriters came up with "You'll Never Know," a song that not only sat well alongside the period songs but also spoke to the loneliness of people separated by World War II.

The song is heard first early in the film: On stage in a Barbary Coast saloon, a set represents New York on one side and San Francisco on the other. John Payne and Jack Oakie are on the right in New York and they place a long-distance phone call to Alice Faye in San Francisco; on the left, June Havoc dressed as a maid answers it. Payne and Oakie sing "Hello Frisco, Hello" and June is soon joined by Alice Faye. Her reply in song is "You'll Never Know."

The words of the song come across with impact because of the simplicity of her performance—no big production, just Alice Faye singing sweetly and directly as she holds the receiver to her ear. Mack Gordon's lyric employs everyday phrases that any lover might use. The singer seems to be responding to her lover's demands to know how much she loves him. She answers tenderly but at times this wistful tenderness turns to something like annoyance—she has told him how much she loves him "a million or more times," suggesting the kind of phrase often used by an exasperated mother who wonders how many times she has told her delinquent child something. The ending of the song repeats the title but adds another touch of exasperation: "You'll never know if you don't know now."

The melody is used frequently on the soundtrack to underscore some of the romantic scenes and John Payne even whistles a few bars. Soon it becomes apparent that the song has become a comment on the relationship between Payne and Alice Faye. It seems that he is blind to her feelings for him, that he will never know how much she loves him.

Eventually all is resolved when Jack Oakie contrives to get them back on stage together. This time the set is reversed and she rings him from New York and he takes the call in San Francisco. But as Alice sings "You'll Never

Know" just for him, he receives the message loud and clear. They ignore the artificial boundaries and stand together center stage; he joins in the song, they kiss and the film ends.

This cleverly constructed ballad was the deserving winner of the Oscar even though it was up against some other excellent numbers. Sheet music sales made it Harry Warren's most successful song and it was one of the biggest hits of the war. Unfortunately for Alice Faye, 20th Century–Fox wouldn't allow her to record it. A recording by Dick Haymes and the Song Spinners sold well over a million copies; it was No. 1 for four weeks and remained on the U.S. charts for 16 weeks. This was Haymes' first million-seller. Frank Sinatra hit

Alice Faye in *Hello, Frisco, Hello* (Fox, 1943)

the top ten with his version. Alice Faye reprised it in the 1944 film *Four Jills in a Jeep* and Ginger Rogers sang in it *Dreamboat* (1952). Alice Faye's original recording was used in 1975 under the opening credits of the Martin Scorsese movie *Alice Doesn't Live Here Anymore.*

Harry Warren died in 1981 and is buried at Westwood Memorial Park, Los Angeles. The first four bars of "You'll Never Know" are his epitaph.

1944

Grauman's Chinese Theatre in Hollywood was the venue for the 1944 Oscar presentations. Bob Hope was back as host for the main awards though film director John Cromwell hosted the first half of the evening when the Technical Oscars were presented. The number of nominations for Best Song increased to 12 and Hope presented the Oscar himself.

The Nominations

Jimmy McHugh and Harold Adamson for "I Couldn't Sleep a Wink Last Night" from *Higher and Higher* (RKO)

Jule Styne and Sammy Cahn for "I'll Walk Alone" from *Follow the Boys* (Universal)

James Monaco and Mack Gordon for "I'm Making Believe" from *Sweet and Low Down* (Fox)

Jerome Kern and Ira Gershwin for "Long Ago (and Far Away)" from *Cover Girl* (Columbia)

Harold Arlen and Ted Koehler for "Now I Know" from *Up in Arms* (Goldwyn)

Harry Revel and Paul Francis Webster for "Remember Me to Carolina" from *Minstrel Man* (Producers Releasing Corporation)

Ary Barroso and Ned Washington for "Rio de Janeiro" from *Brazil* (Republic)

Lew Pollack and Charles Newman for "Silver Shadows and Golden Dreams" from *Lady, Let's Dance* (Monogram)

M.K. Jerome and Ted Koehler for "Sweet Dreams, Sweetheart" from *Hollywood Canteen* (Warner)

Jimmy Van Heusen and Johnny Burke for "Swinging on a Star" from *Going My Way* (Paramount)

Walter Kent and Kim Gannon for "Too Much in Love" from *Song of the Open Road* (United Artists)

Ralph Blane and Hugh Martin for "The Trolley Song" from *Meet Me in St. Louis* (MGM)

I Couldn't Sleep a Wink Last Night

from *Higher and Higher*
Music: Jimmy McHugh
Lyrics: Harold Adamson

RKO chose the 1940 Rodgers and Hart Broadway musical *Higher and Higher* for Frank Sinatra's first screen starring role. The show had flopped but it did contain one of Rodgers and Hart's finest songs, "It Never Entered My Mind." Nevertheless, RKO discarded this and most of the other original songs, retaining only the novelty number "Disgustingly Rich." Jimmy McHugh and Harold Adamson were contracted to write the new score.

Victor Borge had a small role in the film, as did Dooley Wilson of *Casablanca* fame. Another fine American singer made his screen debut in *Higher and Higher*—Mel Torme. The film was poorly reviewed, the *New York Times* critic Bosley Crowther opining that it should have been called *Lower and Lower*. But Sinatra himself was praised for his acting as well as his singing, even though the character he plays—a singer called Frank Sinatra—is quite unimportant to the flimsy plot. But he received prominent billing on the posters and his performance of "I Couldn't Sleep a Wink Last Night" is especially good.

Michele Morgan and Frank haven't met but he often waves to her from the window of his house across the square. Michele plays the part of Millie, one of the servants, and Frank becomes concerned when he hasn't seen her for a few days. He calls on her, bringing as gifts a large bunch of roses and a new song he has written that he describes as "a torch ballad." That song is "I Couldn't Sleep a Wink Last Night" and he proceeds to sing it to her. Dooley Wilson, as Oscar, the chauffeur, is at the piano, apparently playing the accompaniment for Frank.*

Frank's song is a ballad of reconciliation, the lovers having had a "silly fight." Frank sings that he has been awake the whole night through nursing a breaking heart, and was even deprived of his favorite dream, the one in which he holds her in his arms.

The song has little relevance to the plot—Michele and Frank are not in love and certainly haven't had a quarrel. In fact, she loves Mike (Jack Haley) and Frank ends up in the arms of Katherine (Barbara Hale).

Dooley was not a pianist even though he appears to play the piano in 1942's Casablanca. It is not his playing that we hear but Elliot Carpenter's. Carpenter sat at a piano out of camera range so that Wilson could watch and copy his hand movements.

Soon after Frank has finished the song, the master of the house, Cyrus Drake, played by Leon Errol, comes downstairs and asks, "Who was that singing down here—Bing Crosby?" When told it was Sinatra, he replies, "Ah well, he'll never get any place." This is one of a number of similarly feeble in-jokes about Sinatra in the film.

The melody of the song is very pleasant and the simple, conversational words have a certain poignancy, especially in Sinatra's deeply felt performance of the song. His recording of it topped the American charts. Because of the musicians' union strike, a vocal group—the Bobby Tucker Singers—backs Sinatra on the record. It was the first of eight songs introduced in films by Sinatra to be nominated for an Oscar.

Helen Forrest also recorded the song with the Harry James band. It is associated with Frances Langford as well—she sang it in two films: *Radio Stars on Parade* in 1945 and *Beat the Band* in 1947.

I'll Walk Alone

from *Follow the Boys*
Music: Jule Styne
Lyrics: Sammy Cahn

Dinah Shore sings "I'll Walk Alone" and it was one of the biggest hits of the war years. *Follow the Boys* is another all-star concoction based around the organization of entertainment for the troops by a group of stars known as the Hollywood Victory Committee. But it does give insight into the way entertainment for servicemen and servicewomen was organized, and some footage shows the audience at actual shows.

The threadbare plot, involving George Raft and Vera Zorina as his wife, is very tedious but there are some enjoyable cameo appearances by a host of stars including the Andrews Sisters, Marlene Dietrich and Orson Welles in a magic act, and Sophie Tucker. W.C. Fields performs his hilarious pool table act, and George Raft dances with style to "Sweet Georgia Brown," played by jazzman Louis Jordan.

The opening verse of "I'll Walk Alone," with the singer vowing to resist advances from all others while her man is away, echoes "They're Either Too Young or Too Old" but in a more serious vein. The words of the chorus are poignantly simple: She doesn't mind if she's lonely because she knows that he will be lonely too. The repetition of "alone" and "lonely" is simple but effective, the long note on the "o" sounding like a soft murmuring of subdued pain. This is reinforced by the rhyming "oo" sounds of "you" and "too" in the last line.

Dinah Shore's soft and gentle delivery of the song in the film is just right. She sings it during a radio broadcast to servicemen overseas and during her performance shots of them listening to the radio in their war zones are superimposed. The song and the way it is presented clearly aim to reassure "the boys" that their wives and sweethearts are being faithful to them.

The stoic acceptance of the loved one's absence makes the song infinitely preferable to the usual run of sugary sentiment that marks most other ballads of wartime separation. It was well-liked by servicemen: During the Allied advance into Germany, songwriters Jule Styne and Sammy Cahn received a photograph from the front showing a group of soldiers who had painted the words "I'll Walk Cologne" on a German fence.

Shore's recording of "I'll Walk Alone" was a number one in the U.S. for four weeks and the sheet music sold over a million copies. Mary Martin and Martha Tilton also recorded successful versions of the song while Vera Lynn cornered the British and Commonwealth markets. "I'll Walk Alone" turns up again in the biopic of Jane Froman, *With a Song in My Heart* (1952). Susan Hayward performs the song with Froman's dubbed voice and this revival gave the song a new lease on life, leading to more recordings by a number of singers including Don Cornell, Margaret Whiting and Richard Hayes.

I'm Making Believe

from *Sweet and Low Down*
Music: James Monaco
Lyrics: Mack Gordon

"I'm Making Believe" is yet another of the hundreds of songs of separation that were churned out in wartime. Lynn Bari, who plays band singer Pat Sterling, performs this one (her voice dubbed by Lorraine Elliott) with the Benny Goodman Orchestra in *Sweet and Low Down*. The film doesn't have much of a plot but what there is involves Johnny Birch, a trombonist (James Cardwell) who has an inflated idea of his own talents. Joe Harris dubs his trombone playing.

Benny Goodman recruits Cardwell for his band when he hears him playing the melody of "I'm Making Believe." Goodman asks him about the tune and Cardwell tells him that it's just "a little thing I fool around with." From here on, the melody is used extensively to underscore Cardwell's romantic scenes with Linda Darnell, who plays Trudy Wilson. Lynn Bari later performs the song during a band concert and Cardwell's trombone is heavily showcased, so much so that when the record is released and sells a million copies, *Down Beat* magazine features him on its cover.

Cardwell is now convinced that he is a star and sets up a band of his own, poaching most of Goodman's band. When the new band fails, all the musicians return to Goodman—except for Cardwell, who is too proud to apologize. But his pal, Popsie (Jack Oakie) contrives a reconciliation and Cardwell rejoins his old boss as they play a reprise of "I'm Making Believe."

The song has a pleasant melody but the lyrics are undistinguished and describe how the singer, alone in her gloomy room, uses her imagination to bring her loved one close.

There were a number of recordings of the song, including versions by the Hal McIntyre band (vocal by Ruth Gaylor), Bing Crosby, the Mills Brothers and Doris Day with the Les Brown band. But easily the most successful version was by Ella Fitzgerald and the Ink Spots, a double-sided hit with "Into Each Life Some Rain Must Fall." It topped the U.S. charts for ten weeks in 1944.

Long Ago (and Far Away)

from *Cover Girl*
Music: Jerome Kern
Lyrics: Ira Gershwin

Apart from "Long Ago (and Far Away)" and "Sure Thing," a song that deserves to be better known, Jerome Kern and Ira Gershwin's songs for *Cover Girl* are not particularly memorable. Rita Hayworth had proved herself an excellent dancer when paired with Fred Astaire in *You Were Never Lovelier*; in *Cover Girl* she matched steps with another great screen dancer, Gene Kelly, who also did the choreography with assistance from Stanley Donen. One of the best sequences they devised was the "Alter Ego Dance" where Gene partners his own reflection that has stepped out of a shop window. Kelly plays a character named Danny McGuire, which is also the name of the character he played in *Xanadu* in 1980.

The tune of "Long Ago" is used extensively as a love theme for Kelly and Hayworth and a jazzed-up, almost surrealistic version of it accompanies much of the "Alter Ego Dance." The romantic sequence in which the song is first sung is one of the best in the film. Kelly runs a small Brooklyn nightclub and is in love with Rita Hayworth, who plays Rusty Parker, a dancer in his show. But now she has hit the big time as a cover girl model and has been offered a chance to star in a Broadway show. Kelly is certain that this will finish their romance. It is after hours in the nightclub; Phil Silvers is quietly playing the tune of "Long Ago (and Far Away)" on the piano while Kelly is stacking the chairs.

The atmosphere is heavy with Kelly's sadness. Then Rita enters looking absolutely stunning in a long, off-the-shoulder blue dress. She begins to sing "Long Ago (and Far Away)" to Kelly, telling him in song that she will stick by him. He is too far into his melancholy to respond and she walks away despondently. But then he takes up the song and she rushes back to him. They kiss and go into a sensuous dance sequence. Martha Mears dubs Rita Hayworth's singing voice for the film.

Later in the film, Kelly uses the song almost as a weapon against Rita: Knowing he must not stand in the way of her big break but also knowing that she loves him, he forces her to go by giving "Long Ago (and Far Away)" to Leslie Brooks to sing in his new show. Rita finally returns to Gene at the end of the film and finds him sadly singing their song to himself. She joins in and they are joyfully reunited.

In his book *Lyrics on Several Occasions,* Ira Gershwin writes that he found it very difficult to fit words to Jerome Kern's soaring and swooping melody, especially the opening phrase, which has seven notes. He was stuck for a title, too, and at one stage was set on calling the song "Midnight Music"—apt because the scene takes place late at night. Kern approved of what Gershwin had written so far and remarked favorably on the alliteration of one line in particular, "the moment midnight music made you mine."

But Gershwin goes on to say that he rejected this version as being too melodramatic. Jerome Kern started to become impatient at the amount of time his lyricist was taking and sarcastically offered him the working title he himself had used on his dummy lyric: "Watching Little Alice P."

Eventually the film's producer Arthur Schwartz, himself a songwriter of note, rang Ira and told him that the shooting schedule demanded that the song be ready straight away. Ira gave him his current working title, one he thought was fairly ordinary: "Long Ago (and Far Away)." But he soon changed his mind, realizing that these simple words complemented the melody perfectly and were very singable. The first three lines of the song are a quiet masterpiece of simplicity, a love lyric that avoids all pretentiousness. Unfortunately the rest of the lyric falls away from this standard into cliché and melodrama, though some originality is restored by the neat word play of the last line of the song, using "long" first as a verb then as an adjective: "...that all I longed for long ago was you."

"Long Ago (and Far Away)" was the most successful song that Ira Gershwin ever wrote in terms of sales, both of records and sheet music. But Ira was not happy with it and felt that he had not achieved much in the way of originality with the lyric. As it happens, even the song's title is not original as Ralph Rainger and Leo Robin used it for a song they wrote in 1936 for *Three Cheers for Love.*

Four different recordings managed a place in the U.S. top ten, the most successful being a duet by Dick Haymes and Helen Forrest. The other chart entries were by Bing Crosby, Jo Stafford and Perry Como, who had his very first hit with the song. Kathryn Grayson sang "Long Ago (and Far Away)" in the film biography of Jerome Kern, *Till the Clouds Roll By* (1946).

Now I Know

from *Up in Arms*
Music: Harold Arlen
Lyrics: Ted Koehler

Up in Arms is the film in which Danny Kaye made his screen debut. He made an immediate and exhilarating impact, especially with his amazing performance of "The Theater Lobby Number," often called "Manic-Depressive Films Present." This is a hilarious spoof on Hollywood: "These musical films are all alike—if you've seen one, you've seen them all," says Danny, introducing the number. Sylvia Fine (Mrs. Kaye) and Max Liebman wrote it for him. They also supplied "Melody in 4F," a tongue-twisting Kaye specialty that he had first sung on Broadway in *Let's Face It!*

Kaye's character in *Up in Arms* is taken from a play, *The Nervous Wreck*, which was filmed in a silent version in 1926 starring an actor called Harrison Ford. The play was also the source of the stage musical *Whoopee!* which contains two famous songs: "Makin' Whoopee" and "Love Me or Leave Me." It was filmed in 1930 with Eddie Cantor repeating his stage role. Sam Goldwyn had had enormous success with musicals in the 1930s and he hoped that Kaye would be a second Cantor.

In *Up in Arms*, Kaye plays Danny Weems, a hypochondriac who also has romantic delusions—he believes himself to be in love with Mary Morgan (Constance Dowling) when Virginia (Dinah Shore) is obviously the one he should be pursuing. In any case, Constance is in love with Joe (Dana Andrews). When Danny and Dana are drafted into the army, the ladies also join up as nurses. On the eve of their departure for the Pacific, they decide to cut a record at a dockside booth, a farewell message as a memento of their last evening. Dinah Shore sings "Now I Know" as her contribution and she is clearly directing the song's message of love to Danny.

This is one of Harold Arlen's finest melodies; it has a sensuous rhythm and a complex, wandering construction which insinuates itself subtly into the listener's consciousness. It does not have a clear and repetitive pattern and seems to flow on and on. It has shifting keys, rising and falling; Ted Koehler must have worked hard to fit his lyric to it. But he succeeds admirably, revealing a sophisticated and deft touch.

In the first lines of the chorus, the "o" sounds in "know," "so" and "glow" fall on long notes so that the sounds are sustained. A similar euphonious effect is achieved in the sixth and seventh lines with no less than seven "i" sounds. This deft assonance and the alliteration of "thrive" and "thrill" give the words a flowing quality which reinforce the quiet, unaccented rhythm of the melody. The words and the music work together inseparably to express the gentle tenderness of Dinah Shore's feelings. "Now I Know" is a song of real quality and it deserves to be better-known. It does not have the instant appeal of many popular songs but it does repay repeated listening.

Later in the film, the song is used for comic effect: Kaye has annoyed his fellow conscripts so much that they have stopped him from using the phonograph to play his precious recording. He borrows it surreptitiously, when caught in the act, mimes to the record in an attempt to cover up his crime. He opens his mouth and out comes the sound of Shore singing "Now I Know." Of course, the needle gets stuck and he is found out.

Shore recorded the song but made little impression on the charts; subsequently "Now I Know" became a favorite with jazz musicians. Among those who recorded it were Duke Ellington, Lionel Hampton and Charlie Parker.

Remember Me to Carolina

from *Minstrel Man*
Music: Harry Revel
Lyrics: Paul Francis Webster

"Remember Me to Carolina" is a rather dull song performed by Benny Fields in the film but the song begs for attention. It is sung four times at key points in the plot, and on every occasion poignancy is laid on with a trowel. The melody is also used extensively on the soundtrack.

Fields is the blackface minstrel man of the title, billed as Dixie Boy Johnson. "Remember Me to Carolina" is his theme song and we first hear it when he sings part of it to his wife Caroline in a scene designed to establish the pair as a happily married couple. Soon afterwards we see him perform the entire song on stage. As he sings, a friend behind the scenes takes a telephone call and learns that Caroline has died in childbirth. Fields receives the tragic news and from now on he will always associate "Remember Me to Carolina" with the loss of his wife and therefore will never sing it again. Pathos oozes like syrup.

His daughter is also named Caroline; and to escape this constant reminder of his wife, he gives her up for adoption and continues his stage career. Soon he has no contact with her at all and goes off on a world tour. He tours Europe, then Latin America; there, in a Havana nightclub, the audience demands that he sing his theme song. Reluctantly he starts to sing it but breaks down halfway through and rushes off. More pathos.

Years later, Fields' daughter (played by Judy Clark) has grown up and, like her father, has become an entertainer (she is billed as Dixie Girl Johnson). At the opening night of her show, Fields arrives at the theater unannounced and watches her from the wings. As Caroline starts to sing her father's hit song "Remember Me to Carolina," Fields, now suddenly back in his blackface and minstrel clothes, joins her on stage and they sing it together in a happy reunion.

In the song, the singer, parted from his sweetheart Carolina, is addressing the stars and asking them to take a message to her. The song is really quite unremarkable—it has an unoriginal tune and the lyric employs all the usual clichés of love ballads. Fields has a pleasant baritone voice but he is not a talented actor.

Rio de Janeiro

from *Brazil*
Music: Ary Barroso
Lyrics: Ned Washington

After Carmen Miranda's success, Hollywood searched Latin America for other possible stars. One of them was Mexican singer-guitarist Tito

Guizar, cast as Miguel Soares, a Brazilian, in *Brazil*. The plot involves a book written by Nicky Henderson (Virginia Bruce) entitled *Why Marry a Latin?* that puts down the image of the hot-blooded Latin lover; Guizar attempts to change Bruce's views.

Republic made the film and the studio included its singing cowboy Roy Rogers in the cast; he sings "Hands Across the Border," another song designed to cement U.S.–South American relations. Carmen Miranda's sister Aurora appears in the dance numbers.

"Rio de Janeiro" is sung first in English and then in Portuguese—composer Ary Barroso translated Ned Washington's lyric. Guizar plays a songwriter who had won the Carnival songwriting contest the year before with "Brazil." This year the very similar "Rio de Janeiro" is his entry. "Brazil" had been introduced in 1943 in the Disney film *Saludos Amigos*.

"Rio de Janeiro" is sung during a very lively sequence showing the Rio Carnival. The filming is excellent and the song has a very infectious and rhythmic Latin American melody. But the words have little importance, other than to make excited exclamations about the attractions of Rio, a place full of "love and romance." Walter Scharf's lively and colorful scoring and Daniel Bloomberg's sound also earned Oscar nominations.

Silver Shadows and Golden Dreams

from *Lady, Let's Dance*
Music: Lew Pollack
Lyrics: Charles Newman

"Silver Shadows and Golden Dreams" is the featured song in *Lady, Let's Dance*. Monogram had made the ice revue *Silver Skates* in 1943 to show off the talents of English skater Belita, hoping that she would be another Sonja Henie. The film made little impact at the box office but the studio tried again in 1944 with *Lady, Let's Dance*. This film has Belita playing herself as a war refugee from England. She is working as a waitress and is "discovered" when Jerry Gibson, a showman played by James Ellison, needs a replacement for his leading lady, who has walked out. Belita just happens to be a multi-talented dancer—we see her ballroom dancing, as a ballet dancer and finally as an ice dancer. She becomes a star, the showman falls in love with her, enlists in the service and ends up in a wheelchair as a result of war injuries

The highlights of the film we are the superbly lavish production numbers. One of them was for the song "Silver Shadows and Golden Dreams" and Dave Gould's staging was surely responsible for its Oscar nomination. (Edward Kay was also nominated for his scoring of the film.)

A chorus of men sings the song, accompanied by the Mitch Ayre band. Belita and her partner Eugen Mikeler skate languorously to the song's dreamy melody. The rather coy lyric describes a pair of lovers enjoying the night, with the moon throwing "silver shadows" as they share their "golden dreams."

Monogram's plans for Belita came to little and she was last seen on the screen playing a very minor role in the 1957 musical *Silk Stockings*.

Sweet Dreams, Sweetheart

from *Hollywood Canteen*
Music: M.K. Jerome
Lyrics: Ted Koehler

After the success of New York's Stage Door Canteen, set up to entertain U.S. troops on leave, Bette Davis and John Garfield established a similar venture in Los Angeles: the Hollywood Canteen. Both establishments were open to servicemen only, the food was free and many stars gave their time free to provide the entertainment. The Warner Bros. film *Hollywood Canteen* was designed to show the general public how the studio and its stars were doing their bit for the war effort. Davis and Garfield were there along with many others, including Eddie Cantor, Jack Benny, Joan Crawford and Barbara Stanwyck. "Don't Fence Me In" was aired for the first time, ten years after Cole Porter wrote it, sung by Roy Rogers and the Andrews Sisters.

The song "Sweet Dreams, Sweetheart" is sung twice in the film. One of the servicemen, Ed "Slim" Green, an Army corporal played by Robert Hutton, has a won a date with Joan Leslie, his favorite movie star. While dancing together at the Canteen, Joan is asked to sing with the Jimmy Dorsey band.

She sings "Sweet Dreams, Sweetheart," gazing all the while into Hutton's eyes. Not surprisingly, he falls heavily in love with her and tells her that her singing made him go weak at the knees. His feelings seem to be reciprocated and Joan suggests they go off to a club together. His unit is later mobilized for combat and he arranges to spend his last evening at the Canteen with Joan, but she is delayed. As he stands disconsolately near the door believing that Joan has rejected him, Kitty Carlisle turns up and offers to sing a request for Robert. There are no prizes for guessing which song he chooses.

As Kitty sings for him, a buddy comforts him with the friendly suggestion that the date was probably part of a publicity campaign. Hutton seems to accept this and writes Joan a farewell note, making it clear that he thinks their romance was a stunt.

It's all heart-rending stuff, but naturally Joan turns up just in time—the highly sentimental finale has her rushing onto the railway platform just as Hutton's train is about to depart. An obliging soldier lifts her up to Hutton as he leans out of the window and they manage one last kiss as the train starts to roll. Over the noise of the engine, she tells him that she will wait for him to come home from the war. Then, as the closing credits roll, the melody of "Sweet Dreams, Sweetheart" plays on.

Hutton's situation of having a beautiful young Hollywood star in love with him was clearly intended as a point of identification for all the lonely servicemen. And in spite of the sentimental clichés, there is a certain moving quality to the closing scene, given the wartime context. The publicity for the film said that it "makes a million dreams come true!"

The song effectively squeezes out every last drop of tear-stained emotion but it has had little life outside the film. It is a very short piece intended as an end-of-the-evening song in the manner of Ray Noble's "Goodnight Sweetheart." The singer bids his sweetheart goodnight, wishes her "sweet dreams" and asks the angels to care for her until the morning.

No doubt it brought tears to the eyes of GIs separated from their loved ones but the banal and repetitive lyric is certainly no match for Ray Noble's better-known song, and the melody is also bland and predictable.

Appropriately, Ray Noble and His Orchestra recorded "Sweet Dreams, Sweetheart" with vocalist Larry Stewart but neither this nor Kitty Carlisle's recording made much of an impact on the charts.

Too Much in Love

from *Song of the Open Road*
Music: Walter Kent
Lyrics: Kim Gannon

United Artists' *Song of the Open Road* starred the 15-year-old Suzanne Burce making her screen debut. A singing star in Portland, Oregon, she and had her own radio program there, and she was also heard over the national networks. Her parents were convinced that she could be a film star so took her off to Hollywood.

In *Song of the Open Road*, Suzanne plays a lonely child star named Jane Powell, dominated by her mother and deprived of the company of young people her own age. As Suzanne's real name was considered inappropriate for a movie star, the studio has her adopt this name as her own.

The film attempts to get the youth of America to contribute to the war effort by picking fruit and vegetables. Jane makes a commercial for the U.S. Crop Corps and encourages young people to do their bit, to join the American Youth Hostels and get picking. She herself runs away from her mother and the film studio to join the pickers.

Her winsome personality and beautiful soprano voice liven up a rather thin film. There are cameo performances from Edgar Bergen and Charlie McCarthy, W.C. Fields (his last screen appearance) and Sammy Kaye and His Orchestra. Jane Powell does most of the singing and though her photograph appears on the song sheet, the Oscar-nominated song is performed by Jack (Jackie Moran). Getting dressed for an evening's dancing, he serenades the photo of his girlfriend with "Too Much in Love." He meets up with her and they go out in the garden to dance. He continues to sing and at the end of the song they embrace and kiss. Jane Powell looks on and sighs at the romance of it all.

The song itself is on the short side: The entire unremarkable refrain consists of two four-line stanzas and a verse that comes after the refrain. The melody is pleasant but there is a certain clumsiness in the lyric, the ecstatic ramblings of a besotted young man. He is in a permanent daze, thinking of nothing else but his girl's eyes and her sighs.

Frank Sinatra, Harry James and His Orchestra and Boyd Raeburn and His Orchestra (vocal by Don Darcy) all recorded "Too Much in Love."

The Trolley Song

from *Meet Me in St. Louis*
Music and Lyrics: Hugh Martin and Ralph Blane

"The Trolley Song" is a perfect vehicle for Judy Garland's exuberant personality and the song is one of the many high spots in *Meet Me in St Louis*. It fits into the film so well in such a specific context that it is surprising that it has had any success as an independent song. Yet it was very popular at the time of the film's release—a number of singers recorded it, including Judy herself, but the best-selling version was by the Pied Pipers, with Jo Stafford.

Songwriters Martin and Blane felt it would be trite to have a song *about* a trolley so they came up with a rousing song to be sung *on* the trolley. But producer Arthur Freed insisted on a song about the trolley and the songwriters were compelled to oblige. Ralph Blane did some research at a public library and found some books about old St. Louis. In one was a photograph of a double decker trolley of 1903 which was captioned "Clang, Clang, Clang went the trolley." The songwriters were off and running and they claim to have completed the song in about ten minutes.

The song occurs when Judy Garland, as Esther Smith, and a group of people are boarding the special trolley car en route to the St. Louis Fairgrounds. Judy is hoping that Johnny Truett, "the boy next door," played by Tom Drake, will be joining the trip and she delays getting on board. "Let her go, motorman!" comes the cry and she has to get on board without young Tom. The trolley starts and the excited crowd starts to sing "Clang! Clang! Clang! went the trolley." The song has the driving tempo of the trolley as it rattles and rolls along the tracks.

As the crowd sings and expresses its excitement, Judy is the only one not enjoying herself. She walks along the aisle, ignoring the singing, then climbs the stairs and leans over the rail looking anxiously for her beau. Suddenly someone shouts, "Hey, look!," and here is Tom Drake rushing after the trolley. Now Judy starts her contribution to the song, and the thrill of riding the trolley merges with the dizziness of the developing romance.

Judy Garland rides the trolley in *Meet Me in St. Louis* (MGM, 1944).

It's a long song but it moves at a fast tempo, full of driving energy propelled by the repetition of onomatopoeic words like "buzz," "thud" and "clang." There is an authentic, period flavor to the lyric and the opening lines make a turn-of-the-century fashion statement as Judy describes her collar, shoes and hair style, and her man's brown derby hat.

The scene was completed in one take and Judy Garland's performance is superb. She seems to be having a wonderful time and a real sense of fun and laughter comes from the screen. She made only one mistake with the complex lyric—at one point she sings "Buzz, buzz, buzz" when she should have sung "Chug, chug, chug." Hugh Martin commented on this to Roger Edens, who was voice coach to Judy, and suggested that another take might be necessary. Edens' response was, "Forget it, the spirit was so marvelous. Don't touch it, she'll never do it that well again!"

Judy's recording reached as high as number four in the charts but Jo Stafford and the Pied Pipers (with the Paul Weston Orchestra) outsold her—their version went to number two. Other popular recordings came from Vaughn Monroe and His Orchestra (vocal by Marilyn Duke), the King Sisters and the Guy Lombardo orchestra. In 1947, MGM used the song again—in a Tom and Jerry cartoon entitled *Cat Fishin.'*

A stage version of *Meet Me in St. Louis* opened on Broadway in 1989 and in this Donna Kane and the company performed "The Trolley Song."

And the Winner Is...

Swinging on a Star

from *Going My Way*
Music: Jimmy Van Heusen
Lyrics: Johnny Burke

"Swinging on a Star" is a sermon-in-song designed to teach young people how to behave well and make the best of themselves. Bing Crosby as a priest sings it with a choir of potential delinquents in *Going My Way*.

Leo McCarey wanted to make a film about Father Joe Connor, a Roman Catholic priest who also wrote popular songs under the name of Pierre Norman. His most successful effort was "When I Take My Sugar to Tea." The film was to be called *The Padre* and McCarey wanted Bing Crosby for the role. Bing had doubts about his credibility as a priest but he believed in McCarey and so agreed to take the part. The film, now entitled *Going My Way*, was the biggest hit of 1944 and Bing earned himself a Best Actor Oscar.

In the film, the priest that Bing plays is called Father Chuck O'Malley. He has progressive ideas that clash with those held by Father Fitzgibbon, the old priest, played by Barry Fitzgerald, to whom he is sent as assistant.

In addition to playing baseball with local delinquents, Bing forms them

In *Going My Way* (Paramount, 1944), Bing Crosby as Father Chuck O'Malley settles a dispute between two of his "choirboys," played by Carl "Alfalfa" Switzer and Stanley Clements.

into a choir and writes songs for them to sing. His songs are intended as simple sermons without a thought of commercial success until he finds that his church has a heavy mortgage debt. With the help of his boys' choir and Genevieve Linden (played by Rise Stevens, the Metropolitan Opera star), he tries to raise funds by selling a little effort called "Going My Way" to a music publisher. The publisher deems the song too classy to appeal to the general public and turns it down.

Disappointed, Bing and the boys decide to lift their spirits by singing their favorite song, "Swinging on a Star." The boys call it "the mule song" and of course the publisher hears it, loves it and buys it immediately.

The song is an amusing warning of the dangers of certain antisocial behaviors. These behaviors are described through the characteristics of animals—a fish, a pig and a mule. The idea for the lyric came to Johnny Burke while he and Jimmy Van Heusen were having a meal at the Crosby home. He overheard Bing reprimanding one of his sons with the words, "You're acting just like a mule!"

The whimsical humor in the lyric and the catchy tune enable the song to avoid heavy-handed moralizing. Bing and the Robert Mitchell Boychoir sing it with great style and the camera emphasizes the light-heartedness of it all by dwelling particularly on one of the lads who has eyebrows that go up and down like a holland blind.

The song was a big hit for Crosby, his ninth million-selling record; it topped the US charts for nine weeks. The Williams Brothers, a group that included 13-year-old Andy Williams, supplied the backing vocals.

Bing sang "Swinging on a Star" again in the 1945 film *Duffy's Tavern* and this version was a very funny parody of the original. Frank Sinatra sang another parody version of it in *The Joker Is Wild* (1957), with lyrics especially written for the film by Harry Harris. In 1963, "Swinging on a Star" was a hit for Big Dee Irwin—the record had Little Eva (of "The Loco-Motion" fame) singing backing vocals, though she is uncredited.

1945

Bob Hope and James Stewart were the hosts at Grauman's Chinese Theatre and this Awards Ceremony was the first at which all the nominated songs were performed. The singers were Frank Sinatra, Dinah Shore, Dick Haymes and Kathryn Grayson—they performed the choruses of the songs as a medley. The evening had started with an orchestra playing the winning songs from previous years.

The Nominations

Harold Arlen and Johnny Mercer for "Ac-Cent-Tchu-Ate the Positive" from *Here Come the Waves* (Paramount)

Jule Styne and Sammy Cahn for "Anywhere" from *Tonight and Every Night* (Columbia)

James Van Heusen and Johnny Burke for "Aren't You Glad You're You?" from *The Bells of St. Mary's* (RKO)

Jay Livingston and Ray Evans for "The Cat and the Canary" from *Why Girls Leave Home* (Producers Releasing Corporation)

Walter Kent and Kim Gannon for "Endlessly" from *Earl Carroll Vanities* (Republic)

Jule Styne and Sammy Cahn for "I Fall in Love Too Easily" from *Anchors Aweigh* (MGM)

Allie Wrubel and Herb Magidson for "I'll Buy That Dream" from *Sing Your Way Home* (RKO)

Richard Rodgers and Oscar Hammerstein II for "It Might As Well Be Spring" from *State Fair* (Fox)

Ann Ronell for "Linda" from *The Story of GI Joe* (United Artists)

Victor Young and Edward Heyman for "Love Letters" from *Love Letters* (Paramount)

Jerome Kern and E.Y. Harburg for "More and More" from *Can't Help Singing* (Universal)

James Van Heusen and Johnny Burke for "Sleigh Ride in July" from *Belle of the Yukon* (RKO)

David Rose and Leo Robin for "So in Love" from *Wonder Man* (Goldwyn)

Ray Heindorf, M.K. Jerome and Ted Koehler for "Some Sunday Morning" from *San Antonio* (Republic)

Ac-Cent-Tchu-Ate the Positive

from *Here Come the Waves*
Music: Harold Arlen
Lyrics: Johnny Mercer

Here Come the Waves was little more than recruiting propaganda for the women's U.S. Navy. It starred Bing Crosby and Sonny Tufts as Johnny and Windy, Navy men in love with Susan and Rosemary Allison, identical twin Waves, both played by Betty Hutton. Crosby is ordered to organize entertainment for naval personnel and "Ac-Cent-Tchu-Ate the Positive" is the show-stopping number from the show he produces.

Harold Arlen and Johnny Mercer had written three reasonably good songs for the film, including the very attractive romantic ballad "I Promise You." But now a bright and breezy number was needed and the songwriters were short of ideas. They decided to go for a drive, hoping that a change of scenery would help. It apparently did the trick and they composed most of the Oscar-nominated song whilst on the road.

The song is written as though a sermon for a Southern revivalist preacher. Mercer grew up in Savannah, Georgia, and often heard black preachers. He borrowed the phrase "Accentuate the positive" from one known as Daddy Grace.

The lyric exhibits Mercer's superb talent for earthy slang, combined with the pretentious, formal vocabulary of a sermon. Though it pokes fun, it does so in a delightfully affectionate way that is never condescending. Unfortunately, the song is presented in the film in a way that is patronizingly racist by today's standards. Bing Crosby and Sonny Tufts are in blackface and dressed as caricatures. Crosby is a comic mailman, complete with a white-haired wig poking out from under his hat, while Tufts is a commissionaire, resplendent in outlandish mock military coat and plumed hat.

The song itself has survived its original screen presentation. Crosby recorded it with the Andrews Sisters and it stayed in the hit parade for three months. There were other 1945 hit recordings, one by Artie Shaw's band, with vocalist Imogene Lynn, and another by the Kay Kyser band that had Dolly Mitchell vocals.

But lyricist Johnny Mercer had the most successful version and it topped the U.S. charts. Decades later, it was heard over the opening and closing credits of the 1997 crime film *L.A. Confidential*; the following year, Clint Eastwood sang it on the soundtrack of his film *Midnight in the Garden of Good and Evil*. This film is set in Savannah, Georgia, Johnny Mercer's birthplace, and Eastwood, who directed, makes great use of his songs—though he's clearly a better director than singer.

Anywhere

from *Tonight and Every Night*
Music: Jule Styne
Lyrics: Sammy Cahn

Tonight and Every Night was intended as a tribute to London's Windmill Theatre which stayed open right through the Blitz. After the war, the theater publicized itself with the slogan "We never clothed," a punning reference to its courage under fire and its nude showgirls. Though set in London, most of the film's cast was American—Rita Hayworth, Lee Bowman and Janet Blair starred. At least director Victor Saville was British. Rita plays the part of Rosalind Bruce, the theater's leading entertainer, while Janet is Judy Kane, a young member of the cast. Bowman plays Rita's fiancé, Squadron Leader Paul Lundy of the RAF.

There are great costumes, and very good use of Technicolor, but the plot is rather thin. The best things in the film are the highly entertaining production numbers, including "You Excite Me" and the title song, brilliantly staged by Jack Cole and Val Raset. The film is well scored; Marlin Skiles and Morris Stoloff received an Oscar-nomination for their work. And though Rita Hayworth performs some of the songs—her voice dubbed by Martha Mears—it is Janet Blair who sings very prettily the Oscar-nominated "Anywhere." Janet was originally signed for the film only as Rita's voice.

The melody is used throughout as a love theme for Rita and her RAF fiancé. At one point an ancient xylophone player, Prof. Lamberti, billed here as The Great Waldo, plays it on stage in bizarre circumstances. As the aged gentleman plays, Rita dances with tasteful suggestiveness.

Towards the end of the film, Rita is in suspense wondering whether Bowman will return from a dangerous mission. Janet is on stage singing "Anywhere" and Rita is watching from the wings. Enter Bowman for a joyful reunion. Janet continues the song and at this point we see that Tommy Lawson, the young male dancer played by Marc Platt, is watching from the other side of the stage. He has been in love with Rita himself but now the reunion he witnesses confirms that he will never win her. But Janet is in love with Marc and is clearly directing the message of the song to him. It seems he will find consolation here. The two meet after the show in the pub opposite the theatre—and just as all seems bright for them, they are killed in an air raid. "Anywhere" has been their requiem.

But the show must go on and Rita fills in for Janet on her big number "Tonight and Every Night." As she sings, the tears stream down her face. Many empathetic members of the wartime audience must have joined her.

The song "Anywhere" had no hit recordings and is rarely heard nowadays but it did turn up again in the 1947 musical *Glamour Girl*, sung by Susan Reed. The tune is attractive but the words break no new ground. The singer tells her man that she will follow him wherever he goes, though it seems his kiss already has the power to magically transport her "Anywhere" at all.

Aren't You Glad You're You?

from *The Bells of St. Mary's*
Music: Jimmy Van Heusen
Lyrics: Johnny Burke

Jimmy Van Heusen and Johnny Burke won the 1944 Best Song Oscar with "Swinging on a Star" from *Going My Way*. *The Bells of St. Mary's* was the 1945 follow-up to that film. Once more Bing Crosby plays Father Chuck O'Malley and this time the opposition to his unconventional ideas comes from Ingrid Bergman as Sister Benedict, the nun in charge of the church school.

"Swinging on a Star" from *Going My Way* is a sermon in song, a piece of lyrical preaching: Van Heusen and Burke wrote a similar sprightly sermon for Bing to sing in *The Bells of St. Mary's*, entitled "Aren't You Glad You're You?" Bing sings it to Patsy, a teenage girl played by Joan Carroll. She is going through unhappy times and finds it impossible to get started on a school essay she has to write on the five senses. Bing offers his help, telling her she should write something different, something unique. He suggests that there is a sixth sense—the sense to appreciate the other five; the song is designed to illustrate this and also to boost her self-esteem. Bing sings of all the joys to be experienced through the senses and ends the song by telling her that these pleasures should make her feel glad to be who she is. A sermonizing tone is avoided by the use of such homey phrases as "Ain't life grand?"

Joan learns the lesson well and sums it up this way: "If you can't appreciate your five senses, then life isn't worth five cents!" She tells Bing that she feels much better now and the song seems to have worked for Bing too: He says that he feels "pretty good" himself. And of course the resulting essay receives an A plus.

The film failed to achieve as high a score from the critics, though it was a box office success. It collected a total of seven Oscar nominations, including Best Actor and Best Actress for Bing and Ingrid Bergman.

The Cat and the Canary

from *Why Girls Leave Home*
Music: Jay Livingston
Lyrics: Ray Evans

Livingston and Evans' first Oscar nomination, for "The Cat and the Canary," resulted in a contract with Paramount. The fact that Johnny Mercer sang the song on his popular NBC radio show also helped.

In *Why Girls Leave Home,* Pamela Blake plays Diana Leslie, a nicely brought-up young lady who feels stifled by suburban family life. She leaves home to make a career for herself as a singer, lands a job in a seedy nightclub, but becomes embroiled with a group of criminals. When she learns too much about their activities, her boss decides to kill her and make it look like suicide. A reporter (Sheldon Leonard) suspects the truth and pursues the story until the facts are made public.

Although it was the launching pad for the movie songwriting careers of Livingston and Evans, the film and the songs it contains have disappeared almost without trace. All the prints have deteriorated and it does not exist in any archive holdings. Ray Evans himself very generously supplied the author of this book with the lyrics for "The Cat and the Canary" and some comments on its use in the film.

Pamela Blake performs "The Cat and the Canary" in a nightclub, her voice dubbed by Martha Tilton. The song is very amusing but it is barely heard in the film and this is perhaps why it escaped the notice of the singers of the time and was never recorded.

The "cat" is a trumpeter and a girl singer is the "canary." They are in a "razz-ma-tazzy, sort of jazzy, kind of snazzy little band" and the cat is "a musician with ambition to audition for her hand." The song is full of such inventive internal rhymes and these and the amusing jazz slang help to make "The Cat and the Canary" a lively song that deserves to be better known.

Walter Greene also received an Oscar nomination for his scoring of the picture.

Endlessly

from *Earl Carroll Vanities*
Music: Walter Kent
Lyrics: Kim Gannon

The annual *Ziegfeld Follies,* the most spectacular revues on Broadway, lasted from 1907 until 1932. A number of other producers attempted to rival Florenz Ziegfeld and the best-known are George White with his Scandals and Earl Carroll and his Vanities. Hollywood paid homage three times to

Ziegfeld with *The Great Ziegfeld* (1936), *Ziegfeld Girl* (1941) and *Ziegfeld Follies* (1946). There were also three versions of *George White's Scandals*, in 1934, 1935 and 1945. And in 1945 Republic put the *Earl Carroll Vanities* on screen.

The star was Constance Moore—she plays Princess Drina, part of an entourage from an obscure European country, in New York to negotiate a bank loan. Whilst there she becomes, almost by accident, the star of Earl Carroll's latest show and falls in love with Danny Baldwin (Dennis O'Keefe), its producer and songwriter.

It is Moore who sings "Endlessly." The first time we hear it is at rehearsal. She drapes herself elegantly across a grand piano and sings the song with simplicity and natural expression. She sings that, just as the seasons change but always return, so her love will last forever—"Endlessly."

There's nothing strikingly original about the lyric but it is pleasant and the flowing melody is attractive. Moore's singing impresses Dennis O'Keefe and he watches entranced as she sings. Later, when they kiss for the first time, the melody plays on the soundtrack. Moore returns to her Park Avenue apartment floating on air, and sweeps the butler into a waltz. Again the melody of "Endlessly" accompanies them, this time *a la* Strauss.

The song is used one last time in the film when Moore performs it in the actual show. The scene is Ziegfeld on a budget. Firstly the usual bevy of chorus girls enters, attempting to walk elegantly in over elaborate costumes and cumbersome headdresses. A male chorus sings the song and then Constance appears, walking down the obligatory celestial staircase clutching an enormous fan of feathers. This time she sings "Endlessly" with over-dramatic affectation and every line is milked for sentimental emotion that overwhelms the simplicity of the song.

I Fall in Love Too Easily

from *Anchors Aweigh*
Music: Jule Styne
Lyrics: Sammy Cahn

When MGM wanted Frank Sinatra for *Anchors Aweigh*, he insisted that the studio hire Sammy Cahn and his then-partner, composer Jule Styne, to write the songs for the film. His demand is understandable—of all lyricists, Sammy Cahn had an extraordinary skill in writing words to suit Sinatra's persona. But MGM felt that it was rather presumptuous of the young star to demand the services of Cahn and Styne, even if they were giving him top billing, but agreed when he threatened to walk out. Sinatra's judgment was proved correct when "I Fall in Love Too Easily," the hit song of the film, was nominated for an Oscar. The film received four other nominations and Georgie Stoll won an Oscar for his scoring of it.

Sinatra plays sailor Clarence Doolittle, also known as Brooklyn, and he

Kathryn Grayson, Frank Sinatra and Gene Kelly in *Anchors Aweigh* **(MGM, 1945).**

and his buddy Joe Brady (Gene Kelly) are on liberty in Los Angeles. The melody of the song is used to underscore Brooklyn's feelings for Susan Abbott (Kathryn Grayson) but the song occurs in full for the first time late in the film. Frank is alone in the Hollywood Bowl and he sings the lovely ballad seated at a piano. He has come to realize that he will never win Kathryn, who is in love with Gene, and he ruefully admits to himself that he is a fool when it comes to romance: He falls in love too easily and too quickly.

But at the end of the song, he confirms the truth of this insight by switching his feelings from Kathryn Grayson to Pamela Britton (who plays a waitress from his old stomping grounds, Brooklyn) and he rushes off to propose to her.

The song perfectly conveys his screen character, naive and girl-shy. The vulnerable, introspective quality that he is able to convey through the song is very much one of the reasons for the enormous following he built up. He seems to be sharing his innermost feelings, asking his audience to share them with him.

"I Fall in Love Too Easily" is quite a short song—it has only 16 bars instead of the usual 32. When challenged on this, Sammy Cahn refused to add another word and, like Jerome Kern before him who faced a similar charge over "Lovely to Look At," said, "That's all the song has to say!"

Sinatra recorded the song but the best-selling version was not his—that honor went to Mel Torme.

I'll Buy That Dream

from *Sing Your Way Home*
Music: Allie Wrubel
Lyrics: Herb Magidson

Sing Your Way Home is a forgettable musical that starred Jack Haley as Steve Kimball, a war correspondent sailing back to America after VE Day. On board he finds himself chaperoning a group of teenage entertainers who have been on tour in Europe but are unable to get back home because of the war. The group continues to put on some musical entertainments on the ship. One of the girls, Kay Lawrence, played by Anne Jeffreys, sings "I'll Buy That Dream." As a vocalist, Jeffreys is really very good and the film is worth catching if only to hear her and the other vocalists sing.

The Oscar-nominated song is easily the best thing in the film and in amongst the romantic platitudes are some inventive ideas and unexpected rhymes ("flow'ry/dowry" and "Cairo/autogyro") which lend the song a slightly tongue-in-cheek quality.

The Harry James Orchestra, with vocalist Kitty Kallen, made a best-selling recording of the song. Almost as successful was a Dick Haymes—Helen Forrest duet.

Linda

from *The Story of GI Joe*
Music and Lyrics: Ann Ronell

"Linda" is sung with significant effect in *The Story of GI Joe*. Directed by William Wellman, the film follows the fortunes of a group of American soldiers during the Allied invasion of Italy. The film is based on the wartime experiences of journalist Ernie Pyle, played here by Burgess Meredith. Pyle was a highly regarded war correspondent, something of a hero to millions of Americans who admired his simply written yet vivid portraits of ordinary men in uniform, stories of ordinary people doing extraordinary things. The credits, as well as the original posters, bill the film as *Ernie Pyle's Story of GI Joe*.

The Story of GI Joe is a decidedly unglamourous, realistic portrayal of warfare. It avoids the pitfalls of jingoistic patriotism, unusual for a film made before the Second World War was over. Robert Mitchum became an important star as a result of his brilliant performance as Lt. (later Cpt.) Bill Walker, the platoon's leader, and he was nominated for Best Supporting Actor.

A number of American soldiers who took part in the Anzio landings acted as extras in the film. Soon after, many of them were killed in action fighting the Japanese in the Pacific. *The Story of GI Joe* had its premiere in July 1945, but Ernie Pyle was not there to see it as he also had been killed by machine-gun fire a few months before.

During World War II, the Germans regularly broadcast propaganda to the Allied soldiers. One ploy was to try to make the troops long to be home with their loved ones by playing romantic love songs. The broadcasts made regular use of a singer known as Axis Sally and she was notorious for her seductive voice. In the film, Shelly Mitchell (later cabaret singer Shelly Cullin) did the voice over as Axis Sally.

Early in the film, as the American troops are advancing, they are settling for the night in their tents and know that they will be facing the enemy the next day. The radio is playing an Artie Shaw record, then the men grow quiet as the voice of Axis Sally evokes memories of home, of their wives and sweethearts, "summer nights ... the juke box down the road ... Cokes ... double malt ... a girl's soft laughter in the moonlight." She identifies the men correctly as the 18th Infantry and speaks directly to them, inviting them to surrender: "Be my guests in Germany," she whispers, "dance with our lovely girls—they know how to entertain nice young men like you. Now I'll sing you Germany's latest hit, the lyrics especially written for my handsome American friends"—and the song that Axis Sally sings at this point is "Linda."*

Ann Ronell's melody for "Linda" is quite lovely though the words of the song are almost unimportant—just romantic, even sensual murmurings, designed to play on the emotions of the homesick soldiers and create doubt about the fidelity of their wives and sweethearts at home. But with great economy, the ordinary words, in only eight lines, do set up an atmosphere very effectively. It is a poignant scene, the lull before the storm of the battlefield.

When Axis Sally finishes the song, one soldier picks up his guitar and claims the song as his own: "It was Nazi music, now it's mine—our first German prisoner," and he begins to play the tune, a small act of defiance that tells us that the morale-reducing ploy has failed. From this point, the melody belongs to the GIs and it is played by them a number of times—by the guitarist, by a soldier with a mouth organ and by another who whistles it.

Axis Sally's real name was Mildred Gillars. She was an American studying music at Hunter College in Germany in the 1930s and fell in love with her professor. He later recruited her for German radio propaganda programs from a Berlin radio station. After the war, she was brought back to the U.S. and in 1949 she was found guilty of treason. She was sentenced to 10–30 years in prison and eventually released in 1962. Until her death in 1988, she was a music instructor at a Catholic girls school in Columbus, Ohio.

In spite of its attractive melody, no recordings of Ann Ronell's "Linda" exist and the song has had no life whatsoever outside of the film. Perhaps its brevity is the reason. Also, it is often confused with the quite different 1947 hit song written by Jack Lawrence that has the same title. Some writers on film history wrongly credit the Oscar nomination for "Linda" to Lawrence, while the normally very reliable Ken Bloom, in his major work *Hollywood Song,* gives Ronell and Lawrence a joint songwriting credit. Lawrence's "Linda," a hit for Buddy Clark, was reputedly written for Linda Eastman, the little girl who grew up to become Mrs. Paul McCartney.

The film's script was also nominated for an Oscar—the writers were Leopold Atlas, Guy Endore and Philip Stevenson. Playwright Arthur Miller was producer Lester Cowan's original choice to write the screenplay and did do some early work on the script. He left when Alan LeMay was brought in as his collaborator in an effort, he felt, to create a storyline that was more acceptable for Hollywood consumption. However, Miller's work on the screenplay was not wasted. He used the research he had done as the basis for his first published book, *Situation Normal,* a book of reportage about Army training.

Producer Lester Cowan gave the job of scoring the film to his wife Ann Ronell. She justified his faith when she received Oscar nominations for both her score and for "Linda."

Love Letters

from *Love Letters*
Music: Victor Young
Lyrics: Edward Heyman

"Love Letters" had little impact on the charts when the film for which it is the title song was screened. Dick Haymes' recording of it was a minor hit in the U.S. but it had to wait until Ketty Lester recorded it in 1962 before it made a real impact on the bestseller lists. Four years later, Elvis Presley's version also sold more than a million copies.

In the film, Joseph Cotten plays Allen Quinton, a soldier serving on the Italian front who pens love letters on behalf of a companion with a writing block. Jennifer Jones plays Singleton, the recipient, and she is swept off her feet with love for the writer. Of course she marries the wrong man and finds out too late that the letters were actually written by Cotten. All is resolved in the most melodramatic and unlikely manner. The film received three other nominations, including one for Victor Young's score.

The song "Love Letters" is sung over the credits by the studio chorus. It has a pleasant tune but the lyrics are nothing special. The night may be dark but it is lit by the glow of love from those wonderful love letters that keep the lovers close even though they are far apart. Alone in that dark night, the singer kisses the signature and memorizes every line.

"Love Letters" is the first Oscar-nominated title song from a non-musical film and it is an indication of things to come—there will be many more and some of them will win the Academy Award.

More and More

from *Can't Help Singing*
Music: Jerome Kern
Lyrics: E Y Harburg

Can't Help Singing is a light-hearted operetta that starred Deanna Durbin in another of her characteristically charming roles. She plays Caroline Frost, a rich young lady from Washington travelling by covered wagon across the West to marry Robert Latham, an Army lieutenant played by David Bruce. On the way she meets Johnny Lawlor (Robert Paige) and opts for him instead.

The musical numbers are enjoyable and the Oscar-nominated "More and More" does have a charming melody by Jerome Kern. Deanna Durbin sings it with controlled and gentle romantic fervor to a moonlit Robert Paige as an expression of her newfound love for him. The warmth of his kisses, his cool blue eyes thrill her, make her tremble with love, and she wants "more and more" of him. Yip Harburg's understated and simple lyrics make the song all the more appealing.

In the grand finale, Deanna sings the song once more as she walks down an ornate staircase, while Paige watches her from a fountain jetting with pink water. As she approaches, he joins in and sings some manly lines, assuring her that he is "more than willing" to work and strive for her.

Pleasantly romantic as the song is, it is rarely heard nowadays. The title song is the one that people remember: it is sung three times in the film and was very popular for a while but it was overlooked for the Oscars.

Deanna released a recording of "More and More" though the better-selling version was by Bonnie Lou Williams, singing with the Tommy Dorsey orchestra. Perry Como also had a minor hit with it. The song spent 15 weeks on *Your Hit Parade* and was the last big hit for Jerome Kern during his life.

Sleighride in July

from *Belle of the Yukon*
Music: Jimmy Van Heusen
Lyrics: Johnny Burke

Appropriately, "Sleighride in July" is about someone who has been deceived. It features in *Belle of the Yukon,* a musical comedy in which all the main characters seem to be pretenders or deceivers of some sort, with the exception of Lettie Candless (Dinah Shore)—she seems to be the *victim* of deception.

Deanna Durbin in *Can't Help Singing* **(Universal, 1944).**

The setting for the film is a saloon in the Yukon at the time of the Gold Rush; Randolph Scott plays the saloon's owner, a con artist known as Honest John Calhoun, while Gypsy Rose Lee plays the Belle of the title. With all the double-dealing and double-crossing that occurs, it is fitting that the Oscar-nominated song is one about a girl who has been deceived by Steve, the man she loves. William Marshall plays the cad concerned. It seems that he has a wife and children back in Seattle and Dinah Shore receives this news from her father (played by Charles Winninger) just before she goes on stage to sing at the saloon.

Marshall attempts to explain the situation away but her eyes have been opened and she tells him so in her song, "Sleighride in July." It expresses her rueful feelings at having fallen for the wrong man—her "big romance" is a confidence trick. And, as in "Blues in the Night," a mockingbird whistles nearby. The song neatly builds on the slang expression for someone who is the victim of such a trick, someone who has been "taken for a ride."

She cries as she sings but makes sure that William Marshall gets the message. Having sung the song once through, she rushes from the stage in tears. In the wings, Gypsy Rose Lee tells her to stop crying and get mad— she has been a sucker but she should get back and carry on. So Dinah does and this time she smiles bravely as she sings "Sleighride in July" once more. But by the end of the movie, she learns that Marshall's apparent wife is actually his sister and that his supposed children are his younger brothers. The obligatory happy ending occurs on schedule.

"Sleighride in July" is an unusually short song with an unconventional form and although it is effective in expressing the singer's plight, it has a forgettable melody and is rarely heard today. Dinah's own recording was the best-selling version, and Bing Crosby was reasonably successful with his. Other popular vocal renditions were by Bonnie Lou Williams with the Tommy Dorsey band, and Gordon Drake backed by Les Brown and His Band of Renown.

So in Love

from *Wonder Man*
Music: David Rose
Lyrics: Leo Robin

Not to be confused with Cole Porter's "So in Love," this song was originally entitled "So-o-o-o-o in Love" and appears as such on the published song sheet. Vera-Ellen (with vocals dubbed by June Hutton) and the Goldwyn Girls sing it in *Wonder Man*. The film was RKO's follow-up to the huge success Danny Kaye had had in *Up in Arms* and it was one of the most popular of 1945. It gathered four Oscar nominations and won for its special effects.

Kaye plays identical twin brothers: one is Buzzy Bellew, a sophisticated and extroverted nightclub performer, while the other is Edwin Dingle, an introvert who hides away in libraries, preferring books to people. He does manage to fall in love with librarian Ellen Shanley (Virginia Mayo), while his brother romances with showgirl Midge Mallon (Vera-Ellen). When gangsters kill the extrovert brother to prevent him from testifying in a murder trial, he manages to transfer his soul to the reclusive brother who saves the day and brings the murdering gangsters to justice.

Mrs. Kaye—Sylvia Fine—wrote three numbers for her husband, notably the "Opera Number" that occurs at the climax. On the run from the gangsters, Kaye somehow finds himself on stage at the Met as the lead tenor in the opera. Spotting the DA in the audience, he spills the beans in a very fast, tongue-twisting operatic parody that reveals the identity of his brother's murderers.

The song "So in Love" has no dramatic function but is performed in a nightclub by Vera-Ellen (her voice dubbed by June Hutton) with a chorus of Goldwyn Girls. The production number is designed to show off Vera-Ellen's considerable dancing talents. The song is in three parts. It begins with Vera-Ellen in the Garden of Love, sitting on a bench. She is dressed in a fetching red blouse with a short white skirt decorated with hearts. She looks at her watch, then tells the audience that she's waiting for someone called Freddy who is already ten minutes late. The lyric of "So in Love" reveals that she is unsure of Freddy's feelings and she has fallen in love with him against her better judgment.

The number continues and at this point a gypsy fortuneteller enters. She offers Vera-Ellen some wise advice on how to get her man—and it will come from the lips of the Goldwyn Girls. The curtain rises to reveal the Girls clad in gauzy Grecian gowns, like a gathering of Delphic oracles. They have all the answers for Vera-Ellen—they tell her to use the time-honored ploy of making him jealous by flirting with someone else.

Now Vera-Ellen goes into an energetic dance routine, to the jazzed up melody of "So in Love," and she is joined by various male dancers. They throw her around and end the number holding her high above their heads.

With its witty internal rhymes and slangy style, the lyric is very appealing and the number as a whole is highly entertaining. But it's not a very singable song and it has had no life outside the film.

Some Sunday Morning

from *San Antonio*
Music: Ray Heindorf and M.K. Jerome
Lyrics: Ted Koehler

San Antonio was one of a series of Westerns made by Warner Bros. to capitalize on the great success Errol Flynn had experienced with *Dodge City* in 1939. No expense was spared—the film was shot in Technicolor and the screen teemed with extras—and though the interior decoration of the film earned an Oscar nomination, it is still not much more than a corny B-Western. Some of the supporting actors are distinctly wooden and the plot creaks. And mixed with the usual goodies-against-baddies conflict were farcical elements such as a whisky drinking cat and a bright green parrot with a Southern drawl. But Flynn, as the dashing and handsome Clay Hardin, lends some style to the proceedings. Alexis Smith provides his love interest and it is she who sings the Oscar-nominated song, "Some Sunday Morning."

Smith plays Jeanne Starr, a beautiful New Orleans singer who has come to town to perform for the unsophisticated folks of San Antonio. At the Bella Union Hotel, she comes on stage to much whooping and hollering, quieting the yokels with her "Some Sunday Morning" rendition.

The songwriters were clearly called upon to provide an appropriately corny song and they succeed only too well. Alexis sings of a girl eagerly looking forward to her wedding. As she sings, Alexis moves through her audience of frontiersmen and cowboys, lingering at Errol Flynn's table where he sits alone. Gazing at him tenderly, she continues to imagine the wedding with friends and relatives, calling the happy couple "a peach of a pair."

After Smith's performance, the song is taken up by a male quartet and their singing continues in the background as Flynn goes to meet his new lady love. From this point on, the tune plays every time they meet, underscoring their romance.

The melody is rather bland and the unoriginal imagery used in the lyric appears in almost every other wedding song but Ted Koehler was only writing to order. The song is designed to fit a specific situation, a sweet, unsophisticated offering for the supposedly unlettered menfolk of a frontier cattle town.

"Some Sunday Morning" was only a very minor hit; the leading version was by Dick Haymes and Helen Forrest, singing with Gordon Jenkins and His Orchestra. Haymes seems to have found the phrase "a peach of a pair" rather too cornball and changes it to "a beautiful pair."

The song rode again in the 1952 Western *The Man Behind the Gun*, which starred Randolph Scott.

And the Winner Is...

It Might as Well Be Spring

from *State Fair*
Music: Richard Rodgers
Lyrics: Oscar Hammerstein II

All the Rodgers and Hammerstein stage musicals were transferred to film but the songs for *State Fair* were the only ones they wrote together directly for the screen. Alfred Newman and Charles Henderson scored the film and they received an Oscar nomination for their efforts.

When Richard Rodgers first wrote the music for "It Might as Well Be Spring," he marked it "bright, medium tempo," but director Walter Lang felt that the scene called for a slow ballad. The songwriters reluctantly agreed but when they saw the finished film, they soon came to see that Lang was right.

Oscar Hammerstein's lyric was intended to be about a girl suffering from the spring fever of love but the scriptwriters pointed out that the Iowa State Fair was always held in autumn. Hammerstein therefore altered it so that the finished song is a self-portrait of a girl who shows all the symptoms of the said fever even though "it isn't even spring."

In his autobiography *Musical Stages*, Rodgers described the song as a good example of the way a melody can amplify the meaning of a lyric. For the first two lines where the girl describes her agitated feelings, the music is "appropriately restless and jumpy." He adds:

> Since the song is sung by a young girl who can't quite understand
> why she feels the way she does, I deliberately ended the main
> phrase on the uncertain sound of the F natural [on the word
> "string"], rather than on the more positive F sharp.

The song occurs early in the film: Jeanne Crain, as Margy Crake, is moping around the house and her mother (Fay Bainter) wonders what is wrong with her. In her bedroom she too is puzzled by her own behavior. She looks at the photograph of Harry Barker, her bespectacled and unprepossessing fiancé, and we realize that part of her discontent is with him. She expresses her feelings in the opening verse of the song: She is full of self-doubt. As she perches on her upstairs windowsill, her mother calls her to come down and help in the kitchen. Now she begins the song proper and expresses her restlessness in a series of images, comparing herself to a willow in the wind, a puppet and a song-less nightingale. She keeps wishing to be elsewhere, meeting the man of her dreams. And this prospect makes her feel so happy, albeit in a somewhat sad way, that "It Might as Well Be Spring."

The song is a slightly melancholy ballad sung by a daydreaming girl. A little later, in the garden, she sings more of the song but this time with a touch of self-mockery as she speculates about the man she is "yet to meet," suggesting that he could be a mixture of her three favorite movie stars: Charles Boyer, Ronald Colman and Bing Crosby. And we hear the voices of these stars as she imagines them, whispering sweet nothings, or in Bing's case, singing them.

Lost in these romantic daydreams, her mood is shattered by the sudden arrival of nerdish Harry, played by Henry Morgan. He prattles on to her about his plans for the modern farm they will have when they are married, along with a wonderful "plastic, prefabricated" house. Jeanne Crain is not impressed: "Life will be just ducky," she says, with heavy irony. She sings new—and bitter—words to her song, envisioning a sterile home with no flowers or any touch of the sentimental. She ends the song abruptly, on a discordant note. Her irony has gone over Harry's head and he raves on about the Fair and the prize animal that Jeanne's father is showing there: "It must be the biggest boar in the world!" he cries. "Depends on how you spell it" is her reply and she gives him a withering look.

The song establishes superbly well the innocent character of this lovesick girl and all her adolescent discontent. The extra lines add a little humor to the scene and establish in our minds that Jeanne will probably find a new and more congenial love at the State Fair.

But this scene is not the last we hear of the song: At the Fair, the melody is played by the fairground organ, especially when Jeanne meets her new romance in the shape of Dana Andrews, who plays Pat Gilbert. We hear her voice on the soundtrack, singing a few lines from the song, and from this point the tune becomes their love theme. Later in the evening, the band playing for dancing at the Fair renders the tune again.

Louanne Hogan dubs Jeanne Crain's singing voice and her sweet and wistful singing of the song conveys wonderfully the innocence of Jeanne's character. With the work that the song does in establishing character and situation, its lively and original imagery and the differing ways the melody is employed on the soundtrack, it is not surprising that "It Might as Well Be Spring" attracted attention and became a big hit, though not for the lady who sang in it the film. It was Dick Haymes who had the best-selling record—he had a role in the film as Wayne, Jeanne Crain's brother. Margaret Whiting's version, backed by the Paul Weston orchestra, was also popular, as was the one by Sammy Kaye and His Orchestra, which had a vocal by Billy Williams.

State Fair was originally made as a non-musical in 1933 when it starred Will Rogers and Janet Gaynor; another version of the Rodgers and Hammerstein treatment was filmed in 1962 starring pop singers Pat Boone and Bobby Darin. Pamela Tiffin, her voice dubbed by Anita Gordon, performs "It Might as Well Be Spring."

1946

The number of songs nominated had been creeping up until it reached an unwieldy 14 in 1945. The Academy solved the problem by ruling that, from 1946, a maximum of five songs only could be nominated. The 1946 awards ceremony was open for the first time to ticket-buying members of the public. To accommodate the bigger audience, the venue was changed to the Shrine Auditorium in Los Angeles, which had seating for nearly 7,000 people. The host was Jack Benny; Van Johnson presented the Best Song Oscar. Once again all the songs were performed as part of the evening's entertainment. Judy Garland attended rehearsals for a performance of "On the Atchison, Topeka and the Santa Fe" but withdrew on the night. Dinah Shore stepped into the breach and also sang "All Through the Day." Bing Crosby declined an invitation to sing "I Can't Begin to Tell You" and Frank Sinatra followed suit by refusing to attend and sing "You Keep Coming Back Like a Song." Dick Haymes and Andy Russell took the great singers' places. Hoagy Carmichael sang his own song "Ole Buttermilk Sky."

The Nominations

Jerome Kern and Oscar Hammerstein II for "All Through the Day" from *Centennial Summer* (Fox)

James Monaco and Mack Gordon for "I Can't Begin to Tell You" from *The Dolly Sisters* (Fox)

Hoagy Carmichael and Jack Brooks for "Ole Buttermilk Sky" from *Canyon Passage* (Universal)

Harry Warren and Johnny Mercer for "On the Atchison, Topeka and the Santa Fe" from *The Harvey Girls* (MGM)

Irving Berlin for "You Keep Coming Back Like a Song" from *Blue Skies* (Paramount)

All Through the Day

from *Centennial Summer*
Music: Jerome Kern
Lyrics: Oscar Hammerstein II

Centennial Summer was the last film that Jerome Kern worked on, and its song "All Through the Day" was the last song he ever wrote before his death on November 11, 1945.

Much of the film is set at the Centennial Exposition in Philadelphia in 1876 and it tries unsuccessfully to emulate the nostalgic charm of *Meet Me in St. Louis*, made two years earlier. Two sisters—Julia and Edith Rogers, played by Jeanne Crain and Linda Darnell, compete for the affections of a handsome Frenchman, Phillipe Lascalles, played by Cornel Wilde. He is in charge of setting up the French section of the Centennial. Dorothy Gish, in one of her rare screen appearances, plays Mrs. Rogers, the sisters' understanding mother, while Walter Brennan is Jesse, their father.

The romantic tenor Larry Stevens sings the Oscar-nominated song. He sings it during a magic lantern slide show: The first slide introduces him as Richard Lewis, Esq., "the voice that thrills," and as he sings, the rest of the slides illustrate the song, showing poses of romantic couples and moonlight.

The words Larry Stevens sings reveal that he spends all his days dreaming about the night when he can be with his sweetheart once more. Then as the sun goes down, he runs to meet her and the moon smiles down on the lovers as they enjoy the kiss that he has dreamed of "all through the day."

After singing it through, Stevens then asks the audience to join in with the words as they appear on the slides. We see all the main characters singing along, including Cornel Wilde (whose actual voice is heard) and Jeanne Crain (her voice dubbed by Louanne Hogan, as it was in *State Fair*).

Kern's buoyant and flowing melody is very attractive and Hammerstein's lyric has a simple, poetic quality with subtly constructed internal rhymes.

Originally, Leo Robin had been contracted to work with Jerome Kern to supply the lyrics but it was not a happy experience for him. Robin was a very competent lyricist, having had ten of his songs nominated for Academy Awards and winning the Oscar in 1938 with Ralph Rainger for "Thanks for the Memory." But he was used to working in a relaxed way and liked to take his time, while Kern demanded instant responses to his melodies. Robin produced lyrics for five songs in reasonable time but had trouble with "All Through the Day." Kern grew impatient and high-handedly called in his old friend Oscar Hammerstein to write the lyric instead.

Frank Sinatra made the most successful recording of "All Through the

Day"—Axel Stordhal arranged it beautifully and Sinatra brought out every nuance of the lyrics. Perry Como and Margaret Whiting both had hits with their versions.

I Can't Begin to Tell You

from *The Dolly Sisters*
Music: James Monaco
Lyrics: Mack Gordon

"I Can't Begin to Tell You," the plea-in-song of an inarticulate lover, features in the Fox musical *The Dolly Sisters*. The Dolly Sisters were brunettes but that didn't stop Darryl F. Zanuck from casting two bombshell blondes— Betty Grable and Alice Faye—as Jenny and Rosie Dolly. Unfortunately for Zanuck's plans, Alice Faye had retired from the screen and couldn't be persuaded back so her part went to another blonde, June Haver.

The Hungarian-born Dolly Sisters were a successful American vaudeville act in the first part of the twentieth century. Though this film version of their lives doesn't let the truth get in the way of a good story, it is a splendidly enjoyable production. Financially it was one of Betty Grable's most successful films.

John Payne sings "I Can't Begin to Tell You" first—he plays Harry Fox, another vaudeville performer. He is rehearsing his song-and-dance act at an out-of-town theatre where he is on the same bill as the young Dolly Sisters, who are just beginning their show business career. He introduces "I Can't Begin to Tell You" as a song he just written and he tells the band leader, "It's a ballad but I want it played lively!" And he proceeds to sing it that way, the bright polka-like rhythm working against the sentiments of the song.

Mack Gordon's basic concept for the song is quite original: The singer is unable to articulate his feelings for his lady and the words that he does manage to use are the usual clichés from run-of-the-mill love songs. But then the singer comes up with a brilliant idea: His loved one should make up her own sweet nothings on behalf of her tongue-tied swain and make believe that he is saying them to her.

As Payne sings these words, Betty Grable watches him from the wings and it's not hard to tell that romance is in the offing. From this point in the film, the tune is used as background to love scenes between the pair. But true love does not run smoothly, of course, and though they marry, the First World War separates them. The second time we hear "I Can't Begin to Tell You," Betty sings it. She has just had a loving letter from her husband and she sings snatches of the song with great joy as she dances at a London ball.

But here come more of the obligatory complications and the pair is estranged through misunderstandings. Payne continues his vaudeville career alone in New York. The Dolly Sisters are performing in Europe where Betty

June Haver and Betty Grable in *The Dolly Sisters* **(Fox, 1945).**

is on the point of marrying into the aristocracy. Payne, now graying at the temples, sings "I Can't Begin to Tell You" as part of his act and when he finishes it he receives the final divorce papers.

The song is sung for the fourth time as the grand finale to the film, when Payne and Grable are reunited at last. She has been almost killed in a car accident but she survives and plastic surgery restores her beauty. The

Dolly Sisters appear together at a New York all-star benefit show and naturally our hero is also on the bill. As he sings "I Can't Begin to Tell You," Betty joins him on the stage and sings with him. Next, June Haver (who is delighted to see her sister happy again) joins them, and a celestial chorus swells the song to supply a rapturous ending for the film.

Bing Crosby, with Carmen Cavallaro on piano, released a very successful recording of "I Can't Begin to Tell You" which rocketed to the top of the U.S. charts. It was his twelfth million-seller and the record enjoyed a run of 17 weeks in the hit parade. Andy Russell also had a hit with the song. Contractual difficulties prevented Grable recording it under her own name; the version by her then-husband Harry James and his band credits a vocalist by the name of Ruth Haag. Betty's real name is Ruth Elizabeth Grable and Harry James had the middle name "Haag."

"I Can't Begin to Tell You" was heard twice more in films, first in 1949's *You're My Everything*, which starred Dan Dailey and Anne Baxter. Then in 1952, Ginger Rogers sang it in the Clifton Webb comedy *Dreamboat*.

Ole Buttermilk Sky

from *Canyon Passage*
Music: Hoagy Carmichael
Lyrics: Jack Brooks

Canyon Passage presents a fairly realistic picture of pioneering life in the Old West. It features Dana Andrews, Susan Hayward and British star Patricia Roc, who was in Hollywood as part of the postwar lend lease scheme between British and American studios. Songwriter Hoagy Carmichael appears in the film too, as Hi Linnet, a folksy character called on to supply a few songs.

In his autobiography *Sometimes I Wonder* Carmichael claims that when he and Jack Brooks wrote "Ole Buttermilk Sky," he didn't feel that it would be suitable for *Canyon Passage*. He pleaded with producer Walter Wanger not to use the song but Wanger liked it and insisted on including it. Carmichael thought that Wanger was just being stubborn but he became very grateful when he received "a fancy piece of paper" from the Academy of Motion Picture Arts and Sciences, the certificate of nomination for the Best Song Award.

Canyon Passage is set in Oregon, where Logan Stuart (Dana Andrews) has had his trading post destroyed by fire. Spurred on by the love of Lucy Overmire (Susan Hayward), he resolves to return to San Francisco to raise credit and start all over again. As this pair ride off to happiness together on their well-shod steeds, Hoagy Carmichael follows behind on his mule and he sings "Ole Buttermilk Sky," a song about a man travelling towards the lady he intends to marry. He searches the sky for signs that the weather will stay fine for his long journey, but as he and his mule amble along, they seem— like Hoagy's melody—to be in no particular hurry to arrive.

It's a pleasing song with a relaxed and charming melody and it has become something of a standard. Carmichael grew up in rural Indiana and there is a feeling in the song of American small-town life, a certain folksiness quite different from the more urbane, sophisticated songs of Broadway and Hollywood.

When the film was released, there were at least six popular recordings of "Ole Buttermilk Sky" including one by Carmichael himself. Four of them were in the top ten at the same time and the most successful of these was the one by the Kay Kyser band, vocal by Mike Douglas and the Campus Kids. It reached the number one position in the U.S. charts. In 1961, Bill Black, guitarist on Elvis Presley's first hit "That's All Right," revived the song. This version reached the number 25 position and was in the charts for eight weeks.

You Keep Coming Back Like a Song

from *Blue Skies*
Music and Lyrics: Irving Berlin

There are 24 Irving Berlin songs in *Blue Skies* but only four of them were specially written for the film. One of them, the haunting ballad "You Keep Coming Back Like a Song," serves as a love theme for Bing Crosby and Joan Caulfield. The melody also plays softly in the background, adding poignancy to several of the scenes between Bing and Joan. The scoring is by Robert Dolan and he also received an Oscar nomination.

Bing plays Johnny Adams, a nightclub owner. Though he and Mary O'Hara (Joan Caulfield) are in love, he is not willing to be tied down in marriage. We first hear the melody of "You Keep Coming Back Like a Song" playing in the background as Joan proposes and Bing refuses her. Joan then goes off with Fred Astaire, who plays a character named Jed Potter. Later Bing sings the song and we know he regrets his earlier decision—his love for her will not go away but keeps returning. Irving Berlin's lyric has simplicity and an effective air of sweet nostalgia.

As he sings, Joan enters the nightclub and Bing leaves the stage to approach her. The lovers embrace and the melody changes to "Always"—"I'll be loving you, always...." Marriage soon follows but unfortunately Bing doesn't settle to married life and the couple divorce. Still later, when Bing has settled down and committed himself to the relationship, he sings the ballad again. Caulfield joins him and heavenly choirs swell the song.

Bing Crosby has most of the best Berlin numbers including the title song, "How Deep Is the Ocean?" and "White Christmas," but Astaire gets the chance to do some clever and inventive dancing in "Puttin' on the Ritz." And Bing and Fred have a very entertaining duet, vaudeville style, in "A Couple of Song and Dance Men." Immediately the film was in the can, Astaire announced his retirement on medical advice.

Bing released a recording of "You Keep Coming Back Like a Song" but two other versions—by Dinah Shore and Jo Stafford—were bigger hits at the time.

And the Winner Is...

On the Atchison, Topeka and the Santa Fe

from *The Harvey Girls*
Music: Harry Warren
Lyrics: Johnny Mercer

It took 20 days of rehearsal to perfect the nine-minute film sequence for "On the Atchison, Topeka and the Santa Fe"—and it was well worth the effort. The sequence introduces every member of the cast and it is the absolute highlight of *The Harvey Girls*.

The film tells the story of Fred Harvey and the chain of Harvey House restaurants he set up across America's West, following closely behind the construction of the railroad. His idea was to provide respectable railway passengers with a good meal in a family restaurant as they travelled through the wild and far-from-respectable West. In this way, the arrival of his restaurant in a Western town indicated that lawlessness was on the way out. Harvey wanted his waitresses, the Harvey Girls, to be paragons of virtue and the film certainly presents them in that light.

The Harvey Girls is set in the town of Sandrock, New Mexico, and the citizens are eagerly awaiting the arrival of Engine No. 49 on the Atchison, Topeka and Santa Fe railroad, which is bringing the Harvey Girls to town. The porter is the first to hear the unmistakable whistle of the approaching train—only Engine No. 49 sounds like that, he sings. The cowboys waiting on the platform for the first glimpse of the Girls take up the song. They sing of the train's reliable punctuality and how the many passengers will want transport to the hotel for refreshment because of the length of their journey. Next we are aboard the train and the train's engineer and fireman contribute a few lines. Soon the train reaches the station in its full glory and the Harvey Girls have arrived at last.

One by one they introduce themselves in song, telling the townsfolk where they come from and what they hope for in Sandrock. (Roger Edens and Kay Thompson contributed the lyric for this section.) The cowboys grow even more enthusiastic as the last passenger alights like royalty—it's mail-order bride Susan Bradley (Judy Garland), who sings to everybody of the wonderful journey she's had. And at this point the train finally pulls out of the station and the ensemble waves it goodbye, hats in the air.

There is a certain makeshift quality to the extra verses written by Edens and Thompson and they are much inferior to Mercer's lyric. But Edens needed

Judy Garland arrives on the Atchison, Topeka and the Santa Fe in *The Harvey Girls* **(MGM, 1946).**

the song to introduce the Harvey Girls individually though for some reason did not ask Mercer and Warren to write the additions. Mercer was livid with anger when he discovered the interpolations and was concerned that people would think that he was responsible for them.

Nevertheless, it is an exhilarating sequence, one of the most enjoyable in musical films. The music of the song is heard once more in the film when Ray Bolger features in some spectacular tap dancing. It is all superbly well-scored; Lennie Hayton received an Oscar nomination.

The song has a driving, rhythmic quality and Mercer's lyric has the feel of real speech, full of contractions and idiomatic phrases. It is an exuberant song that captures perfectly the excitement of the arrival of the train and the Harvey Girls.

Harry Warren was something of a specialist at writing train songs—he wrote "Shuffle Off to Buffalo" for *42nd Street*, "Chattanooga Choo Choo" for *Sun Valley Serenade*, as well as "On the 10:10 from Ten-Ten-Tennessee," used in *Just for You*. He was given his own choice of lyricist for *The Harvey Girls* and he had no hesitation in picking Johnny Mercer. The story of the Harvey Houses and the West is a part of American folklore and Mercer is the folk poet of song par excellence.

In a very good year for film songs with such luminaries as Irving Berlin, Jerome Kern, Oscar Hammerstein and Hoagy Carmichael nominated for Oscars, there was no argument from anyone when "On the Atchison, Topeka and the Santa Fe" won the Award.

Harry Warren heard the news of his Oscar win on the car radio as he was driving to Palm Springs with Harold Arlen. Arlen himself had won an Oscar for "Over the Rainbow" but his friend Harold Warren had two. As they listened to the news of his third award, Warren seemed almost oblivious and Arlen made no comment, but when they got out of the car he said to Arlen with all the mock airs and graces he could summon, "Remember, Harold, you walk two Oscars behind me." This was obviously a quip that Warren enjoyed because he repeated it in 1951 to Dorothy Fields, another single-Oscar-winning songwriter. They were working together at the time on songs for the MGM film *Texas Carnival*.

In 1971, the president of the Santa Fe railroad sent Harry Warren a gold-plated wall plaque to celebrate the twenty fifth anniversary of the song. It was the first Oscar for Johnny Mercer, who went on to win three more. As one of the founders of Capitol Records, he quickly put out his own recording of "On the Atchison, Topeka and the Santa Fe" with the Pied Pipers and it reached the top of the U.S. charts. Unfortunately the advertisements for the recording referred to the song only as Johnny Mercer's, making no mention of Harry Warren. The composer took offense and refused to speak to Mercer for some years.

Judy Garland's version also sold well, as did those by Bing Crosby with Six Hits and a Miss, and the Tommy Dorsey Orchestra (vocal by The Sentimentalists). At one stage there were three different versions in the *Billboard* top ten. The recordings all use the Johnny Mercer lyric as published though it varies slightly from what is sung in the film.

1947

Dinah Shore presented the Best Song Oscar for the 1947 awards at the Shrine Auditorium (and also sang "Pass That Peace Pipe.") Gordon MacRae ("A Gal in Calico"), Dennis Day ("I Wish I Didn't Love You So") and Frances Langford ("You Do") sang the other songs, with Johnny Mercer and the Pied Pipers singing "Zip-a-Dee-Doo-Dah."

The Nominations

Arthur Schwartz and Leo Robin for "A Gal in Calico" from *The Time, the Place and the Girl* (Warner)

Frank Loesser for "I Wish I Didn't Love You So" from *The Perils of Pauline* (Paramount)

Ralph Blane, Hugh Martin and Roger Edens for "Pass That Peace Pipe" from *Good News* (MGM)

Josef Myrow and Mack Gordon for "You Do" from *Mother Wore Tights* (Fox)

Allie Wrubel and Ray Gilbert for "Zip-a-Dee-Doo-Dah" from *Song of the South* (Walt Disney)

A Gal in Calico

from *The Time, the Place and the Girl*
Music: Arthur Schwartz
Lyrics: Leo Robin

Composer Arthur Schwartz wrote the songs for *The Time, the Place and the Girl* not with his usual lyricist partner Howard Dietz but with Leo Robin. But Schwartz and Dietz had written a song together in 1934 that was the basis for the Oscar-nominated "A Gal in Calico" The melody stayed but the original lyric was scrapped and Robin wrote a new one for the film. The stars are Dennis Morgan and Jack Carson as Steve Ross and Jeff Howard, a couple of nightclub owners trying to put on a Broadway show. "A Gal in Calico" is one of the numbers for it, apparently written by Morgan. He and Carson appear on stage as cowboys serenading the glamourous Martha Vickers, who plays Victoria Cassel. It is Martha who wears the calico dress in question. Chorus girls dressed in Western outfits soon surround them and there is much rope-twirling and whip-cracking in the dance sequence that follows.

The song is very singable, with cheerfully swinging words and music, and the unpretentious lyric has a homespun, country feel, just like the calico the "gal" wears. Leo Robin uses the natural sounding speech of a Western character, full of colloquial contractions and cries of "Yippee-Yi!" and "Yes, siree!" The singer is a rodeo cowboy who aims to return to Santa Fe to rope the "gal" he met there, fence her in and settle down to married bliss.

There were many recordings of "A Gal in Calico" but the four most successful were Johnny Mercer's, Tex Beneke's, Benny Goodman's (vocal by Eve Young) and Bing Crosby's. It has been quite a favorite with jazz musicians over the years—Miles Davis recorded an excellent interpretation of it on his 1955 album *The Musings of Miles*. Vocal quartet Manhattan Transfer recorded a popular version in 1978 on their *Pastiche* album.

I Wish I Didn't Love You So

from *The Perils of Pauline*
Music and Lyrics: Frank Loesser

The Perils of Pauline was Paramount's homage to the early days of silent cinema, in particular to the queen of the cliffhanger serials, Pearl White. Betty Hutton plays Pearl with her usual verve and vitality and her high spirits are perfect in carrying off the hilarious slapstick chases and edge-of-the-seat predicaments.

A number of old stalwarts from Hollywood's early years are in the cast, including James Finlayson, who bristled his bushy moustache to great effect in many a Laurel and Hardy film. John Lund supplies the required romantic interest somewhat unconvincingly. He is Mike Farrington, the pretentious actor manager of a group of travelling players. Betty joins the group but is not a success on stage. The pompous Lund gives her his low opinion of her acting abilities and Betty storms off after much angry shouting. But this kind of Hollywood-style antagonism often signals romance to come; snatches of the melody of "I Wish I Didn't Love You So You" are heard on the soundtrack to underline Betty's growing love for him.

When next we see her, she is auditioning for a theatrical agency and the song she sings is "I Wish I Didn't Love You So." The tears in her eyes and the

Betty Hutton and her sewing machine in *The Perils of Pauline* **(Paramount, 1947).**

sob in her voice tell us—in case we didn't know—that she is thinking of Lund as she performs. She sings plaintively and the melody of the song is quite attractive. But the lyric has no special qualities and the rhymes are rather obvious.

It's hard to see why this ordinary song received a nomination, especially when Betty Hutton's slightly strangulated ballad singing doesn't do it full justice. By far the most enjoyable numbers in the film are the comedy songs, "The Sewing Machine" and "Poppa Don't Preach to Me," which are much more suited to her style. But, as we have seen, love ballads often take precedence over comedy numbers when it comes to the Oscars.

"Poppa Don't Preach to Me" became one of Betty's biggest hits and, although her recording of "I Wish I Didn't Love You So" was also quite successful, versions by Vaughn Monroe and Dinah Shore outsold it.

Pass That Peace Pipe
from *Good News*
Music and Lyrics: Ralph Blane, Hugh Martin and Roger Edens

"Pass That Peace Pipe" made a difficult journey to the screen. The songwriting team of Blane, Martin and Edens wrote it originally for *Ziegfeld Fol-*

lies in 1944. MGM studio bosses were not happy with the film, which ran for more than three hours, and delayed its release until 1946, deleting some of the footage. As well as losing numbers by Fred Astaire, Jimmy Durante, Fanny Brice and Lena Horne, MGM also cut the sequence in which June Allyson, Gene Kelly and Nancy Walker performed "Pass That Peace Pipe."

Then in 1945, MGM made its first attempt at a musical version of *Huckleberry Finn* and "Pass That Peace Pipe" was marked down for inclusion. But the film remained unmade until 1960, when Samuel Goldwyn, Jr., produced *The Adventures of Huckleberry Finn*; Burton Lane and Alan Jay Lerner wrote four songs for it.

Filmgoers eventually saw "Pass That Peace Pipe" in the college musical *Good News*. This was originally a very successful Broadway show, opening in 1927. Filmed in 1930, it was one of the earliest talkie musicals; it starred Bessie Love and Stanley Smith. The songs were by the team of DeSylva, Brown and Henderson and included "The Best Things in Life Are Free" and "The Varsity Drag." The 1947 film improved on the original and had June Allyson and Peter Lawford as its stars. The excellent screenplay is by Comden and Green, their first venture in Hollywood. Most of the show's original songs were recycled and a few, written by the team of Blane, Martin and Edens, were added, including "Pass That Peace Pipe."

Lawford plays Tommy Marlowe, a college football hero who ignores his studies and spends his time chasing girls, especially Pat McClellan, a sexy vamp played by Patricia Marshall. In danger of being failed because of his poor academic record, he enlists the help of Connie Lane (June Allyson), portrayed at first as a studious "plain Jane." It's no surprise that Lawford ends up with her, as well as almost single-handedly winning the big football game.

"Pass That Peace Pipe" is the highlight of the film, a very lively dance routine brilliantly performed by Joan McCracken, making her screen debut. Ray McDonald and a whole troupe of college students assist her. The scene is the local drugstore where the students hang out together. Patricia Marshall is having a bit of a tantrum and Joan McCracken (as Babe Doolittle) advises her to cool down. She puts her advice into song and as she sings and dances, another student is seen bearing the said pipe, which is not the Native American variety but a huge meerschaum which Sherlock Holmes would have been proud to own.

The sequence could be seen today as offensive to Native Americans as the students pretend to be Red Indians and whoop and holler their way around the drugstore. The words of the song, too, might give offense to some but there are some amusing rhymes (for example, "wet hen"/"get then"), and the alliterative use of tribal names is very neat. All of them have "Ch" as their first two letters and finding so many of them is a triumph of research.

Charles Walters and Robert Alton brilliantly choreograph this superbly inventive number in the film and it thoroughly deserved its Oscar nomination.

The best-selling recorded version of the song was by Margaret Whiting, outselling another by Bing Crosby.

You Do

from *Mother Wore Tights*
Music: Josef Myrow
Lyrics: Mack Gordon

"You Do" was the hit song from the Betty Grable film *Mother Wore Tights*. It is performed on three different occasions and this strong emphasis ensured its Oscar nomination. Alfred Newman was also nominated for his scoring of the picture, as was Harry Jackson for his cinematography.

The plot concerns a successful vaudeville couple, Myrtle and Frank Burt, played by Grable and Dan Dailey. One of their daughters, Mikie (Connie Marshall), proudly narrates the story of her parents' lives but the other, Iris (Mona Freeman), develops snobbish tendencies and is ashamed of her parents' occupation.

"You Do" is sung twice on the vaudeville stage, first early in the film by

Dan Dailey and Betty Grable in *Mother Wore Tights* (Fox, 1945).

Dailey. The presentation is deliberately crude and raucous and Dailey is dressed in a loud check suit, pink waistcoat and a huge pink bow tie. He sings the song in a bright and breezy way, hamming it up with pratfalls and leers at the chorus girls. One of these is Betty Grable; during the number, she is horrified to see her grandparents come into the theatre. They think she is at business college and, though her straight-laced Grandma (Sara Allgood) is appalled, Granddad (George Cleveland) is rather pleased to see his beautiful granddaughter on stage. The number continues and Betty is propositioned by a couple of sailors, but Grandma rushes to the rescue and fends them off with her umbrella.

Later, when Dailey and Grable are married and their careers have advanced to the legitimate theatre, Betty performs the number but this time as a tender love ballad. The presentation is very classy to demonstrate that she has left the crudities of vaudeville behind. She is dressed in a sumptuous gown while four suave young men of the chorus dance around her in full evening dress. Dan watches her fondly from the wings.

The third version of "You Do" occurs at the end of the film. The priggish daughter is at a prestigious music school; one evening her friends go to see her parents' show, love every minute of it and return to school singing its praises. Now young Mona sees the folly of her ways and she sings "You Do" at her school graduation as a gesture of newfound pride in her parents. The sentiment of the occasion is laid on as thickly as treacle, with the proud parents clutching hands, while sister Connie Marshall cries buckets.

The song itself has a pleasant tune but the words are unremarkable and they include such trite images as love turning December into May and making dreams come true. The song enjoyed much popularity for a while with Dinah Shore's recording reaching the U.S. Top 10. There were also versions by Vaughn Monroe, Margaret Whiting, Vic Damone and Bing Crosby.

And the Winner Is...

Zip-a-Dee-Doo-Dah

from *Song of the South*
Music: Allie Wrubel
Lyrics: Ray Gilbert

This infectiously happy song marks the transition from live action to animation in the Disney feature *Song of the South*. James Baskett as Uncle Remus is telling the first of his Brer Rabbit stories to Johnny (Bobby Driscoll), an unhappy youngster whose parents have just separated. He tells him that the story happened "on one of those zip-a-dee-doo-dah days—now that's the kind of day when you can't open your mouth without a song jumpin' out of it." Immediately he begins to sing "Zip-a-Dee-Doo-Dah" and the background behind him becomes an animated landscape with brilliant blue skies. As Uncle Remus ambles down the tree-lined lane, birds and butterflies flutter around his head, all the animals skip alongside and that actual Mr. Bluebird perches on his shoulder.

All the stories that Uncle Remus tells serve to teach Johnny (Bobby Driscoll) a lesson relevant to his problems. "Zip-a-Dee-Doo-Dah" is a general purpose, do-it-yourself recipe designed to show the boy how to defeat any trouble that might come his way.

"Zip-a-Dee-Doo-Dah" is sung again at the end of the film, this time by Driscoll. The stories that Uncle Remus has told him have calmed all his fears and anxieties, his parents are reunited and he can see plenty of sunshine coming his way too. He sings the song with two of his playmates as Uncle Remus looks on fondly. Again animation is combined with live action; much to Uncle Remus' amazement, Brer Rabbit himself makes an appearance and joins in the song. Soon the birds and butterflies appear, along with Mr. Bluebird and many of the other creatures from the stories. The studio chorus finish the song as the film ends with the obligatory sunset.

James Baskett was given a Special Award for his role as Uncle Remus; Ingrid Bergman presented the Oscar to him at the Awards Ceremony. The citation read, "To James Baskett for his able and heart-warming characterization of Uncle Remus, friend and story-teller to the children of the world in Walt Disney's *Song of the South*." He died of a heart attack only a few months afterwards.

Three people were nominated for the scoring of *Song of the South*: Charles Wolcott, Paul Smith and Daniele Amfitheatrof.

Johnny Mercer's record of "Zip-a-Dee-Doo-Dah" with the Pied Pipers was the best selling version though one by Sammy Kaye and His Orchestra and another by The Modernaires with Paula Kelly also sold well. Bob B. Soxx and the Blue Jeans revived it in 1962—their revamped rocking version reached No. 8 in the U.S. charts. It was the vocal group's only big hit.

Carmen Miranda included a parody of "Zip-a-Dee-Doo-Dah" in her nightclub act under the rather backward title of "Eedapiz Ooh Dad."

1948

Robert Montgomery acted as host for the 1948 Oscars, held at the Academy Theatre, Hollywood. With far fewer seats than the previous year's venue, there was an outcry from Academy members who could not get a ticket. Those who did get in saw Kathryn Grayson present the Best Song Oscar. Jane Russell ("Buttons and Bows"), Gloria Wood and Harry Babbitt ("The Woody Woodpecker Song"), Doris Day ("It's Magic"), Gordon MacRae ("For Every Man There's a Woman") and Jo Stafford ("This Is the Moment") sang the nominated songs.

The Nominations

Jay Livingston and Ray Evans for "Buttons and Bows" from *The Paleface* (Paramount)

Harold Arlen and Leo Robin for "For Every Man There's a Woman" from *Casbah* (Universal)

Jule Styne and Sammy Cahn for "It's Magic" from *Romance on the High Seas* (Warner)

Frederick Hollander and Leo Robin for "This Is the Moment" from *That Lady in Ermine* (Fox)

Ramey Idriss and George Tibbles for "The Woody Woodpecker Song" from *Wet Blanket Policy* (Walter Lantz)

For Every Man There's a Woman

from *Casbah* Music: Harold Arlen
Lyrics: Leo Robin

The original version of *Casbah* was *Pepe-le-Moko*, a 1937 French film that starred Jean Gabin. United Artists remade it as *Algiers* in 1938 with

Charles Boyer and Hedy Lamarr. The musical version, *Casbah*, was made in 1948 with Tony Martin as the romantic thief Pepe-le-Moko and Marta Toren in Hedy Lamarr's role as Gaby. Yvonne De Carlo plays Inez, Marta Toren's rival for Martin's affections, and Peter Lorre is excellent, as Slimane, a policeman rather than his usual villain. He is also in pursuit of Martin but for legal rather than romantic reasons. Martin's character, Pepe-le-Moko, is exiled in the Casbah where he is safe from arrest. If caught outside, he can be arrested and taken back for imprisonment in his native France.

The most popular of the film's songs at the time was "Hooray for Love," though in the film it is practically thrown away as background music to a loud party scene. Johnny Mercer told Leo Robin that "It Was Written in the Stars," another song from the film, was one of his favorites. But these two were passed over for nomination in favor of "For Every Man There's a Woman." It attracts attention mainly because it is used three times, though the minor key melody with its neat harmonic changes is quite haunting. Composer Harold Arlen gives it a convincing Middle Eastern flavor.

Tony Martin sings "For Every Man There's a Woman" for the first time early in the film. It is his first appearance and we see him standing on an Algerian balcony, wearing a shirt of gleaming white and gazing over the Casbah. The song expresses his philosophic certainty that he will find love because there's a prince for every princess, a woman for every man. And though the words are full of romantic yearnings, Martin seems to be addressing the song to two washerwomen on a rooftop below him. At the end of the song, he jokingly proposes marriage to one of them. The song has successfully established his character as a charming, carefree vagabond. He sings the song with great style and he is very effective in the role of the romantic thief.

Next we discover that Yvonne De Carlo loves him but for Martin the relationship is only casual. He finds the woman meant for him in the shape of Marta Toren and he sings the song again to her as they dance together. This time the romantic yearnings are fully meant.

As the song ends, we see that Yvonne has been jealously watching the encounter. Later she sings "For Every Man There's a Woman" at Martin, a mocking comment on his love for Marta Toren, and it gives the song a tawdry spin.

The love triangle reaches the inevitable melodramatic conclusion as Lorre uses Marta as bait to lure Martin out of the Casbah. He is shot as he watches Marta's plane fly off to Paris. This climactic scene of lovers parting forever at the airport has echoes of the ending of *Casablanca*. The North African setting and the presence of Peter Lorre in both films emphasize the similarities.

Tony Martin's record of the song sold well, as did versions by Peggy Lee, reunited with the Benny Goodman band, and Frank Sinatra.

It's Magic

from *Romance on the High Seas*
Music: Jule Styne
Lyrics: Sammy Cahn

Doris Day made a spectacular film debut in *Romance on the High Seas*. She had already achieved great popularity as band singer with the Les Brown orchestra, with two million-selling records to her name, "Sentimental Journey" and the double-sided hit "Confess" and "Love Somebody," on which she duetted with Buddy Clark. Though she received only fourth billing behind *High Seas* stars Jack Carson, Janis Paige and Don DeFore, hers was the lead role. She made a huge impact on audiences and critics with her fresh charm and naturalness but it was her beautiful rendition of the Oscar-nominated "It's Magic" that really got her noticed.

She was cast in the film almost by accident. Her domestic life in shambles, she was about to leave California and head back home to Cincinnati when she was persuaded to attend a party at composer Jule Styne's home. There she was persuaded to sing a few songs; Styne and his songwriting partner Sammy Cahn were so impressed with her voice that they asked director Michael Curtiz to consider her for the important role of Georgia Garrett in *Romance on the High Seas*, the film for which they had just written the songs. Warner Bros. was having trouble casting the role—Judy Garland had been first choice but she was having personal problems and declined. Warners then cast Betty Hutton but she was pregnant so Curtiz was more than willing to audition Doris. The subsequent screen test was a success and her performance in the film made her an international star.

Romance on the High Seas is a lightweight musical set mainly on a cruise liner and ashore in Latin America. There are a few amusing scenes and some good musical numbers, the most enjoyable of which are "Put 'em in a Box (Tie 'em with a Ribbon and Throw 'em in the Deep Blue Sea)" and "The Tourist Trade," a cynical commentary on the effects of tourism in developing countries. Ray Heindorf's scoring is good and he was nominated for an Oscar.

The plot has the usual farcical convolutions: Elvira Kent (Janis Paige) suspects her husband Michael (Don DeFore) of infidelity. She persuades nightclub singer Georgia Garrett (Day) to take her place on a cruise ship, so that she can stay behind in New York and spy on her husband. DeFore is just as suspicious and hires private eye Peter Virgil (Jack Carson) to take his place on the cruise to spy on his wife. Naturally, Doris and Jack fall in love but he thinks that Doris is married to Don DeFore. As his personal slogan is "never kiss a client's wife," it takes them a while to get together.

Doris sings "It's Magic" on three occasions. When the ship stops in Havana, she and Jack Carson go ashore together. Hearing a local group singing "It's Magic" in Spanish, they track the sound to a nearby restaurant.

Doris asks the leader of the group to teach her the song and conveniently he has a copy of the lyrics in English. She sings and her performance is so heartfelt that Jack is entranced. The songwriters wrote an opening verse in which the singer puts her lover's magic above Houdini's. Doris does not sing it in the film or on her recording.

Later, on a beach in Rio, Doris sings part of the song to Carson's guitar accompaniment, and then in the film's romantic finale she sings "It's Magic" to the accompaniment of Oscar Levant on piano and a full orchestra in a classy Rio hotel. By this time, all the complications are resolved, the main characters forgive each other for the deceptions and assumed identities, and "It's Magic" indeed. To take advantage of the song's popularity, the film was released as *It's Magic* in many countries, including Britain and Australia.

Despite its effusive lyric with its inflated poetics, Doris sings "It's Magic" with such fervent sincerity that the song has strong appeal. Her recording was very popular, remaining in the American charts for 21 weeks, reaching number two. It was the third million-selling record for Doris Day, as popular overseas as it was in the U.S.A. The song was so popular that five other versions reached the U.S. Top 20: These were by Dick Haymes, Gordon MacRae, Tony Martin, Sarah Vaughan and Vic Damone. The Platters revived it with only moderate success in 1962.

"It's Magic" was Sammy Cahn's sixth losing Best Song nomination. Some years after the event, he was asked for his recollections of the 1948 awards. He recalled that he and Nicholas Brodszky were seated behind rival songwriters Jay Livingston and Ray Evans and...

> ...I watched the lips of the presenter after he had opened the envelope, and sure enough his lips formed the letter "B" so Brodsky and I started to rise when he said "Buttons and Bows." Of course we slunk back in our seats, Brodsky snarling in my ear, "It's a fix!" I smiled my customary loser's smile and said, "If it were a fix, we would be up there!" [Quoted in *70 Years of the Oscar* by Robert Osborne]

It's a shame to let the facts get in the way of a good story but Sammy Cahn's memory was letting him down and he confuses 1948 with 1950. Livingston and Evans did win the 1948 Oscar for "Buttons and Bows" but it wasn't until two years later that Cahn wrote a song with Nicholas Brodszky—that was "Be My Love," the year Livingston and Evans won with "Mona Lisa."

This Is the Moment

from *That Lady in Ermine*
Music: Frederick Hollander
Lyrics: Leo Robin

Leo Robin received two nominations in 1948, the second for "This Is the Moment." *That Lady in Ermine* was based on a German operetta, filmed in a silent version in 1927 as *The Lady in Ermine* and remade in 1930 as *Bride of the Regiment* with a cast including Walter Pidgeon, Myrna Loy and Lupino Lane.

The 1948 version starred Betty Grable as Francesca, the lady of the title, the ruling countess of an imaginary principality. Douglas Fairbanks, Jr. is her love interest–he plays a dashing Hungarian hussar, Col. Ladislas Karolyi Teglas. It was the last film to be directed by Ernst Lubitsch, who died during production. Otto Preminger completed the film. He refused a credit as a tribute to Lubitsch, although cynical critics have maintained that the real reason was because he turned what Lubitsch intended as lighthearted, romantic operetta into a confusing mishmash.

But the film does have its moments and one of them occurs when Betty Grable sings the Oscar-nominated song. The plot is slightly confusing and there are dream sequences and time shifts between the sixteenth and ninteenth centuries, with Grable and Fairbanks playing roles in both. In the sixteenth century, Angelina, the original "lady in ermine," saves her people from the Hungarian invaders by flirting with their leader, then stabbing him in the back. Three hundred years later, Betty, her descendant, is suffering from a similar invasion.

The original "lady" emerges from her portrait and advises Grable to do what she did—pretend to fall in love with the invader and then kill him. Some tension is generated by uncertainty—will she follow her predecessor's advice? She makes a dramatic appearance at the top of a magnificent staircase, dressed like a bride in an opulent white gown. Has she come to give herself to her Hungarian conqueror or to kill him? This certainly is the moment of truth and as she glides down the stairs, she begins to sing to him. There is a reference to danger in the second verse, a reminder of the sixteenth century stabbing. The last phrase of the song is "you are the one" but does she mean that he is the one to be killed or kissed?

The couple drinks champagne, dances, then Fairbanks, Jr. takes up the song, singing in a high operatic tenor at top volume. Deafened, Betty tries to quiet him and does so by taking over the singing. Now that it's clear that she has fallen in love with Fairbanks and will not stab him after all, she sings different words for the last three lines—telling him that "this is the moment" for love and kisses. Fairbanks finishes the line by speaking the final words—"you are the one."

The melody is lushly romantic and the lyric has an operatic ring befitting the melodramatic plot. There were very few recordings of the song and the best of them was by Jo Stafford.

The Woody Woodpecker Song
from *Wet Blanket Policy*
Music and Lyrics: Ramey Idriss and George Tibbles

For months on end in 1948, it was impossible for radio listeners to escape from the incessant "ha-ha-ha *ha*-ha" of "The Woody Woodpecker Song," a sound so inanely infectious it was almost a disease. Even *Time* magazine felt compelled to comment on the phenomenon.

The song was first heard in the Woody cartoon *Wet Blanket Policy* in which Woody buys a life insurance policy and names Buzz Buzzard as beneficiary. Buzz spends the rest of the cartoon trying to kill Woody.

The song is an accurate account of the bird's annoying character as he pecks out holes in the redwood tree—and perhaps in your head—all day long. But the lady woodpeckers find his tune appealing and one of them marries him while the choir sings along to his song. The amusing words and insistent rhythm of the tune perfectly suit the indefatigable bird. But, like Woody himself, they quickly wear out their welcome.

The animated cartoon character Woody Woodpecker was the brainchild of Walter Lantz and he first appeared on screen in *Knock, Knock* in 1940. Mel Blanc voiced him for his first few films, then Ben "Bugs" Hardaway took over in 1941. Legend has it that Lantz got the idea for Woody when a woodpecker tapping on the roof of their honeymoon cabin continually disturbed him and his wife. But this story was apparently the invention of a Hollywood press agent—the Lantzes' honeymoon actually took place a year after Woody's first appearance on screen.

In 1948, Lantz decided that the character needed a new voice and he arranged for 50 actors to audition on tape. Lantz saw none of the actors' faces but listened carefully to all the recorded tryouts and made his selection. The winning actor turned out to be his wife, Grace Stafford, and she remained the chirpy voice of Woody Woodpecker for the next 24 years.

She was uncredited at her own request as she thought children might be disillusioned to find that the famous bird's voice was a woman's. But in 1952, Walter Lantz prevailed on her to change her mind and from 1952, with *Termites from Mars*, Grace Stafford's name appeared in the screen credits.

Wet Blanket Policy was the third 1948 Woody Woodpecker cartoon made with Grace Stafford's voice and it was the one that introduced his signature tune. The song was the first from a short subject to be nominated for an Oscar.

The song's first recording and the top-selling version in the U.S.A. was by Kay Kyser and His Orchestra, which had vocals by Harry Babbitt and Gloria Wood. It was 15 weeks in the hit parade and in the number one spot for six of them. By 1949 it had sold a million copies. Danny Kaye with the Andrews Sisters also made a popular recording as did Mel Blanc, the original voice of Woody Woodpecker.

Even Frank Sinatra was forced to sing the painful song: As host of radio's *Your Hit Parade*, he had to sing whatever was top of the charts. He must have watched with growing apprehension as "The Woody Woodpecker Song" soared towards the #1 spot. It reached that peak in July 1948, and in the program that went out on the tenth of that month the great singer, assisted by a vocal quartet, gave listeners his reluctant rendition.

And the Winner Is...

Buttons and Bows

from *The Paleface*
Music and Lyrics: Jay Livingston and Ray Evans

Bob Hope was convinced that the immense success of *The Paleface* had a great deal to do with "Buttons and Bows." It was released before the film and by the time *The Paleface* opened, Dinah's Shore record of the song had been at the top of the Hit Parade for several weeks. The song was so popular that the marquee of the Paramount Theater in Hollywood billed the song alongside the names of Bob Hope and Jane Russell.

There are some very funny moments in *The Paleface* in which Jane Russell plays Calamity Jane and Bob Hope is Painless Peter Potter, an incompetent dentist. Jane has been released from jail to undertake a dangerous undercover operation: She has to join a pioneer wagon train to find out who is selling guns to the Indians. She marries Bob as a cover and he spends the rest of the film trying to claim his marital rights. Whenever he kisses Jane, she surreptitiously slugs him on the back of his head with the butt of her gun. He chooses to believe that he has been rendered unconscious by the power of her passion.

Bob sings "Buttons and Bows" to Jane as he drives a wagon and it is an expression of a city boy's aversion to the West. Accompanying himself on a concertina, he lounges lazily on his wagon, leaving his horses to find their own way along the pioneer trail. They take the wrong track, head deeper into Indian country, and the rest of the wagon train follows, heading straight for an ambush.

Director Norman McLeod had asked songwriters Livingston and Evans for a song to fit the scene and they came up with one they called "Skookum" which they avowed was an actual Indian expression, which roughly translates to "okay." McLeod rejected this effort, arguing that the Indians were supposed to be menacing and threatening and a humorous song about the Indians would work against the scene. The songwriters lost the argument and went away to try again, this time coming up with "Buttons and Bows."

The song is a good one, well-contrived musically and lyrically, thoroughly deserving its Oscar. The neat use of internal rhymes adds to the humor of the piece and Bob Hope's performance, complete with exaggerated Western drawl, is excellent. His recording of the song was very popular but he was easily outsold by Dinah Shore, whose version was her second million-seller. It was in the U.S. charts for 24 weeks, ten of them in the number one spot. Dinah recorded "Buttons and Bows" (with a group billed as Her Happy Valley Boys) only just in time before a musicians' strike began—she finished the

Bob Hope in *The Paleface* **(Paramount, 1948).**

recording minutes before the midnight deadline. This was the last song recorded before the strike took effect. When Bob Hope made his record later, Capitol beat the strike by recording the music in Mexico. Bob listened to the music on earphones and sang along.

The Dinning Sisters also sold a million copies of their disc on which the Art Van Damme Quartet backed them. Betty Garrett and Betty Rhodes also had popular versions. One of the most recent versions is by songwriter Jay Livingston himself: He sings it on Michael Feinstein's CD *Livingston and Evans Songbook*, issued in 2002.

The song was used again in the sequel to this film, *Son of Paleface*. This time it is sung as a duet between Jane Russell and Roy Rogers, with extra lines interpolated by Bob Hope. Ray Evans and Jay Livingston later wrote parody lyrics for Bob that he often used in personal appearances.

For a long while *The Paleface* held the record as the most successful film ever released in Australia, based on tickets sold rather than actual revenue. It remained in continuous circulation for more than 15 years, mostly screening at minor theaters. It was withdrawn only when Gulf and Western bought out Paramount in 1966.

1949

The venue for the awards ceremony was changed yet again, this time to the grandiose RKO Pantages Theatre, the biggest movie house in Hollywood. Paul Douglas was host and Cole Porter presented the Best Song Oscar. Guests thoroughly enjoyed a rendition of "Baby, It's Cold Outside" by three of the stars who sang it in *Neptune's Daughter*, Arlene Dahl filling in for Esther Williams. Paul Douglas introduced the song as "the bachelors' anthem" and Red Skelton forgot some of the words. Dean Martin ("Through a Long and Sleepless Night"), Jack Smith ("It's a Great Feeling"), Gene Autry ("Lavender Blue") and Ann Blyth ("My Foolish Heart") were the other performers. Donald O'Connor, who presented a special award to Bobby Driscoll, came on stage to the strains of "Mule Train," which would be nominated for Best Song in 1950. The musical reference was to the first of O'Connor's films about Francis the Talking Mule, that had just been released.

The Nominations

Frank Loesser for "Baby, It's Cold Outside" from *Neptune's Daughter* (MGM)

Jule Styne and Sammy Cahn for "It's a Great Feeling" from *It's a Great Feeling* (Warner)

Eliot Daniel and Larry Morey for "Lavender Blue (Dilly Dilly)" from *So Dear to My Heart* (Walt Disney)

Victor Young and Ned Washington for "My Foolish Heart" from *My Foolish Heart* (Goldwyn)

Alfred Newman and Mack Gordon for "Through a Long and Sleepless Night" from *Come to the Stable* (Fox)

It's a Great Feeling

from *It's a Great Feeling*
Music: Jule Styne
Lyrics: Sammy Cahn

After her great success in *Romance on the High Seas* and *My Dream Is Yours*, Warner Bros. moved Doris Day up two places and gave her second billing for her third film, *It's a Great Feeling*. Top billing went to Dennis Morgan; Jack Carson also starred.

The film is a gentle satire on the ways of Hollywood film making with Carson playing the part of a director. Doris Day, as Judy Adams, a waitress at the Warner Bros. commissary, is hoping to be discovered as an actress. With this setting, the producer was able to have almost all the stars contracted to Warners make guest appearances and Doris has brief scenes with Gary Cooper, Ronald Reagan, Edward G. Robinson, Jane Wyman and many other luminaries. She also sings most of the agreeable Jule Styne-Sammy Cahn songs and has great fun with a song called "At the Cafe Rendezvous" which she performs with a heavy French accent. There is also a lovely ballad entitled "Blame My Absent-Minded Heart" but it was the title song that received the Oscar nomination. Doris sings "It's a Great Feeling" over the opening credits and it's a happy-sounding song that does its job of setting a light-hearted mood, but it has a fairly undistinguished lyric—the "great feeling" is being in love.

There is a convoluted plot which gets a little tedious but the ending of the film is very funny. Frustrated by all the wheeling and dealing she has encountered, she resolves to return to her hometown, Gerkey's Corner, Wisconsin. There she intends to marry her childhood sweetheart who has the unpromising name of Jeffrey Bushfinkle. We see the happy pair in church from the rear. When they have taken their vows, they kiss and turn towards the camera. Mr. Bushfinkle is played by Errol Flynn.

It's a Great Feeling was a hit and on the strength of it and her blossoming popularity, Doris Day decided to remain in Hollywood and pursue her careers in movies and records. Other 1949 recordings of the song were made by Kay Starr, and by Pearl Bailey duetting with Hot Lips Page.

Lavender Blue (Dilly Dilly)

from *So Dear to My Heart*
Music: Eliot Daniel
Lyrics: Larry Morey

The avuncular Burl Ives sings "Lavender Blue" in the Disney feature *So Dear to My Heart*, a film that starred Bobby Driscoll. Like a number of child stars exploited by their studios, he was dropped when he lost his appealing "little boy" looks. He became a drug addict, and died penniless in New York at the age of 32. But in his happier days he did win a special Juvenile Academy Award for his work in films, including his role as Jerry Kincaid in Disney's *So Dear to My Heart*.

Like *Song of the South*, *So Dear to My Heart* has a mix of live action and animation and stars Ives as kindly old Uncle Hiram, a white version of Uncle Remus, with Beulah Bondi as Grandma Kincaid, Bobby's grandmother, a role similar to that of Hattie McDaniel in the earlier film.

Set in rural Indiana just after the turn of the century, the film is full of nostalgia for an idealized country life and has a certain charm.

An Oscar nomination went to Eliot Daniel and Larry Morey for their reworking of a bawdy English folk song, "The Kind Country Lovers," sometimes known as "Diddle Diddle." In the film the song comes over very innocently as befits a Disney production and there is no sign of its seventeenth century origin as a story of sexual seduction.

In a charming scene, Ives is visiting Beulah Bondi and the two children (Bobby Driscoll and Luana Patten). The four gather around the hearth and Burl takes up his guitar and sings "Lavender Blue." The song is now quite suitable for the children and amounts to a marriage proposal in song. It describes how Great Grandfather proposed to Great Grandmother. He seems to have had a limited vocabulary, describing everything—his heart, the wedding day, the bridal dress—as "dilly, dilly." Burl's voice has a rough but pleasing quality and his appealing performance of the song is gentle and intimate.

There were three popular versions of "Lavender Blue" apart from Burl Ives' recording. The others were by Dinah Shore, Sammy Kaye and His Orchestra (vocal by Don Cornell and the Kaydets) and Jack Smith.

My Foolish Heart

from *My Foolish Heart*
Music: Victor Young
Lyrics: Ned Washington

The film *My Foolish Heart* is an out-and-out tearjerker about a warblighted romance between Eloise Winters (Susan Hayward) and Walt Dreiser (Dana Andrews). The title song is not confined to the credits but is also sung twice during the film. Victor Young's score makes extensive use of the melody and it is heard in all the key scenes. The song's enormous popularity contributed mightily to the film's box office.

The melody is played first over the opening credits, then at a dance. Susan Hayward has gone there with Lew Wengler (Kent Smith) but as the orchestra plays "My Foolish Heart" she meets and falls for Dana Andrews. She is a "good girl" and at first resists his advances but when he is drafted into the Army Air Force she succumbs. Pregnant, she refuses to tell him, afraid that he will feel trapped into marriage. They spend their last evening together in a cocktail lounge and it is here that the song is sung for the first time, by Martha Mears, as the nightclub singer. Hayward and Andrews are very miserable—she because of her pregnancy and the parting, he because his squadron is going overseas to the war. He comments on the singer, "I wish she'd shut up—I don't need her to tell me I feel low. Everyone else is babbling away—what's wrong with us?"

When Andrews is killed in a flying accident, Susan now faces the shame of unmarried motherhood. But then she meets her old flame Kent Smith again at a dance in the place where she fell in love with Andrews, and the song is sung again there in the background. Smith takes her for a drive and, to the sound of "My Foolish Heart" playing on the car radio, tells her that he still loves her. She sees her chance and seduces him to get a father for her child. The couple lead an unhappy married life until Smith leaves her and she is left alone with her daughter, a perpetual reminder of Andrews.

The film reflects the loosening of morals in the postwar years and audience acceptance of a premarital sexual relationship. Most young women in the audiences at the time would have identified strongly with Susan Hayward—she does describe herself as a "good girl" and she certainly goes in for much soul-searching before she succumbs to Andrews' charms. This soul-searching is the basis of the song's lyric. By the end of the film, conventional morality has reasserted itself as the premarital affair leads to years of tragedy.

In "My Foolish Heart," the singer expresses the age-old dilemma of how to distinguish between love and lust. The lyric coyly decides the emotion that Susan feels is genuine, excusing her premarital pregnancy. The moonlit night is like a "lovely tune" and the lovers are on the point of making love but she wonders if this can be the real thing and warns her "foolish heart" to take care. She knows that it is difficult to distinguish between "love and fascination" but when "eager lips combine" she realizes the truth—this time it really is love.

The lyrics are rather overblown in their poeticism but Victor Young's flowing melody is very romantic and it's easy to hear why the song was so popular. There were a number of recordings of it that sold well, the two most popular being by Billy Eckstine, and by the Gordon Jenkins orchestra, with vocals by Sandy Evans.

The film's plot was actually based on *Uncle Wiggily in Connecticut*, a short story by J.D. Salinger originally published in *The New Yorker*. After the success of *My Foolish Heart*, producer Samuel Goldwyn tried to buy screen rights for Salinger's best-selling novel *The Catcher in the Rye*. Salinger, having seen what had been done to his short story, vowed never to sell anything else to Hollywood.

Through a Long and Sleepless Night

from *Come to the Stable*
Music: Alfred Newman
Lyrics: Mack Gordon

"Through a Long and Sleepless Night" is a hymn-like song from *Come to the Stable*, a film about a group of nuns and their good works. Rarely sceened nowadays, it is a charming film in which Loretta Young and Celeste Holm—as Sister Margaret and Sister Scholastica, nuns from a French order—arrive in America to build a children's hospital. The site they choose is near the appropriately named town of Bethlehem, New England. Though they encounter many obstacles, their essential innocence and naïve faith in the goodness of others wins through. The film was a popular success in the U.S. (though it flopped in Britain and Australia), and it received seven Oscar nominations, including one for the writers of "Through a Long and Sleepless Night."

The song plays an essential part in the plot—it is the indirect means by which the nuns raise the last bit of money they need to start their hospital.

Hugh Marlowe plays Robert Masen, a successful songwriter who has written "Through a Long and Sleepless Night" for a forthcoming show. We hear it first in Marlowe's home where he performs the song for his leading lady Kitty (Dorothy Patrick) and his agent. Ken Darby dubs his voice. In this relentlessly cheerful and optimistic film, the melody for the song is surprisingly dirge-like and the very sad words tell the depressing tale of a lovers' quarrel.

Dorothy Patrick, her voice dubbed by Eileen Wilson, reprises the song later in the film. She sings it for Marlowe's houseguests and as the song finishes we hear the voices of the nuns from nearby. They are singing a Gregorian plain chant and the melody bears a striking similarity to the one that Marlowe has composed. One of his guests accuses him of plagiarism but he is able to show that he was inspired to write it four years earlier whilst in Normandy, France, during the war. But he is soon to discover that the nuns came originally from that area and he realizes that he owes his inspiration for the hymn-like melody to them. To assuage his conscience, he makes the final financial contribution that enables the hospital to go ahead. The film concludes with the hospital's dedication that includes the nuns singing the chant that has proved to be the source of "Through a Long and Sleepless Night."

Mack Gordon was an accomplished lyricist responsible for such gems as "You'll Never Know" and "The More I See You," but this song is largely forgotten. It is a very sad-sounding song, with a solemn and melancholy melody, but it does manage to evoke quite well the tossing and turning of a lover, sleepless because of a quarrel. The image of the "tick-tock silence" is vivid, and some of the rhymes are very striking.

The song had little popularity in 1949 in spite of a good version by Peggy Lee. Its composer Alfred Newman also recorded an instrumental version with his orchestra. Since then it has turned up regularly as an album track from such singers as Sarah Vaughan, Dean Martin and Bobby Darin.

And the Winner Is...

Baby, It's Cold Outside

from *Neptune's Daughter*
Music and Lyrics: Frank Loesser

"Baby, It's Cold Outside" is one of the wittiest songs in all film musicals. It started life not in a film but as a party piece that Frank Loesser and his wife Lynn used to perform at New York gatherings. Loesser wrote it in 1944 and held onto it for these private performances. Lynn Loesser described the impact the song made the first time they performed it: She and Frank became "instant parlor room stars" and were invited to "all the best parties for years." When the Loessers moved to Hollywood, they continued to perform at parties there, sitting at the piano and acting out the lyrics in great style. They even made a private recording of it that has become a collector's item.

Understandably Lynn Loesser loved the song—it was theirs alone to perform and she delighted in the audience's applause. Then Frank Loesser dropped a bombshell by selling the song to MGM for the 1949 film *Neptune's Daughter* where Esther Williams and Ricardo Montalban would sing it. Lynn was devastated:

> I felt betrayed as if I'd caught him in bed with another woman. I
> kept saying "Esther Williams and Ricardo Montalban!!!" He
> finally sat me down and said, "If I don't let go of 'Baby' I'll begin
> to think I can never write another song as good as I think this one
> is." [Quoted in *A Most Remarkable Fella* by Susan Loesser]

The fact that the song had been written some years before it appeared in *Neptune's Daughter* and therefore not expressly for the film led to some protests about its eligibility. But the Academy ruled that it had never before been performed commercially and was therefore eligible.

In the film, Montalban plays Jose O'Rourke, a stereotypical Latin lover trying to seduce Eve Barrett (Williams). The song is a contrapuntal duet, with Montalban attempting to make Williams stay the night with him while she nervously insists on hurrying home. It is an amusing scene and as fast as Williams puts on her hat and coat, Montalban, like a conjurer, is taking them off again. The singers take alternate lines, each dovetailing neatly with the next. In the original song sheet, these alternate lines are labelled "The Mouse"

Ricardo Montalban and Esther Williams in *Neptune's Daughter* **(MGM, 1949).**

and "The Wolf." The song is *tour de force* in the way it sustains the conversational flow. Every line sounds like natural speech, as though the singers are making it up on the spot. The rhymes are used to great comic effect and they never seem contrived.

Later in the film, Red Skelton and Betty Garrett reprise the song with broader comic intent and Skelton even mimics Montalban's Latin accent. In this version, it is the lady who is trying to seduce her bashful man into staying longer. They have a similar routine with the coat and hat but Skelton is so confused and disconcerted by Garrett's assault on his virtue that he leaves the house wearing her outdoor clothes, mincing his way down the path before noticing his mistake and rushing back in again.

The song was immensely popular. The version by Williams and Montalban was taken off the film soundtrack and issued as a single. It sold more than a million copies and there were three other hit recordings in 1948 and 1949: Johnny Mercer with Margaret Whiting, Dinah Shore with Buddy Clark, and Ella Fitzgerald with Louis Jordan. In 1952, Louis Armstrong and Velma Middleton recorded it, followed by Pearl Bailey and Hot Lips Page, then Carmen McRae and Sammy Davis, Jr. Ray Charles and Betty Carter also sang it on their classic 1961 album, and the track was released as a single.

Bette Midler and James Caan sang it in the 1991 movie *Follow the Boys* and, strangely for a song of seduction, it has often turned up on Christmas albums. Amongst these are versions by Ann-Margret with Al Hirt, Petula Clark with Rod McKuen and Vanessa Williams with Bobby Caldwell. And, in keeping with the idea that "Baby, It's Cold Outside" is a suitable song for Christmas, it turns up twice in the 2003 movie *Elf*: Zooey Deschanel sings it superbly with the Elf, Will Ferrell, then she sings it again over the closing credits, this time with Leon Redbone.

1950

The 1950 awards ceremony, held again at the RKO Pantages Theatre, began with the orchestra playing a medley of the nominated songs. Fred Astaire acted as host and Gene Kelly presented the Best Song Oscar. The singing of the nominated songs provided some highlights: Dean Martin sang most of "Bibbidi-Bobbidi-Boo," with Jerry Lewis supplying all the "Boos." Frankie Laine came along to sing "Mule Train" but his whip failed him and he couldn't make it crack as on his recording. Gloria De Haven and Alan Young ("Wilhelmina"), Lucille Norman ("Be My Love") and Robert Merrill ("Mona Lisa") performed the other songs without a hitch.

The Nominations

Nicholas Brodszky and Sammy Cahn for "Be My Love" from *The Toast of New Orleans* (MGM)

Al Hoffman, Jerry Livingston and Mack David for "Bibbidi-Bobbidi-Boo (The Magic Song)" from *Cinderella* (Walt Disney)

Jay Livingston and Ray Evans for "Mona Lisa" from *Captain Carey, U.S.A.* (Paramount)

Fred Glickman, Hy Heath and Johnny Lange for "Mule Train" from *Singing Guns* (Republic)

Josef Myrow and Mack Gordon for "Wilhelmina" from *Wabash Avenue* (Fox)

Be My Love

from *The Toast of New Orleans*
Music: Nicholas Brodszky
Lyrics: Sammy Cahn

When producer Joe Pasternak approached Sammy Cahn to write the lyrics for the Mario Lanza vehicle *The Toast of New Orleans*, Nicholas Brodszky had already written the music for "Be My Love." Brodszky was born in Russia but had lived in Hungary where he wrote operettas in the Viennese style. He played his soaring melody for "Be My Love" in a very florid, over-decorated manner and Cahn had difficulty in distinguishing the tune. Before he could write the words to go with it, he asked for a pianist who could play it for him in a simpler style.

Lanza plays Pepe Abellard Duvalle, a rough and ready Cajun fisherman, while Kathryn Grayson is Suzette Micheline, a genteel opera singer from New Orleans. She and the opera house director, Jacques Riboudeaux (David Niven), visit the bayou on the day of the blessing of the fishing boats, and during the evening's open air festivities, Grayson treats the locals to a couple of songs. Lanza looks on appreciatively and while she is singing "Be My Love," he leaps uninvited onto the stage and duets with her. Grayson barely controls her annoyance but finishes the song; Lanza assures her: "You sing

Mario Lanza, Kathryn Grayson and J. Carrol Naish in *The Toast of New Orleans*.

real good." As the local mayor reprimands him for his ill-mannered intrusion, Grayson expresses her anger to Niven—but he has enjoyed Lanza's singing and plans to have him join the opera company.

Later, at a classy New Orleans restaurant where Lanza, Grayson and Niven are dining, the orchestra plays "Be My Love." Lanza joins in and forces Grayson up onto the stage with him to duet once more. Again, Grayson is filled with anger but in such cliched circumstances are celluloid romances begun and we know that by the end of the film she will indeed be his love.

From this point, the melody of "Be My Love" is played on the soundtrack to underscore the developing romance, and when they finally kiss each other passionately, a few notes of it sound out ecstatically and "The End" appears on screen.

Sammy Cahn builds on Brodszky's booming melody and his lyric burns with operatic intensity, almost to the point of parody. He makes full use of melodramatic words and phrases—the singer wants burning kisses and pledges eternal devotion. Lanza and Grayson sing with full power, culminating in the huge, extended climax in the last lines, especially on the word "eternally."

Brodszky and Cahn wrote six songs in all for the film and Lanza and Grayson also sing a number of operatic arias by Verdi, Bizet and others, but it was "Be My Love" that attracted most attention. Lanza recorded it (without Grayson) and it gave him his first-million seller. It topped the U.S. hit parade, staying in the charts for a total of 34 weeks. It was the biggest-selling record that RCA Victor had ever had and Lanza made it the theme song for his very popular radio show sponsored by Coca-Cola. Billy Eckstine also made a popular recording of the song and in Australia Bobby Limb had a local hit with it.

The song was used again in the 1952 Lanza film *Because You're Mine* where it is sung by Doretta Morrow; Connie Francis sings it *Looking for Love* (1964).

Mario Lanza was born Alfredo Arnold Cocozza on January 31, 1921, in Philadelphia and he died on October 7, 1959, in Rome. He took the male version of his mother's maiden name, Maria Lanza.

Bibbidi-Bobbidi-Boo (The Magic Song)

from *Cinderella*
Music: Al Hoffman and Jerry Livingston
Lyrics: Mack David

As a song that consists largely of just nonsense words, "Bibbidi-Bobbidi-Boo" is hardly a great example of the songwriting art. But the scene in which it occurs in Disney's *Cinderella* is very enjoyable and inventive: Cinderella has just had her lovely ball gown ripped to pieces by Anastasia and Drusilla, her horrible stepsisters, and she has rushed out into the garden in tears. There she meets her Fairy Godmother (with the voice of Verna Felton) who puts everything right. "Bibbidi-Bobbidi-Boo" is the magic word of transformation: A pumpkin turns into an elegant coach to take Cinderella to the ball, and with just a wave of her stick to finish the trick, Fairy Godmother changes four mice into coachmen. Then an old carthorse becomes the coachman and all that remains is to create a new dress for the ball.

After warning Cinderella that the magic spell will be broken at the stroke of midnight, the Fairy Godmother waves her off to have a good time and off she goes with "a bibbidi-bobbidi-boo!"

The lively song is a perfect expression of the Fairy Godmother's breezy personality and through its infectious high spirits the audience is able to share Cinderella's joy at something good happening to her at last.

Verna Felton was a stalwart of Disney films and, in addition to supplying speech for an elephant in Dumbo, she was also the voice of the Queen of Hearts in *Alice in Wonderland*, Aunt Sarah in *Lady and the Tramp* and Flora in *Sleeping Beauty*.

There were many recorded versions of "Bibbidi-Bobbidi-Boo," notably by Perry Como, Dinah Shore and a duet by Jo Stafford and Gordon MacRae.

The Walt Disney Studio Sound Department was nominated for their sound recording of *Cinderella*; Paul Smith and Oliver Wallace were nominated for their scoring of the picture.

Mule Train

from *Singing Guns*
Music and Lyrics: Fred Glickman, Hy Heath and Johnny Lange

Trombonist, bandleader and singer Vaughn Monroe had a string of hits in the 1940s, including cowboy songs like "Cool Water" and "Riders in the Sky." With the public accepting him as a Western balladeer, it seemed logical to cast him in a Western movie. He had had small parts in films earlier, appearing as himself and singing with his band in *Meet the People* (1944) and *Carnegie Hall* (1947). But Republic Pictures, known in Hollywood as the "cowboy studio," now hoped to make him a star in the Roy Rogers mold. They found what they considered a suitable vehicle with the Max Brand novel *Singing Guns* and assembled an excellent cast around him, including Walter Brennan, Ella Raines and Ward Bond.

Monroe sings three songs in *Singing Guns*, including "Mule Train." But his acting performance is rather wooden and it's clear why he never became a big star. He made only one more film—*Toughest Man in Arizona* in 1952.

In *Singing Guns* he plays the outlaw Rhiannon, pursued by the local sheriff, Jim Caradoc, played by Ward Bond. Both stars are slightly overweight, bulging over their gun belts, and Monroe looks too comfortable and cuddly to be convincing as a deadly and dangerous desperado. Brennan is the local doctor-cum-preacher who tries to save the outlaw's soul, while the love interest is supplied by the sultry Raines.

By a complicated twist of the plot, Monroe becomes the deputy sheriff helping Bond to hunt himself down. The scene in which he sings "Mule Train" occurs shortly after Bond, Brennan and Raines have learned Monroe's real identity. The outlaw is riding shotgun on a wagon drawn by two mules, heading towards town. He sings without a care in the world, not knowing that shortly he will be unmasked. As he sings, the wagon driver supplies the accompanying whip cracks and yells of encouragement to the mules. The musical mules keep the steady clip-clopping beat and the lyric lists all the goods on board the wagon, including those "rheumatism pills" and Bibles.

It's a very effective song with its driving rhythm, a big hit even before *Singing Guns* was released. But Monroe's recording was overshadowed by Frankie Laine's: Released in November, 1949 it shot to the top of the charts and stayed there for six weeks. It was a best-seller for 13 weeks, giving Laine his third gold record. Laine's recording is very dramatic, making good use of the sound of a whip cracking, a feature unaccountably omitted from Monroe's version.

There were other hit recordings of the song by Bing Crosby, Tennessee Ernie Ford and Gordon MacRae. All five versions were in the *Billboard* Top 20 at some stage in 1949. In 1966, TV cowboy Lorne Greene revived "Mule Train" on his album of Western songs, *Portrait of the West*. Gene Autry also sang the song in a film and this time the studio had the sense to call it *Mule Train*.

Wilhelmina

from *Wabash Avenue*
Music: Josef Myrow
Lyrics: Mack Gordon

Coney Island was a moderate success for Betty Grable in 1943 so 20th Century–Fox rehashed it in 1950 as *Wabash Avenue*. George Montgomery co-starred in the earlier film; in the new one, Betty Grable's partner was Victor Mature.

Ralph Rainger and Leo Robin wrote the songs for *Coney Island*, including "Cuddle Up a Little Closer." *Wabash Avenue* is packed with songs but uses none of the originals. Instead the studio brought in 26 oldies from the turn of the century; one of the highlights is Betty Grable's performance of "I Wish I Could Shimmy Like My Sister Kate." James Barton almost steals the film as a tipsy Irishman singing "Harrigan."

Fox also commissioned Josef Myrow and Mack Gordon to write some new numbers. They turned in a solid score and duly received an Oscar nomination for "Wilhelmina," sung in the film by Grable with the Freddy Martin Orchestra. Dressed as Hollywood's version of a Dutch girl in a frothy white dress and her hair in pigtails, Grable sings the amusing little song with her usual brassy verve but it has had hardly any life outside of the film. The lyric describes Wilhelmina as the cutest girl in Copenhagen with all the boys "crazy in the noggin" for her. Her kisses are as sweet as Mother's Danish pastry and her cheeks are like roses. Betty is surrounded by a troupe of male dancers who demonstrate the craziness that the boys feel for Wilhelmina, while she finishes off the song with an enjoyable dance routine.

And the Winner Is...

Mona Lisa

from *Captain Carey, U.S.A.*
Music and Lyrics: Jay Livingston and Ray Evans

"Mona Lisa" is unique in Oscar history: In its film, it is sung neither in English, nor in full, but sung in Italian by a singer who is given no screen credit. The film in question is *Captain Carey, U.S.A.* Ray Evans and Jay Livingston wrote the English lyric and then a professor of Italian at UCLA translated it. The fact that the song is sung only in Italian in the film led to a rule change: After 1950, only a song sung in English could be nominated for an Oscar.

The melodramatic World War II spy drama stars Alan Ladd as Capt. Webster Carey, an American agent working with Italian partisans in Northern Italy, trying to track down an informer who betrayed his O.S.S. team and also caused the death of several villagers.

"Mona Lisa" is used at various points as a coded warning that danger is imminent. A blind accordion player sings it—David Leonard plays the role though the Italian singer who dubs for him is not credited. And though we never hear it in full, the song is given strong emphasis. This is in accordance with the wishes of Paramount executive Troy Sanders, who wrote on the composition sheet that the song "is unusual and good and it is hoped that it will be exploited in the film."

The lyric, in Evans and Livingston's English version, has the singer wondering about a beautiful but apparently cold woman and he compares her with the Mona Lisa, "the lady with the mystic smile." Is she smiling to attract a lover or is this her way of hiding a broken heart? The enigma is never solved and the song ends with an unanswered question: Is she real or just a work of art?

The songwriters must have felt tempted to produce a dark and menacing piece to suit the mood of the film, but instead they had the neat idea of working against the dramatic context and writing a love ballad in the Italian style.

When they were first given the songwriting assignment by Paramount, the film was entitled *O.S.S.* Livingston recalls that he wrote most of the melody as he drove to the studio, though he planned that the opening words should be "Prima donna, prima donna." At the studio he and Evans finished the song quickly, still with the same opening. Then they were told that the movie's name had been changed to *After Midnight* (the title of the novel on which it was based) and the song had to be rewritten to fit the new title. Now the opening phrase became "After midnight, after midnight." And though Louis Lipstone, the head of music at Paramount liked it, Ray Evan's wife persuaded the songwriters that the song should be about the famous painting by da Vinci. When the songwriters discovered that film had been renamed again, this time to *Captain Carey, U.S.A.*, it was easy for them to convince Lipstone to use the more graceful "Mona Lisa" lyrics for the Italian song.

But how is it that a song sung in a foreign language and then heard only in snatches managed to win the Best Song Oscar? The explanation may be found in the phenomenal sales of Nat King Cole's record of the song. It shot to number one in the American hit parade and stayed there for five weeks. There were six other versions that also had reasonable sales but Cole's record remained in the charts for 27 weeks and sold more than three million copies. It was his biggest ever hit and only eight other records sold more copies in the first half of the twentieth century. Many people still believe that Cole sings "Mona Lisa" in the film.

Cole almost missed recording the song. Paramount had seen two years earlier what a hit record could do for a film when "Buttons and Bows" boosted audiences for *The Paleface*. They wanted similar publicity for *Captain Carey, U.S.A.* Livingston and Evans thought that all the American-Italian singers would jump at the chance to record "Mona Lisa" but Frank Sinatra, Perry Como and Vic Damone all turned it down.

The studio now decided that the song would be ideal for Cole's voice and an executive approached Capitol Records and Nat's agent, Carlos Gastel. Gastel was not very impressed by the song but he took it to Cole, who asked his wife Maria for an opinion. She disliked it and felt very strongly that "an offbeat thing about an old painting" wouldn't sell. Nat himself referred to it disparagingly as "the Italian song." But in spite of all the negativity, Nat did decide to record it and it became his most successful recording. His expressive voice brings out all the poignancy of the melody and there is real tenderness in his singing. The orchestra behind him is Les Baxter's and the excellent arrangement is by Nelson Riddle (one of his earliest hit recordings).

When the record was finally released, Capitol executives—like others before them—had little faith in its commercial possibilities. They put it on the back of a recording by Nat King Cole and His Trio, a swinging gospel number entitled "The Greatest Inventor of Them All." This was the song that Capitol pushed, including the placing of full-page advertisements in the trade papers, all of which failed to mention "Mona Lisa." But then their sales-

men began to report that it was "Mona Lisa" that the disc jockeys were playing.

The record also marked a turning point in Nat King Cole's career: Previously better known as a first class jazz pianist and singer, this was his first
without his trio. Now he was set on a career as a ballad singer and jazz fans
everywhere were dismayed.

When Cole's "Mona Lisa" reached the top of the *Billboard* charts, there
was also a recording of the song in the *Billboard* top 20 by Victor Young and
His Orchestra. The vocalist on this was Don Cherry. Conway Twitty revived
"Mona Lisa" successfully in 1959 and the song was once more at the top of
the American charts. And in 1986, *Mona Lisa* was the title of a movie starring Bob Hoskins, Michael Caine and Cathy Tyson. Nat King Cole's recording of the song was used extensively on the soundtrack.

Captain Carey, U.S.A. was released in the U.K. under the novel's title *After
Midnight.*

1951

Danny Kaye hosted the 1951 Oscars at the RKO Pantages Theatre, with Donald O'Connor presenting the award for Best Song. Once again the orchestra played O'Connor onto stage with "Mule Train" and he had to put up with more jokes about Francis, as he did at the 1949 Awards. Jane Powell ("Too Late Now"), Kay Brown ("A Kiss to Build a Dream On"), Dick Haymes ("Never") and Howard Keel ("Wonder Why") performed the nominated songs. With Jane Wyman's help, Kaye sang "In the Cool, Cool, Cool of the Evening."

The Nominations

Hoagy Carmichael and Johnny Mercer for "In the Cool, Cool, Cool of the Evening" from *Here Comes the Groom* (Paramount)

Bert Kalmar, Harry Ruby and Oscar Hammerstein II for "A Kiss to Build a Dream On" from *The Strip* (MGM)

Lionel Newman and Eliot Daniel for "Never" from *Golden Girl* (Fox)

Burton Lane and Alan Jay Lerner for "Too Late Now" from *Royal Wedding* (MGM)

Nicholas Brodszky and Sammy Cahn for "Wonder Why" from *Rich, Young and Pretty* (MGM)

A Kiss to Build a Dream on

from *The Strip*
Music: Bert Kalmar and Harry Ruby
Lyrics: Oscar Hammerstein II

In *The Strip*, Mickey Rooney plays Stanley Maxton, a jazz drummer just released from the Army. He becomes embroiled with some shady characters

189

but manages to find employment with Louis Armstrong in a band that also includes Jack Teagarden and Earl Hines. There's some great jazz but the melodramatic plot, with Rooney wrongly implicated in a murder, is very thin.

The film is now chiefly recalled for introducing "A Kiss to Build a Dream On," one of Louis Armstrong's biggest hits. The song had its origins in 1935 when Bert Kalmar and Harry Ruby wrote the appealing melody and gave it the title "Moonlight on the Meadow." Later that year, MGM decided to use the song in the Marx Brothers movie *A Night at the Opera* and Oscar Hammerstein was contracted to write a new lyric. In spite of his excellent efforts, the song was rejected and stayed buried for 16 years until it reemerged in *The Strip*. Bert Kalmar's Oscar nomination was posthumous as he had died in 1947.

In the movie, William Demarest plays "Fluff," the owner of the club where much of the action takes place. He is also a pianist and would-be songwriter and he it is who first sings "A Kiss to Build a Dream On." Mickey Rooney joins him on the vocals to delightful comic effect as they get badly off-key in their attempts at close harmony. Later the song is given a more tuneful treatment by Kay Brown as Edna, the club's hatcheck girl; she has ambitions to become a singer. After this, the melody is heard a number of times on the soundtrack before Louis gives the song its definitive treatment in the final scene.

The chorus has an unusual rhyme pattern in that it is the second and third lines that rhyme. The lyric is beautifully structured, the chorus starting and finishing with the same phrase and sustaining the conceit of the singer asking for a parting kiss to fantasize on during the separation. The bridge is especially fine, with its internal rhyme of "fancies" and "romances."

Although a recording by the Hugo Winterhalter orchestra sold more copies than Louis Armstrong's, the song has become closely associated with Satchmo. He recorded it with Sy Oliver's orchestra and the hit song became a regular part of his repertoire. His recording was heard on screen as part of the soundtrack for the 1993 movie *Sleepless in Seattle*.

Never

from *Golden Girl*
Music: Lionel Newman
Lyrics: Eliot Daniel

Mitzi Gaynor (born Francesca Mitzi de Czanyi Von Gerber) began her film career in 1950. Her first starring role was in *Golden Girl*, the 1951 biopic of Lotte Crabtree, the singer who rose to fame in the years after the American Civil War.

In the film, Mart Taylor (Dennis Day) is deeply in love with Lotte but she prefers the mysterious charms of Tom Richmond (Dale Robertson). When

Richmond is revealed as a Confederate agent, he manages to escape back to the South, vowing to return to claim Lotte after the War. Taylor continues to worship her and he gets the chance to tell Lotte what he feels in song. She has just wowed the audience at San Francisco's Bella Union Theatre and as the applause dies down, a bewhiskered gentleman requests that Taylor sing something "for the ladies." He obliges with "Never," expressing in the song all that he feels about Lotte but is too diffident to say directly: His love is as deep as the ever-flowing sea and as bright as the ever-shining sun; whatever happens to the world, his love will never die. These are the conventional phrases of run-of the-mill love ballads—there is nothing remarkable about the lyric or the melody.

Day sings the song in his high tenor voice with a flowery fervency, but his efforts go unrewarded. As Mitzi sits in her dressing room, her mother points out, "He's singing this to you," but Mitzi's thoughts are all with Dale Robertson.

It is difficult to understand why such an inferior song, with its cliched imagery, should have received an Oscar nomination, especially when another song in the film—only marginally more appealing—receives much more attention. "California Moon" is sung three times and its melody is used as background music on a number of occasions. But in spite of this emphasis, "Never" was the one to be nominated for the Oscar. Day's record was the leading version but very few singers recorded the song and he had little competition.

Too Late Now

from *Royal Wedding*
Music: Burton Lane
Lyrics: Alan Jay Lerner

Three years after the marriage of Princess Elizabeth to Philip Mountbatten, there was still enough public interest for MGM to make *Royal Wedding*, though to avoid any taint of commercialism or exploitation the film was released in Britain with the title *Wedding Bells*. The flimsy plot concerns Tom and Ellen Bowen, a brother-and-sister song-and-dance team, played by Fred Astaire and Jane Powell, invited to take their act to London at the height of royal wedding fever. And just as Fred's real life sister Adele did some years earlier, Jane's character also meets and falls in love with a British aristocrat: Lord John Brindale, played by Peter Lawford.

Jane and Peter seem to be falling in love but have admitted earlier to having a light-hearted approach to romance so Lawford starts to worry when he feels himself getting very serious about Powell. Nervously, he tells her, "Something might happen ... you might look over your shoulder and see someone else." Jane hastens to reassure her man and demonstrates her commitment to him by singing "Too Late Now": Now she will never forget his

Jane Powell and Peter Lawford in *Royal Wedding* (MGM, 1951).

smile, his voice and all the things they've done together. She will never be the same again—it's "Too Late Now."

Burton Lane's melody is superb, simple yet eloquent; the lyric is beautifully structured, with the title phrase beginning and ending the song, and Jane Powell's quietly emotional singing does it full justice. In his autobiography *The Street Where I Live*, Alan Jay Lerner describes Burton Lane's music for *Royal Wedding*'s songs as "spiffy" but says that his own contribution left him "in such a state of cringe that I could hardly straighten up." The great lyricist is being unduly modest.

"Too Late Now" was actually the last song written for the film—Lerner had already returned to New York when the producers decided they wanted one more song. Burton Lane quickly wrote the melody and phoned Lerner, who copied it down. He completed the lyric in three days and phoned it back to Lane in Hollywood.

The song was a minor hit though even bigger was the song with the longest title of any in film: "How Could You Believe Me When I Said I Loved You When You Know I've Been a Liar All My Life." It is often referred to as "The Liar Song" for brevity's sake and was actually the only million-selling record that Fred Astaire had. He sings it in the film as a duet with Jane Powell.

Powell's record of "Too Late Now" was the best-selling version but Toni Arden, Dick Haymes and Dinah Shore also did well with it.

Wonder Why

from *Rich, Young and Pretty*
Music: Nicholas Brodszky
Lyrics: Sammy Cahn

"Wonder Why" runs through *Rich, Young and Pretty* as the love theme for Jane Powell and Vic Damone. The latter, making his movie debut opposite one of MGM's most popular stars, gets to sing "Wonder Why" first.

Jane plays a girl who has grown up on a Texas cattle ranch owned by her father (Wendell Corey). Father and daughter visit Paris and there Jane meets Vic Damone, as well as her mother (Danielle Darrieux), who left her husband to return to Paris many years before when Jane was a small child.

When Jane and Vic meet, there is an instant attraction; he asks her out and as she gets ready in her room, he sits at the piano and sings "Wonder Why?" Is it just a song he is singing to pass the time or does it express his feelings for Jane? There is no doubt that it is the latter as the words reflect on the strange and inexplicable sensations he is experiencing. The song comes up with the simple explanation for the mystery—he has fallen in love.

Later in the film, when the romance is well underway, Vic and Jane are dancing together in a Paris nightclub. As they step around the floor, they begin to sing "Wonder Why" to each other. The rest of the dancers stop to watch the attractive couple in a world of their own. It is only at the end of the song that the applause they receive brings them out of their romantic trance and they return, embarrassed, to their table.

Though it's not a great ballad, the simple lyric and minor key melody make it appealing. It has become a favorite with jazz singers and musicians, with recordings by Sarah Vaughan, Carmen McRae and pianist Bill Evans.

The song turns up again in another Jane Powell film, *Small Town Girl* (1953). On this occasion, Bobby Van sings a few lines of it as he tries to impress Ann Miller with his singing abilities. "Wonder Why" was also used in a 1952 film about the New Orleans Mardi Gras, *Holiday for Sinners*.

And the Winner Is...

In the Cool, Cool, Cool of the Evening

from *Here Comes the Groom*
Music: Hoagy Carmichael
Lyrics: Johnny Mercer

"In the Cool, Cool, Cool of the Evening" is a very funny song given excellent treatment in *Here Comes the Groom* and it was a thoroughly deserving winner of the 1951 Best Song Oscar. Liam O'Brien and Robert Riskin were also nominated for their excellent script for the film.

Here Comes the Groom is an enjoyable film that has some similarities with *The Philadelphia Story* and its musical offshoot *High Society* in that the main character, Pete Garvey, played by Bing Crosby, is trying to prevent the woman he loves from marrying a high society blue blood. Jane Wyman is Emmadel Jones, the woman in question, while Franchot Tone plays Wilbur Stanley, Bing's rival. The wedding is planned for the following Saturday and extra spice is added as Bing has until that day to get married and so provide a home for a pair of French orphans he wishes to adopt. If he fails, they will be sent back to Paris.

The song is used as a very unusual love theme throughout the film—unusual because such songs are usually heavily romantic and not nonsensical comedy numbers like this one. Snatches of the song are heard early in the film, sung by one of the Parisian orphans. Bing and Jane eventually sing the song in full in the most enjoyable sequence of the film.

The words of the song have no dramatic significance—they merely concern a couple of partygoers accepting an invitation: "You can tell 'em we'll be there!" But it clearly has had a very significant place in the history of Bing and Jane's relationship. Set on rejecting Bing, Jane is determined to marry her new and very rich fiancé. Bing tries to stir up her memories of happy times together by singing a snatch of the song and then persuades her to perform their complete routine with him. It is a very funny sequence, full of hilarious business and comic dance steps.

The sequence begins in an office, then Bing and Jane clown and sing their way out into a corridor, into an elevator car, down to the main entrance hall and then out into the street. Director Frank Capra brought off quite a technical coup in that the orchestra was playing live, back on the studio sound stage. Bing and Jane were a few blocks away on the set and they had tiny radios in their ears so that they could pick up the sound of the orchestra via antenna loops on the floor.

The lyric again shows Johnny Mercer's skill with the vernacular and is full of cleverly humorous rhymes such as "teepee/RSVP," "jackass/fracas" and "hair/guerre." Mercer's delight in language and his talent for the unexpected and comic rhyme show up superbly well throughout this enjoyably absurd song. Jane Wyman comments that it's "the silliest song anyone ever did sing" and it's hard not to agree. But it's silliness of the highest order, almost worthy of Lewis Carroll.

Bing later uses the song to remind Jane of what they once were to each other and he sings the song in the background as she is introduced to her fiancé's lordly relatives. He even teaches it to Winifred Stanley (Alexis Smith), Franchot Tone's cousin, in an effort to make Jane jealous. His machinations succeed and as Bing and Jane drive off after their wedding, they and their adopted children sing "In the Cool, Cool, Cool of the Evening" to close the film.

Ray Evans and Jay Livingston wrote the rest of the film's songs but Frank Capra wanted a comedy song-and-dance number to show off the neglected talents of Jane Wyman. Hoagy Carmichael and Johnny Mercer actually wrote "In the Cool, Cool, Cool of the Evening" for Betty Hutton to sing in *The Mack Sennett Girl* (also known as *The Keystone Girl*) but the film was never made and the song was buried in Paramount's files. One of Frank Capra's assistants knew of it and brought it to the director's attention by means of a small try-out recording made by the songwriters—Mercer singing with Hoagy Carmichael on piano. Capra and Crosby listened to it, loved it and quickly grabbed it for the film. It became the fourth and last film song introduced by Bing Crosby to win an Oscar. Bing and Jane's recording of the song was very popular, as was a version by Frankie Laine and Jo Stafford.

Hoagy Carmichael was delighted by the way his song was presented in the film, despite initial reservations about the talents of Jane Wyman as a singer. In his autobiography *Sometimes I Wonder* he makes these very revealing, if cynical comments about the 1951 Best Song Oscars:

> The betting and the studio pressure play had been for "A Kiss to Build a Dream On" by Harry Ruby and Oscar Hammerstein II. Advertising and press agent gall doesn't make an Oscar race pure as the driven snow. But we had planted our song not once but several times in the film, and I carried home, fairly won, the golden nude statue with the sword. Many are cynical about Hollywood awards, and rightly so. There is too much jockeying and lunch buying, gift giving and ad taking. But I didn't do anything but sit back and wait after writing the music—a creative item often overlooked in that busy place.

When Hoagy went up to receive his Award at the 1951 Oscars, he made a sardonic quip about the fact that Sam Goldwyn had called him Hugo Carmichael at the 1946 ceremony when he was nominated for "Ole Buttermilk Sky."

1952

The 1952 awards ceremony was the first to be televised. NBC decided to hold a parallel celebration at the International Theatre in New York for nominees who were unable to get to Hollywood for the evening. Bob Hope hosted at the RKO Pantages Theatre, while Conrad Nagel was his counterpart in New York. Walt Disney presented the Music Awards, including Best Song, and managed to get quite a few things wrong. He found it impossible to pronounce Dimitri Tiomkin's name and misread "Am I in Love?" as "I Am in Love." Bob Hope and Marilyn Maxwell performed that song on the night. Celeste Holm sang "Thumbelina" to a face painted on her thumb, while Billy Daniels ("Because You're Mine"), Peggy Lee and Johnny Mercer ("Zing a Little Zong") and Tex Ritter ("High Noon") sang the other songs.

The Nominations

Jack Brooks for "Am I in Love?" from *Son of Paleface* (Paramount)
Nicholas Brodszky and Sammy Cahn for "Because You're Mine" from *Because You're Mine* (MGM)
Dimitri Tiomkin and Ned Washington for "High Noon (Do Not Forsake Me)" from *High Noon* (United Artists)
Frank Loesser for "Thumbelina" from *Hans Christian Andersen* (Goldwyn)
Harry Warren and Leo Robin for "Zing a Little Zong" from *Just for You* (Paramount)

Am I in Love?

from *Son of Paleface*
Music and Lyrics: Jack Brooks

Son of Paleface is a sequel to *The Paleface* with Bob Hope as Peter "Junior" Potter, Jr., the son of the character he played in the earlier movie. This time,

Jane Russell plays Mike "The Torch" Delroy, the boss of a gang of robbers. "Buttons and Bows," the Oscar-winning song from *The Paleface,* is reprised this time as a duet by Roy Rogers and Jane Russell, with interruptions from Hope.

"Am I in Love?" is an up-tempo comedy number sung by Bob and Jane late in the movie. They are holed up in a deserted saloon with hordes of Indians poised to attack. Lawman Roy Barton (Rogers) is hot on their trail too, so what does Jane decide to do? She gives her man a shave with a cutthroat razor so that he can meet his fate looking clean and tidy. As she wields the razor, he begins to sing, expressing his puzzlement at his feelings for her. He wants to sigh every time he is near her and feels like Humpty Dumpty about to take his fall. It's as though love is a sickness for which there is no cure.

The lyric has a simple pattern and the song's cheerful simplicity gives it an immediate appeal. Joni James had the best-selling recording; there was another by Debbie Reynolds, and one by the Freddy Martin orchestra.

Because You're Mine

from *Because You're Mine*
Music: Nicholas Brodszky
Lyrics: Sammy Cahn

By 1952, Mario Lanza was one of the most popular of MGM's stars. After the success of *The Great Caruso,* his third film, he was convinced that the studio should star him in a series of filmed operas. Instead they offered him *Because Your Mine.* MGM's rationale was to rush out a cheap film as quickly as possible to cash in on Lanza's success; Joe Pasternak outlined the story to Lanza and the singer thought it was junk, unworthy of his talents. But his contractual obligations forced him in front of the cameras. Lanza may have been correct in his judgment but *Because You're Mine* did well at the box office, the title song received an Oscar nomination and Lanza's record of it sold a million, reaching number seven in the U.S. charts.

Lanza plays Renaldo Rossano, an operatic tenor who is drafted into the Army. In charge of his unit is Sgt. Batterson (James Whitmore), an opera fan; the sergeant's sister Bridget (Doretta Morrow) has ambitions to be a singer. Lanza offers to help with her career, falls in love, but the usual complications keep them apart until the properly romantic conclusion.

Mario Lanza in *Because You're Mine* (MGM, 1952).

Part of "Because You're Mine" is sung by Lanza over the opening credits but we hear it in full for the first time when he asks Doretta Morrow to play the piano for him, to play the song she loves best. Of course she plays "Because You're Mine" and Mario sings, making it a declaration of his passion for her.

The melody is floridly operatic and the lyric becomes a little ludicrous in places, particularly when Lanza is concerned that Doretta might mistake the beating of his heart for thunder. The climax of the song is made slightly awkward by the near-rhyme of "applause" and "because," especially as the same note is used on the second syllables of both words. This emphasis only draws attention to the clumsiness of the rhyme.

Nevertheless, Lanza sings with great vigor and feeling and the song works its magic on Doretta. She joins in and the two of them gaze with passionate intensity into each other's eyes. At the end of their duet, they embrace and kiss.

But soon those obligatory complications begin and it is not until Lanza is performing on stage for a group of foreign generals that harmony is restored. He roars out "Because You're Mine," accompanied by the huge MGM Orchestra and with flags of all nations unfurled behind him. It is, perhaps, rather over-dramatic treatment for such a tender love ballad, but then Mario sees Doretta half-hidden at the door of the concert hall and calls out to her that the song will sound better as a duet. She joins in him on stage and they sing the words only for each other. The End.

"Because You're Mine" is in similar vein to the same songwriters' "Be My Love," written for Lanza's 1950 film *The Toast of New Orleans*. The producers decided to reprise the earlier song in this film but this time Lanza does not sing it: He has arranged an audition for Doretta Morrow with his impresario but he is confined to barracks and cannot go to help her with her rehearsal. Instead she sings the song over the telephone; her audition piece is "Be My Love."

Lanza's record of "Because You're Mine" sold more than a million copies, his third and last to do so. It was in the U.S. charts for 17 weeks, reaching number seven. It did even better in the U.K. where it spent 24 weeks in the bestsellers, with number three its highest position. Nat King Cole also recorded the song with some success on both sides of the Atlantic.

Thumbelina

from *Hans Christian Andersen*
Music and Lyrics: Frank Loesser

Producer Sam Goldwyn enjoyed every minute he spent on the set of *Hans Christian Andersen* and he loved all the songs, especially "Thumbelina." For months after the film had been completed, he could be heard humming the tune to himself. This probably explains why "Thumbelina" rather than any of the other excellent songs Frank Loesser wrote received the Oscar nomination. The film was nominated for five other Oscars but failed to win any.

"Thumbelina" has a bright and lilting tune but the repetitious words, though charmingly simple, are not the most outstanding example of Loesser's songwriting skills. Loesser himself often referred to it as an insignificant little ditty, not a real song. When discussing the art of songwriting he would use "Thumbelina" as an example of a cheap song. He should have given himself more credit for writing exactly what the scene required: a charming "little ditty" meant to entertain a small child.

The song occurs when Danny Kaye, as Hans, is in a prison cell, locked up for showing "disrespect for the King's statue." As he looks glumly out of his cell window, a little girl (Beverly Washburn) comes by and the pair begins a conversation. She is concerned that Kaye is lonely but he, never able to resist trying to charm children with his tales, tells that he is never alone: "I'm expecting company right now," he tells her. Tiny Thumbelina arrives on the scene—a puppet made from his thumb, draped with his pocket handkerchief. He tells Beverly that Thumbelina is very unhappy because she is so little; his song is designed to convince her that "when your heart is full of love, you're nine feet tall."

It is a delightful scene, as are others involving Andersen stories turned into songs: "The Ugly Duckling," "Inchworm" and "The King's New Clothes." "The Little Mermaid" is used as the basis for a 17-minute ballet and the songs and dance sequences take up almost half of the film's running time. Roland Petit of the Ballet de Paris choreographed the dancing, and his wife Jeanmaire was the featured ballerina in the film.

The album of the film's song was a best-seller and topped the charts on both sides of the Atlantic. The other excellent songs, any of which deserved nomination, include the lighthearted love duet "No Two People" (a song very much in the vein of Loesser's "Two Sleepy People"), the magical "Anywhere I Wander," the tourism-boosting "Wonderful Copenhagen" and the title song. Danny Kaye had some chart success with "Thumbelina"—it reached number 28. "Wonderful Copenhagen" sold even better, especially in Britain where it reached number five.

Before this film, the Danish storyteller was usually known as Hans Andersen, but Frank Loesser had trouble fitting that to his melody line and hit on the idea of including Andersen's middle name. Since the release of the film, he has been known almost invariably as Hans Christian Andersen. A 1974 London stage adaptation starring Tommy Steele tried to turn the tide by reverting to the title *Hans Andersen*, but the battle was lost.

Zing a Little Zong

from *Just for You*
Music: Harry Warren
Lyrics: Leo Robin

Just for You re-teams Bing Crosby and Jane Wyman as a follow-up to *Here Comes the Groom* the previous year, and "Zing a Little Zong" is clearly an attempt to emulate the success of the Oscar-winning song from the earlier film, "In the Cool, Cool, Cool of the Evening."

"Zing a Little Zong" is a bright and lively number but it plays no part in the story: Bing is Jordan Blake, a highly successful Broadway producer and songwriter, and "Zing a Little Zong" is the hit number from his new show. He and Carolina Hill (Wyman), the show's leading lady, sing the song together at the opening night party.

The song itself is spoof Dutch, about a romantic couple who imagine they are taking a moonlit stroll in Holland. Bing sings first, then invites Jane to join him; she obliges with a chorus while he adds some musical comments of his own. They sing the last lines together and are joined in song by a chorus of party guests. The lyric mentions a couple of classic food dishes, wiener schnitzel and apple strudel, which are Austrian rather than Dutch, but it's near enough for Hollywood.

It is a very enjoyable song with an infectiously catchy melody. It gave Harry Warren his ninth Oscar nomination. He had written the music for many songs for the Warner and Fox musicals but this was his first assignment for Paramount. It came about through a phone call from Bing Crosby at six o'clock in the morning. Warren thought it was someone playing a practical joke, then realized that it really was Bing asking him to write a score. Warren was delighted to accept and to work with the great entertainer for the first time. Bing suggested as lyricist Leo Robin, a man who had written many hits for Crosby and who had worked with Warren on such films as *The Gang's All Here*.

Warren and Robin wrote a huge score for *Just for You*—a total of 11 songs—and all except one were used in the final cut. Apart from "Zing a Little Zong," the only one that has survived to any degree is another of Harry Warren's train songs: "On the 10:10 from Ten-Ten-Tennessee."

And the Winner Is...

High Noon (Do Not Forsake Me)

from *High Noon*
Music: Dimitri Tiomkin
Lyrics: Ned Washington

The use of this plaintive ballad in the Western *High Noon* is masterly, adding considerably to the film's myth-like quality. But it is hard to believe that preview audiences giggled and laughed at the song. The reason was that the song was used too frequently in the original version. Every time that the tight-lipped Gary Cooper strode the dusty streets, his footsteps were followed on the soundtrack by Tex Ritter's voice singing, "Do not forsake me, oh my darling.... " It was musical overkill. Once the number of uses was reduced, the true effectiveness of the song became evident and it gave a focus and direction to the film.

The melody of the song is used extensively to heighten the drama but the song is sung in full only once, over the opening credits. These play over a scene of three desperadoes gathering outside the town to wait for their leader, Frank Miller, played by Ian MacDonald. The song sets the scene for the story to come.

The words have the feel of natural speech, drawn from the setting of the film, yet they are lyrical and expressive. The vocabulary and homespun phrases, as well as rhymes such as "prison/his'n," perfectly suit Gary Cooper's screen character and his everyday speech patterns.

The action all takes place in 90 minutes (approximately the length of the film) on a hot Sunday morning. Will Kane (Cooper), the town's marshal, is marrying Amy Fowler (Grace Kelly), his "fair haired beauty." News arrives that Frank Miller, an outlaw he sent to jail, is arriving on the noonday train and seeking revenge. The marshal's efforts to deputize some of the townspeople are unsuccessful as one by one they make their excuses. He is left alone to face Miller and his three men on the deserted streets.

The song is sung by Tex Ritter on the soundtrack but his record label Capitol showed little interest in a releasing a record. The reaction of preview audiences to the first cut of the movie was not encouraging and the movie's eventual success was not expected. Then news came through that Frankie Laine was about to record the song and Capitol's producer Ken Nelson now brought Ritter to the studio. This recording was actually released a week before Laine's but it was not nearly as popular perhaps because there were no drums, a big feature of the movie version. This prompted Nelson to overdub Ritter's record and a new version, now with drums, was released. Later in 1952, Ritter recorded "High Noon" in the U.K., with an orchestra directed by Johnny Douglas, and most critics believe that this is Ritter's best version, much closer to the soundtrack than the others. It was released only in the U.K.

In spite of all these efforts, Frankie Laine easily outsold Ritter, selling over a million copies, his ninth record to do so. It was in the U.S. charts for 19 weeks, reaching number five. In Britain it reached the number seven spot and was a bestseller for seven weeks.

Dimitri Tiomkin won two Oscars for his work on *High Noon*, one for the title song and the other for his score. He had also started a new trend in Hollywood songwriting: This was the first time the composer of a film's background music also wrote the theme song. Tiomkin had realized that such songs could achieve independent popularity and earn substantial earnings from royalties.

In addition to Tiomkin's Oscars, Gary Cooper won for Best Actor, with Harold Gerstad and Elmo Williams also winning for their editing. *High Noon* was nominated in three other categories: Best Picture, Best Direction and Best Writing.

Gary Cooper in *High Noon* (United Artists, 1952).

At the party given by *High Noon*'s producer Stanley Kramer after the 1952 Oscars, "High Noon" lyricist Ned Washington said he felt like the mother of twins, "only prouder." But he might not have been quite so proud of his lyrics had he heard Pearl Bailey's parody of the song at another post–Oscars celebration.

1953

Joint venues were used again for the 1953 awards with Donald O'Connor hosting at RKO Pantages Theatre in Hollywood and Fredric March at the NBC Century Theatre, New York. Arthur Freed presented all the Music awards. Mitzi Gaynor joined O'Connor to sing "The Moon Is Blue" and Dean Martin performed "That's Amore." The other singers were Ann Blyth ("Secret Love"), Margaret Whiting ("My Flaming Heart") and Connie Russell ("Sadie Thompson's Song").

The Nominations

Herschel Burke Gilbert and Sylvia Fine for "The Moon Is Blue" from *The Moon Is Blue* (United Artists)

Nicholas Brodszky and Leo Robin for "My Flaming Heart" from *Small Town Girl* (MGM)

Sammy Fain and Paul Francis Webster for "Secret Love" from *Calamity Jane* (Warner)

Lester Lee and Ned Washington for "Sadie Thompson's Song (Blue Pacific Blues)" from *Miss Sadie Thompson* (Columbia)

Harry Warren and Jack Brooks for "That's Amore" from *The Caddy* (Paramount)

The Moon Is Blue

from *The Moon Is Blue*
Music: Herschel Burke Gilbert
Lyrics: Sylvia Fine

Hollywood's Production Code maintained strict control over what could be shown on screen but there was a gradual loosening in the 1950s and one of the films that began the downfall of the old industry censorship rules was *The Moon Is Blue*. Director Otto Preminger defied the Code by including some frank—for the times—dialogue, with words such as "pregnant," "mistress" and "seduce" which had hitherto been banned. The most shocking word in the film, though, occurred when Maggie McNamara, as Patty O'Neill, described herself as a "virgin." Under the old rules the word could not be used at all unless it was capitalized and followed by the name "Mary."

In Britain, *The Moon Is Blue* was the first film to receive the new "X Certificate" censorship rating, meaning that no one under the age of 16 years could see it legally. In America, the Roman Catholic Church condemned the film as having an unacceptably light attitude toward seduction and this only added to the publicity; filmgoers flocked to see *The Moon Is Blue*. And many an adolescent, aroused by the controversy, sneaked into the cinema with high anticipation to see this reputedly sexy film, only to be disappointed by the fairly innocuous reality. This subject was dealt with hilariously in an episode of TV's *MASH*.

In *The Moon Is Blue*, David Niven and William Holden play aging playboys David Slater and Donald Gresham, the would-be seducers of Maggie McNamara. She refuses their advances, declaring that she intends to remain a virgin until her wedding night. Both men determine to find a way to overcome her scruples.

The Sauter-Finegan Orchestra plays the title song over the opening titles. The singer is uncredited but Sally Sweetland was the vocalist on the top-selling recording released by the Sauter-Finegan Orchestra.

The jaunty melody and the quirky lyric, with its surrealistic images, work well to set the tone for the mildly amusing proceedings to come. The lyric poses the occurrence of unlikely activities such as the desert freezing over, cats barking and a month of Sundays in June. But these things do happen when "the moon is blue"; therefore it is quite possible that the singer will find romance.

My Flaming Heart

from *Small Town Girl*
Music: Nicholas Brodszky
Lyrics: Leo Robin

"My Flaming Heart" is the song that sets alight the romance between Jane Powell and Farley Granger in *Small Town Girl*. The film was made originally by MGM in 1936 featuring Janet Gaynor. The 1953 remake has Jane Powell in Janet Gaynor's role and the cast includes Ann Miller as well as Fay Wray of *King Kong* fame, who made something of a comeback in the 1950s playing character parts.

The songs written for the remake are not outstanding but they are well orchestrated by Andre Previn and given brilliant staging by Busby Berkeley. *Small Town Girl* was one of the last films he made as dance director in MGM's employ. The most notable routine in the film is the athletic jumping dance performed by Bobby Van.

Jane plays Cindy Kimbell, the small town girl of the title, and Farley Granger is Rick Belrow Livingston, a smooth-talking charmer from the big city. Though obviously destined for each other, Rick is engaged to Lisa Bellmount (Miller), and everyone in the small town expects Cindy to marry Ludwig Schlemmer (Van). When Jane visits New York, Granger takes her out on a tour of the nightclubs. In one of them, the star turn is Nat King Cole, and he it is who sings "My Flaming Heart."

The song smoulders with intensity and the glances that the pair exchanges during Nat's performance are a clear indication that they are falling for each other. The lyric that Nat sings is very short, consisting of two five-line verses, but the word "burn" occurs six times and "flaming" four, and the image of the fires of passion being damped down so that they don't burn out too soon is intense.

When Cole finishes the song, the music continues and the pair gets up to dance. The evening ends with the inevitable passionate kiss. We hear the song once more: Jane has taken to her bed with a cold and daydreams about Granger as she listens to Nat King Cole's recording of "My Flaming Heart." The song is undistinguished and Nat King Cole's singing does it more justice than it deserves. He did record it as a single but only as the B-side of "I Am in Love."

Sadie Thompson's Song (The Blue Pacific Blues)

from *Miss Sadie Thompson*
Music: Lester Lee
Lyrics: Ned Washington

Rain, Somerset Maugham's story of "sultry sex in the South Seas," spawned three film versions: the 1928 silent *Sadie Thompson* which starred Gloria Swanson, the 1932 *Rain* with Joan Crawford as Sadie and the semi-musical *Miss Sadie Thompson.* This film, originally released in 3D, has Rita Hayworth in the title role, with Jo Ann Greer dubbing her singing.

Sadie Thompson is a lady with a doubtful past who falls foul of the local missionary Alfred Davidson, played by Jose Ferrer. He sees her as the embodiment of all the fleshly sins and is determined to drive her from the island. In cliched Freudian terms, it's only too apparent that this stern-faced missionary lusts after Sadie just as strongly as the U.S. Marines stationed there.

As the film begins, "Sadie Thompson's Song" is the first thing we hear, played over the opening credits. On a palm-fringed beach, a U.S. Marine is playing the bluesy tune on his mouth organ while his three comrades swim.

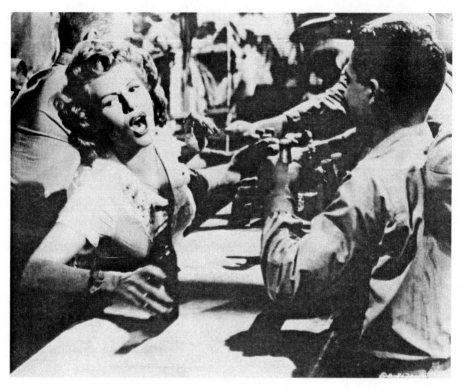

Rita Hayworth in *Miss Sadie Thompson* (**Columbia, 1953**).

(The performer is Leo Diamond.) The swimmers include Aldo Ray and Charles Bronson—billed under his real name, Charles Buchinsky. The tune establishes the mood of steamy tropical languor.

Later in the film, Hayworth performs the song for these same Marines in her hotel room. The tropical rain pours down but gives no relief from the heat. Rita stretches sensuously on her bed while the mouth organist plays. She is wearing a skimpy red dress that emphasizes her bust and shows a great deal of leg. As the three Marines drool, she sings of her sultry and sleepless nights, the pounding rain and the howling tropical wind. Night thoughts in the tropical heat lead to the feeling that nobody cares for her and she is full of those "blue Pacific blues."

It is an effective song that captures the sultry mood and reflects the character of Sadie but perhaps the lyric is too specific to the situation in the film and its setting. The record-buying public ignored the vocal versions of "Sadie Thompson's Song" and the best-seller was an instrumental by Richard Hayman and His Orchestra.

That's Amore

from *The Caddy*
Music: Harry Warren
Lyrics: Jack Brooks

Comedian Jerry Lewis had great respect for Harry Warren and had him write the songs for a number of his films of the 1950s and early 1960s, including *The Caddy*. The respect was not reciprocated—Warren often referred to Lewis as "a pain in the ass" and later in life described his humor as "crass."

"That's Amore" occurs in *The Caddy* when Joe Anthony (Dean Martin) returns home to his family. They are Italian migrants, part of the San Francisco fishing community, and played in the film as stereotypical Italian comic figures. At his welcome home party, Dean is called upon to sing a song. Director Norman Taurog's original idea was to use a well-known Italian song like "Come Back to Sorrento" or "O Sole Mio." But the songwriters prevailed on him to take a more original approach, offering to write a "traditional" Italian

Jerry Lewis and Dean Martin sing "That's Amore" in *The Caddy* (Paramount, 1953), flanked by Donna Reed and Argentina Brunetti.

song of their own. Their effort was the very catchy "That's Amore." The lyric is full of Italian words and phrases and the prominent internal rhymes emphasize the swinging dance rhythms of the melody.

Dean didn't take to the song at first, disliking what he thought of as its corny Italian-ness, and he was quite happy for his partner to contribute a chorus. In his screechy voice, Jerry Lewis sings two new lines, rhyming "oil" with "goil" and "pet" with "spaghett." Then Dean sings with him and they revert to the original lyric, and finally the whole family joins in, singing and dancing around the table.

Apparently, Martin disliked the song so much that he refused to record it. Paramount ignored his feelings by giving the soundtrack rights to Capitol and soon the record started to climb the charts. Ironically, "That's Amore" established Martin as a singing star and remains one of his biggest hits. It was his first million-seller, spending 22 weeks in the American charts, reaching number 2. By 1964, it had sold more than four million copies.

Martin's recording was used very effectively on the soundtrack on the 1987 comedy of Italian manners, *Moonstruck,* where the song's opening line reinforces the film's moon motif.

And the Winner Is...

Secret Love

from *Calamity Jane*
Music: Sammy Fain
Lyrics: Paul Francis Webster

Doris Day's career received a big boost from her performance as legendary sharpshooter Calamity Jane. Paul Francis Webster and Sammy Fain wrote some highly enjoyable songs for the film, including "The Deadwood Stage" and "Just Blew in from the Windy City," both of which are superbly staged by Jack Donohue. There's also the lovely ballad in the folk style, "The Black Hills of Dakota," but the hit of the film was the wistful ballad "Secret Love." The record was top of the U.S. and British charts and sold well over a million copies.

Calamity Jane has some similarities to *Annie Get Your Gun*, made three years earlier: Doris Day's characterization of the gunslinging, buckskinned "Calam" was perhaps modelled on Betty Hutton's Annie Oakley. Howard Keel supplied the romantic interest for both women, and both films have a love-hate duet for the leads—"Anything You Can Do" and "I Can Do Without You."

"Secret Love" occurs late in the film. For most of it, Doris has imagined herself in love with Danny Gilmartin, an Army lieutenant played by Philip Carey. All the while she has been conducting a friendly feud with Keel, who plays Wild Bill Hickok. Neither of the men takes her seriously as an object

Her secret love no secret any more, Calamity Jane (Doris Day) drives off with Wild Bill Hickok (Howard Keel) after their wedding in *Calamity Jane* (Warner, 1953).

of romance until she goes to the ball at the fort. Suddenly, the mud-stained Calamity emerges as a beautiful, well-soaped lady. But it is all too late: her lieutenant has already fallen for Katie Brown (Allyn McLerie). However, Keel claims her and Doris realizes that their feud has hidden her real feelings for him—her love has been a secret even from herself. To express all this, she sings "Secret Love" with shining eyes as first she rides a horse, then stops beside a babbling brook, picks a daffodil and walks alone in an idealized country setting on the morning after the ball. The film closes with a double wedding and Doris sings part of the song again there.

Sammy Fain's melody flows gently and Paul Francis Webster's choice of long sustainable sounds for the rhymes make "Secret Love" a very singable song. At first it moves quietly and slowly, with Doris Day musing wistfully almost to herself. Then the long vowel sounds on the rhyming words "now" and "shout" in the line about shouting her love from the "highest hills" force the singer to project more loudly. The next line quietens things down again, the rhyme of "told" and "golden" making the singer slow up and enunciate clearly. She has moved from the large scale of the "highest hills" down to the smaller scale of the "golden daffodils."

"Secret Love" was a worthy winner of the 1953 Best Song Oscar, even though the competition was not very strong that year. Ray Heindorf was nominated for his scoring of the picture and William Mueller for his sound recording.

Doris Day's recording of "Secret Love," her sixth million-seller, was her biggest hit to date and her first U.S. number one. It also topped the British charts for nine weeks. The *Calamity Jane* soundtrack album from was one of the bestsellers of 1954. Many artists have recorded it since and it has become something of a coming-out anthem for the gay and lesbian community, declaring a once "secret love." There were some who claimed to detect gay undertones in the song and in *Calamity Jane* at the time of its first release.

Doris was asked to sing "Secret Love" at the 1953 Oscars but she had another secret: She confessed to the show's producer, Johnny Green, that she was terrified of singing in front of an audience. Ann Blyth took her place though the fact that she was pregnant attracted controversy as people wondered if it was appropriate for her to be singing about a "secret love" being revealed. In their book *Inside Oscar,* Mason Wiley and Damien Bona wrote, "High level meetings were held, and it was decided that since Blyth was married, no impressionable young viewers would be corrupted."

1954

Bob Hope hosted the awards ceremony at RKO Pantages in Hollywood, with Thelma Ritter doing the honors at New York's NBC Century Theatre. Bing Crosby gave out the music Oscars. Judy Garland had given premature birth to a son two days before the awards and so Rosemary Clooney performed her song "The Man That Got Away." Tony Martin ("Hold My Hand"), Peggy King ("Count Your Blessings [Instead of Sheep]), Johnny Desmond and Muzzy Marcellino ("The High and the Mighty") and Dean Martin ("Three Coins in the Fountain") sang the others.

The Nominations

Irving Berlin for "Count Your Blessings (Instead of Sheep)" from *White Christmas* (Paramount)

Dimitri Tiomkin and Ned Washington for "The High and the Mighty" from *The High and the Mighty* (Warner)

Jack Lawrence and Richard Myers for "Hold My Hand" from *Susan Slept Here* (RKO)

Harold Arlen and Ira Gershwin for "The Man That Got Away" from *A Star Is Born* (Warner)

Jule Styne and Sammy Cahn for "Three Coins in the Fountain" from *Three Coins in the Fountain* (Fox)

Count Your Blessings (Instead of Sheep)

from *White Christmas*
Music and Lyrics: Irving Berlin

President Dwight D. Eisenhower helped "Count Your Blessings" to become a hit song, returning a favor that Irving Berlin had done him two years earlier. In 1952, Berlin helped Eisenhower to win the Presidency with a song he wrote for his Broadway show *Call Me Madam*. The song was "They Like Ike" and it alluded to Eisenhower's campaign. At a Madison Square rally, Berlin got up and sang a new version of his song "I Like Ike," and that phrase became one of the most successful political slogans in America's history.

Eisenhower was duly elected in 1953; a year later Irving Berlin began to put together the score for his film *White Christmas*. He based it around an idea that had been in his mind for some time, the story of a much-loved general who is forgotten after the war. Dean Jagger, who bore a slight resemblance to Eisenhower, was cast as Gen. Thomas F. Waverly. The lead role of Bob Wallace went to Bing Crosby. Fred Astaire was cast originally as Phil Davis, Bing's partner in song and dance, but he declined the role. Donald O'Connor was considered as a replacement but he was ill, so Danny Kaye was drafted. Rosemary Clooney and Vera-Ellen supplied the romantic interest for Crosby and Kaye, as sisters Betty and Judy Haynes.

The plot is basically a reworking of *Holiday Inn*. Crosby and Kaye turn up at Dean Jagger's Vermont hotel to find that their wartime general has fallen on hard times. Without snow, he has no guests and faces ruin. Crosby decides to help him out with a soldiers' reunion and a big plug on national television.

"Count Your Blessings" was the biggest new hit from the film ("White Christmas" was in the film and Bing's 1942 recording of the song shot up the charts yet again). The melody of "Count Your Blessings" is used extensively in *White Christmas*, its poignancy underscoring the developing romance between Crosby and Clooney. It is used also to create a melancholy atmosphere when the inevitable complications threaten the course of true love.

The song occurs when Rosemary Clooney has difficulty in sleeping. She gets up to find something to eat in the hotel and discovers Bing, who is also sleepless. Bing offers her his own remedy for insomnia: to think of former penniless times, of children sleeping in their beds—to "count your blessings instead of sheep."

There is a story that Irving Berlin got the idea for the song from his doctor. Dogged by insomnia, he went for medical help and told the doctor that he had tried the old remedy of counting sheep but it hadn't proved effective. The doctor asked, "Did you ever try counting your blessings instead?"

The sentiment of the song is a simple one but it has a certain charm and the gentle melody is very attractive.

In her 1999 biography *Girl Singer*, Rosemary Clooney makes some interesting observations about the pleasure she found in singing the song with Bing:

> Singing together came as naturally to each of us as breathing. We had the same range: mine was an octave and five notes, while

Bing's was probably larger, but at least that. That meant we could do the duet dramatically, the way that fit the story best. Bing would sing a line, and because my next line would be in exactly the same range of notes, I could sing whatever lyrics it made sense for me to sing with him. We didn't have to make concessions to accommodate our voices.

But in spite of this, the two stars were not able to record it together, being under contract to different labels. They put out separate versions—Paramount's Joseph Lille Orchestra accompanied Bing, while Rosemary Clooney's version was recorded with Buddy Cole and the Mellomen. Both were minor hits but Eddie Fisher outsold them both thanks to the big plug it got from Eisenhower.

Fisher was asked to sing the National Anthem to open a banquet celebrating the arrival of the first Jewish migrants to America 300 years earlier. President Eisenhower was to make the after-dinner speech. The singer arrived late, after the program had already begun. In his autobiography, Fisher says that Eisenhower sent for him. The President said he was sorry that Fisher had missed singing the National Anthem and asked him to sing something else. He chose "Count Your Blessings," a song he thought appropriate for the occasion. After the song, the President sent for him again and said:

"How would you like me to introduce you on television, singing that song?" His address was being broadcast nationwide, and about thirty seconds later the lights and cameras went on and the President stood up and said, "Fellow Americans, I heard a song a few moments ago and I liked it so well that I wanted Americans everywhere to hear it. Mr. Fisher, would you mind singing one more verse of that song?" [From *Eddie—My Life, My Loves* by Eddie Fisher]

This was probably the only time that a President had introduced a performer on television and Fisher's recording, which hadn't been selling too well, suddenly took off. Some years later, at a banquet given in the former President's honor, Fisher related what had happened to the record after Eisenhower had introduced the song. The ex–President grinned broadly and said, "Pretty good press agent, huh, Eddie?"

The High and the Mighty

from *The High and the Mighty*
Music: Dimitri Tiomkin
Lyrics: Ned Washington

The "high and the mighty" referred to in the film's title is Dan Roman, an aging airline pilot with a tragic past, played by John Wayne in a role which had been previously offered to Spencer Tracy. Wayne, as Dan Roman, plays second in command of a passenger jet to Robert Stack, who plays John Sullivan. In an emergency situation Stack cracks under pressure and Wayne is forced to take control. The plane looks doomed to crash but Wayne's bravery wins the day. As he brings the plane and its passengers down to a safe landing, the studio chorus gives voice to the film's haunting theme.

In the song's lyrics, the "high and mighty" character is a man who is too far above the common herd to be concerned with romance until falling in love taught him differently.

The music has a haunting quality but the lyric is rather clumsy and forced, with over-emphasised rhymes—Hollywood songwriters were expected to contrive a song out of the most unpromising film titles. In this case, the words that Ned Washington wrote were a very hasty addition. The original version of the film had an instrumental version only, though it was played on the soundtrack a great deal, and also whistled often by John Wayne. But an instrumental is ineligible for the Best Song Oscar, so the studio commissioned Ned Washington to supply the lyric. The song was added to the closing credits, sung by the studio chorus.

Composer Dimitri Tiomkin was also nominated for Best Music Score and won the award. In his acceptance speech, he thanked those who had inspired him: "Brahms, Beethoven, Richard Strauss and Johann Strauss." William Wellman received an Oscar nomination for his direction of *The High and the Mighty*; Jan Sterling and Claire Trevor were nominated for Best Supporting Actress, and Ralph Dawson for his editing.

There were many instrumental recordings of the tune, notably from Les Baxter and His Orchestra and Chorus, Victor Young and His Orchestra, with the whistling of Muzzy Marcellino, and Leroy Holmes and His Orchestra, featuring the whistling of Fred Lowery. The latter was the top-selling version—it was in the U.S. charts for 14 weeks and sold more than a million copies. The leading vocal version was by Johnny Desmond.

Hold My Hand

from *Susan Slept Here*
Music and Lyrics: Jack Lawrence and Richard Myers

Susan Slept Here is a non-musical film despite the presence of Dick Powell and Debbie Reynolds. But there are two songs in it—a title song (with music and lyric by Jack Lawrence) and "Hold My Hand." Richard Myers had written the melody for the Oscar-nominated song some years before and had played it for Lawrence then. He loved it immediately but as neither songwriter had an immediate use for it, it stayed on the shelf for a few years. When Lawrence thought of using it in *Susan Slept Here*, he had to find a reason for its inclusion. It was his idea to have Susan (Debbie Reynolds) fall in love with a record of it she hears on the radio.

"Hold My Hand" is used twice—on both occasions as a recording. The incredible plot has 50-year-old Dick Powell playing Mark Christopher, a 35-year-old Hollywood scriptwriter trying to write a drama about juvenile delinquency. Two vice squad detectives have arrested Susan Landis, a 17-year-old miscreant, played by Debbie Reynolds, and trustingly leave her in Powell's bachelor apartment over Christmas to help him with his research.

On Christmas morning, Debbie turns on the radio and the announcer introduces Don Cornell's recording of "Hold My Hand." As his soulful baritone fills the air, Debbie performs a mock swoon and puts her head in the freezer to cool her passions. Cornell sings of the bliss of love, a bliss that takes lovers to the Promised Land. Biblical imagery is sustained right through the song with references to angels, the Garden of Eden and Adam and Eve. The lyric is rather overwrought and uses slightly archaic words like "threshold" and "portal," while merely holding hands brings a climactic reward of heavenly bliss and immortality. Jack Lawrence's intention is surely to create a parody of the kind of song that might make a teenage girl swoon; Debbie's reaction bears this out.

From this point, the melody is used extensively as background music. Then, late in the film, when the romance between Powell and Reynolds has run the gamut of complications, Debbie puts on a record of "Hold My Hand"; the label showing the word "Coral" is clearly visible, providing good publicity for the record company.

Coral Records campaigned long and hard in pursuit of a Best Song Oscar for "Hold My Hand," even sending Don Cornell's record to every member of the Academy. Though this frantic lobbying was unsuccessful, the song did give Cornell his third million-seller. "Hold My Hand" topped the British charts and reached number five in the U.S. Ironically, Cornell recorded "Hold My Hand" only because Jack Lawrence was unable to find anyone else willing to do it. Cornell had not had a hit for some time and "Hold My Hand" gave his career a much-needed lift, as well as boosting attendance for the film.

The Man That Got Away

from *A Star Is Born*
Music: Harold Arlen
Lyrics: Ira Gershwin

"The Man That Got Away" is crucial to the plot of *A Star Is Born*. When Norman Maine, the character played by James Mason, sees and hears Esther Blodgett (Judy Garland) singing this song, he must be convinced that she is a great singer, one with "that little something extra—star quality." Judy's performance does exactly that—her singing is mesmerizing. And "The Man That Got Away" is one of the finest of all film songs, a perfect vehicle for revealing "Esther's" talents as well as encompassing the themes of the film.

A Star Is Born was Judy Garland's first film after she was dropped by MGM because of her unreliability during the making of the 1950 film musical *Annie Get Your Gun*. But then she had sensational success with her stage concerts, notably at the London Palladium and on Broadway. Hollywood began to show revived interest in her and Warner Bros. signed her to play the lead in *A Star Is Born,* with her husband, Sid Luft, as producer.

Moss Hart wrote the script and Harold Arlen was contracted to write the songs with Ira Gershwin as lyricist. Hart met with Arlen and Gershwin to discuss the placement of songs. The outline they produced in these first discussions lists something entitled "The Dive Song"; this eventually became "The Man That Got Away."

Arlen soon produced a melody for the opening bars. As he played it, Gershwin expressed his approval and immediately came up with a possible title: "The Man That Got Away." Arlen liked it and the work was off to a great start. When it was completed—in very quick time—both songwriters knew they had an excellent song. But even at this stage, Ira was reluctant to show the song to anyone else, not least because of the speed with which they had produced it. He made Arlen promise not let anyone hear what they had written for the time being.

That Saturday, Arlen met up with Sid Luft and Judy Garland on the Palm Springs golf course. As he followed them around the course, he found himself whistling a few bars of the new song and Judy immediately wanted to know if it was one of the songs for the film. Arlen, remembering his promise, tried to extricate himself but Judy was persistent and marched him off to the clubhouse where he played her "The Man That Got Away." She loved it immediately, called in her husband to hear it, and then all three of them went to Moss Hart's house where Arlen demonstrated it again. Soon, it seemed, everyone in Palm Springs was whistling the song.

When Ira Gershwin got news of how well the song was being received, he forgave Harold and they sat down to complete the rest of the score.

"The Man That Got Away" occurs early in the film: Judy is the girl singer with a dance band and in the early hours of the morning she and some musicians are having a jam session in an empty Sunset Boulevard night club. James Mason, playing the film star whose career is in decline, wanders into the club just as Judy begins to sing. The song is a powerful, bluesy number, a heart-wrenching hymn to lost love. The opening lines, with their harsh consonants rhyming "bitter" with "glitter," set the mood. It is the stars that have ceased to "glitter" and this is a clear and deliberate allusion to James Mason's situation as a fading Hollywood luminary.

Harold Arlen marked the music, "Slowly, with a steady insistence," and certainly it has an almost doom-laden beat as though the singer, in the depths, knows that there is "just no let-up" from the loneliness and despair that has engulfed her now that her man has gone. In feeling, if not in form, "The Man That Got Away" is the saddest of blues songs.

It is full of the everyday phrases and the contractions of ordinary speech. These and the natural but highly effective rhymes give the song a directness, full of emotional power. Ira of course knew that Judy would be singing it and it is easy to find a number of parallels with her own life in the lyric. Just as much as "Over the Rainbow," this great American song became identified with her—and it was her biggest-selling record since the *Wizard of Oz* song.

Frank Sinatra liked "The Man That Got Away" so much that he asked Ira Gershwin to adapt the lyric for him to sing. It was easy enough to change the title and "his" to "her." But Gershwin had to rewrite part of the ending so that the "one-man woman" became a "lost, lost loser" looking for "The Gal That Got Away."

Many other singers have recorded the song and occasionally it suffers revision from some who consider the title grammatically incorrect. In their hands it becomes "The Man *Who* Got Away." Ira Gershwin himself wrote that he intended the title to be a paraphrase of the fisherman's lament: "You should have seen the one that got away."

"The Man That Got Away" was not only the best film song of 1954 but also one of the finest of all time. But the great songs don't always win the Oscars and this year proved no exception. Jack Warner had been disappointed at the film's early failure at the box office and his studio made no effort to lobby for it in the trade papers at the time of the Oscars. On the other hand, the papers were full of advertisements for the rest of the Best Song nominees.

And the Winner Is...

Three Coins in the Fountain

from *Three Coins in the Fountain*
Music: Jule Styne
Lyrics: Sammy Cahn

Frank Sinatra's career was revived by his brilliant performance as Private Maggio in *From Here to Eternity*. The film was a huge success—with the critics and at the box office—and suddenly the studios were clamoring for Sinatra's services. 20th Century–Fox offered him the chance to co-star with Marilyn Monroe in a musical to be called *Pink Tights*. Sinatra signed on but Monroe wasn't interested. Fox had her under contract and started shooting the musical anyway, positive that this was just a show of temperament and that she would soon come around. For more than two weeks, the film crew, actors—and the songwriters under contract for *Pink Tights*, Jule Styne and Sammy Cahn—sat around the set waiting in vain for Marilyn to start work.

At this point, producer Sol Siegel turned up with a problem of his own. He had just finished a film for Fox that the New York moneymen wanted to call *We Believe in Love*. Siegel and Hollywood studio boss Darryl F. Zanuck hated this title and the only way to change New York's mind was to come up immediately with a surefire hit song with the title they preferred. Siegel appealed to Styne and Cahn to help: he described the film's plot concerning three American women who throw coins into Rome's Trevi Fountain, wishing for romance. When they went away to write the song, Sammy Cahn had the opening lines that are also the song's title in no time flat. Two hours later the song was completed, words and music.

Sammy Cahn sang it to Siegel and Zanuck and they were overjoyed—this was exactly the song they needed. Now they had to make a demonstration disc to send to New York. No problem—Frank Sinatra was on the set and so was the studio orchestra. Sinatra ran through the song with Cahn, and then recorded the song in less than ten minutes. Siegel sent the disc to New York and *We Believe in Love* duly became *Three Coins in the Fountain*. The demo was the disc actually used on the soundtrack, over the opening credits, and it was also this Sinatra recording that stayed in the charts for 12 weeks.

The film is a romantic comedy in which three American women working in Rome as secretaries wish for the men of their dreams as they throw coins into city's magnificent Trevi Fountain. Dorothy McGuire, Jean Peters and Maggie McNamara play the women, and their dreams come true in the shape of Clifton Webb, Rossano Brazzi and Louis Jourdan.

The credit sequence during which Sinatra sings the title song is a travelogue of the sights of Rome, especially the Trevi Fountain. The sequence is so long that the song has to be continued by a studio chorus. The photography is superb—the best part of the film—and photographer Milton Krasner deserved the Academy Award he won for it. The song turns up once more in the film, right at the end when the three sets of lovers are reunited at the Trevi Fountain. The studio chorus sings it on this occasion.

The great popularity of *Three Coins in the Fountain* owed much to the success of the title song, and Frank Sinatra was billed prominently on the film poster. But it was not Sinatra's record that hit the charts initially—The Four Aces' recording was the first to be released. Their version—on which they are credited as "The Four Aces featuring Al Alberts"—became a big seller before the release of the film; it was in the American charts for 18 weeks, in the top position for one, and it brought thousands of fans into the cinema to see what was otherwise a fairly ordinary romantic comedy. Sinatra's version reached as high as number four in the charts and there was another popular version by Julius La Rosa. In Britain, Sinatra's version sold better than The Four Aces' and reached the top of the charts there. The Four Aces only managed the number five spot.

The song and the film were also responsible for a boost in tourism to Rome, where all visitors wanted to see the Trevi Fountain.

"Three Coins in the Fountain" is a pleasant enough song. It has a very attractive melody and Sammy Cahn's lyric is effective: The hopeful lovers have thrown their coins into the fountain and it is as though the coins represent their hearts. Only one of these hearts will "wear a valentine," only one wish will be granted—whose will it be? The Four Aces overdo the drama in their recording, particularly on the last line, turning "Make it mine!" into a screeching demand. In comparison, Sinatra's much more appealing version is positively restrained and his ending is gently pleading, as though he lacks confidence in the possibility of his wish being granted.

"Three Coins in the Fountain" was the first of three Oscar-winning songs with lyrics by Sammy Cahn and introduced by Frank Sinatra. For Sammy Cahn, this was his first win after nine previous nominations, going back to 1942. When asked for his comments on his winning his first Oscar, he said that he had lost so many times that he was beginning to feel like the eternal loser.

1955

Jerry Lewis hosted the awards ceremony from the RKO Pantages Theatre, while Claudette Colbert and Joseph L. Mankiewicz officiated in New York. Maurice Chevalier presented the Best Song Oscar and also sang "Something's Gotta Give." Dean Martin ("The Tender Trap"), Harry Belafonte and Millard Thomas ("Unchained Melody"), Jane Powell ("I'll Never Stop Loving You") and Eddie Fisher ("Love Is a Many-Splendored Thing") sang the other nominated songs.

The Nominations

Nicholas Brodszky and Sammy Cahn for "I'll Never Stop Loving You" from *Love Me or Leave Me* (MGM)

Sammy Fain and Paul Francis Webster for "Love Is a Many-Splendored Thing" from *Love Is a Many-Splendored Thing* (Fox)

Johnny Mercer for "Something's Gotta Give" from *Daddy Long Legs* (Fox)

Jimmy Van Heusen and Sammy Cahn for "The Tender Trap" from *The Tender Trap* (MGM)

Alex North and Hy Zaret for "Unchained Melody" from *Unchained* (Warner)

I'll Never Stop Loving You

from *Love Me or Leave Me*
Music: Nicholas Brodszky
Lyrics: Sammy Cahn

When Brodsky and Cahn were commissioned to write an original song for *Love Me or Leave Me*, it would have to stand comparison with songs written by

America's greatest songwriters, songs performed by torch singer Ruth Etting, one of the most popular singing stars of the 1920s and early '30s. Doris Day would play the part of the legendary singer and whether "I'll Never Stop Loving You" stands comparison with such songs as Rodgers and Hart's "Ten Cents a Dance" or Walter Donaldson's and Gus Kahn's "Love Me or Leave Me" is questionable. But certainly the Cahn-Brodszky song does play a crucial role in the plot.

Doris Day had made 17 films at Warner Bros., most of them lightweight, but now MGM gave her the chance to play a dramatic role that cast her against type. In *Love Me or Leave Me*, her role required that she should wear sexy clothes, drink alcohol and become involved with hoodlums. Some of her fans were distraught.

Hoodlum Martin Snyder, played by James Cagney, dominates torch singer Ruth Etting's career. Early in their relationship, she meets Johnny Alderman, a musician and songwriter (Cameron Mitchell). This is the man Ruth really loves but she marries Snyder and under his management her career blossoms. When Ruth is offered a role in the *Ziegfeld Follies* on Broadway, Johnny takes off for Hollywood and it is some years before they meet again. Ruth is now breaking into the movies and the musical director for the picture is none other that Johnny.

When they meet, Ruth is cool, determined not to let the relationship develop any more. Alone with Johnny to run through some songs for the film, he asks her to sing a song he describes as "an old one of mine" and Ruth says she remembers it. At this point the audience is way ahead but the fact that they have never stopped loving each other is laboriously underlined when the song turns out to be "I'll Never Stop Loving You." She sings it to Johnny's simple piano accompaniment.

Later, the jealous Snyder shoots Johnny but fortunately he survives and the way is cleared for the happy pair to wed. The film ends with Ruth singing "I'll Never Stop Loving You" in a nightclub, with full orchestral accompaniment.

Doris sings the song with quiet understatement, avoiding the emotional wallow that the slightly feverish melody suggests. Sammy Cahn's lyric is simple and unpretentious, though it does become tautologous in the last chorus with the phrase "last and endure."

Doris' recording was reasonably popular and reached the Top 20. But it was the soundtrack album that proved to be an enormous critical and commercial success, spending 17 weeks at number one on the *Billboard* Album charts.

Love Me or Leave Me received five other Oscar nominations including one for the Percy Faith—Georgie Stoll score. Daniel Fuchs, who wrote the script, was the only winner.

Something's Gotta Give

from Daddy Long Legs
Music and Lyrics: Johnny Mercer

In 1952, 20th Century–Fox commissioned composer Alec Wilder and lyricist William Engvick to provide a score for a musical version of Jean Webster's novel *Daddy Long Legs*. The pair duly wrote 14 numbers but the film was never produced and they remain in the Fox archives. Three years later, Fox commissioned the Fred Astaire-Leslie Caron version—in Cinema Scope, perhaps an unsuitable treatment for such a slight story.

When Fox signed Astaire, he requested that Johnny Mercer write the songs. Better known as a lyricist, Mercer was also a composer and he supplied words and music for the film. Quite the best of these was "Something's Gotta Give," a song perfectly tailored to Astaire's style, justifying his faith in the great songwriter.

Fred plays the part of Jervis Pendleton III, a rich man on a business trip to France where he is enchanted by Julie Andre (Leslie Caron), a French orphan girl. He sponsors her education in America; he is in his fifties, she only 18, and he makes it a condition of the arrangement that they never meet. But of course they do and romance has its way.

Fred wanted Mercer as songwriter because he thought he could solve the central problem of this romance with Leslie: their age difference. He felt that audiences would see him as an evil old man seducing a young girl unless he had the right lyric to sing to her. Mercer understood completely and produced the perfect solution in the charming and unusual "Something's Gotta Give."

The song is an excellent illustration of the difficulties involved in a romance between youth and age, as well as a lyrical exposition of a well-known scientific principle, than when an "irresistible force" encounters an "immovable object," then "Something's Gotta Give."

The setting is the terrace of the New York hotel at which Leslie is staying. They have just dined together and have reached the coffee stage. Leslie questions Fred about his love life and suggests that he will never marry. He is not so sure, and tells of her "an old theory" which he expounds in the song. This is the beginning of their courtship ritual, and as the words of the song end, the melody continues as they dance, she tentatively, he with suave confidence. He dances her out of the hotel and they are framed against a backdrop of New York scenes. They dance the night away through a succession of nightspots. The melody of "Something's Gotta Give" plays up-tempo all through the sequence. They return to the hotel with the morning newspapers and Fred sings again the first line of the song about the "irresistible force" and Leslie repeats the second concerning the "immovable object." With aplomb, Fred leaves her at her door and completes the sequence, showing his elation by riding a trolley along the corridor of the staid hotel.

Leslie Caron dances with Fred Astaire in *Daddy Long Legs* (Fox, 1955).

The song is memorable, full of the intelligence and wit for which Johnny Mercer is renowned. The use of such long words as "irresistible" and "implacable," as well as erudite and refined phrases such as "en garde" and "vast mysterious store" fit perfectly with the urbane and debonair character played by Astaire. The reversion to the more colloquial, cheerful optimism of "something's gotta give" suggest neatly that the older man has come to terms with his concerns over the age difference with Leslie's character and is now confident of winning her.

Astaire recorded "Something's Gotta Give" but the McGuire Sisters outsold him. Sammy Davis, Jr.'s' version was also successful and his was the most popular one in Britain where it spent seven weeks in the charts, reaching the number 11 spot. The song turned up again on screen when Joanne Woodward sang it in *The Stripper* (1963).

In 2000, writer-director Nancy Meyers used Sammy Davis, Jr.'s' version in her film *What Women Want*. In 2003, she borrowed the title for a romantic comedy starring Jack Nicholson and Diane Keaton, though the song is not heard there.

The Tender Trap

from *The Tender Trap*
Music: Jimmy Van Heusen
Lyrics: Sammy Cahn

This bright and bouncy song comes from the film of the same name and its breezy, witty lyric sets the tone for the film and neatly suggests the character of Charlie Reader, played by Frank Sinatra. He is a Casanova, determined to have his fun and never to be caught in "the tender trap." But he meets his match in Julie Gillis, played by Debbie Reynolds. She is so determined to hook herself a husband that she even has a timetable for getting one.

Frank Sinatra sings to Debbie Reynolds in *The Tender Trap* (MGM, 1955).

"The Tender Trap" is the only song in the film and it is sung first by Sinatra in the pre-credits sequence. First in a distant long shot, he strolls towards the camera looking very inch the swinging playboy. As he reaches the last words, the title sequence begins. Parts of the song are heard three more times during the film, then at the end, when both Sinatra and co-star David Wayne have been tenderly trapped. They and their brides-to-be, Debbie Reynolds and Celeste Holm, sing a chorus together and the closing credits roll.

Sammy Cahn's words are colloquial and down-to-earth and any poetic phrases are merely points of reference to the usual trappings of typical love ballads, the romantic situations the determined playboy must beware of—her laughter-filled eyes, her tingling kisses. The use of long vowels as in "trees" and "soon" in the early lines set the romantic tone and Sinatra's voice almost caresses the word "music." But then comes the jolt supported by words with short vowels—"snap" and "trap." An internal rhyme of "smart" and "heart" has an abruptness, completed with the "whap," that snaps shut "the tender trap."

In his autobiography, Sammy Cahn relates that, because the title of the song came first, he had to write the lyrics before the music. At first all was clear sailing and as soon as he heard the word "trap" he also heard the word "snap." He felt he was almost home. He quickly wrote the first section of the song and handed his efforts over to Jimmy Van Heusen.

This was early in their songwriting relationship and they were still feeling each other out. Cahn pressurised Van Heusen to come up with something quickly but was chagrined to find himself presented with "one of the worst melodies I'd ever heard." Loath to offend his new partner, Sammy said nothing and started to write the second section, agonising over the tune that he'd been given. The next day he went back to Jimmy's home, wondering what to say. But Van Heusen now agreed with him and produced a new melody, the one that they used, and it sounds as though it has always been there.

Like other title songs before and after, the success of "The Tender Trap" turned the film into a box office success and Frank Sinatra's record stayed in the charts for four months.

Unchained Melody

from *Unchained*
Music: Alex North
Lyrics: Hy Zaret

"Unchained Melody" was one of the most successful songs of the twentieth century though the film it comes from is now almost forgotten. *Unchained* is set in a Californian open prison and tells the stories of some of the inmates and the women who visit them. The prison has an enlightened approach, aiming for rehabilitation rather than punishment. The guards are unarmed and there are no uniforms.

The stars are Elroy Hirsch, Barbara Hale and Chester Morris, while baritone Todd Duncan sings the famous song on the soundtrack with a simple guitar accompaniment. Duncan became famous for his portrayal of Porgy in *Porgy and Bess* and he is also noted for being the first African-American in the New York City Opera. His song describes the loneliness of a prisoner separated from the one he loves and it has a lushly romantic melody. He wonders what slowly passing time will do to their relationship—will she stay true? He is as lonely as the rivers and the mountains as he dreams of his distant love. It is one of those rare songs in which the title is not part of the lyrics.

Les Baxter, with his orchestra and chorus, had his first million seller with "Unchained Melody" and it reached number two in the U.S. charts. It was one of the ten top-selling records of the year. Al Hibbler's version, with the Jack Pleis Orchestra, also sold more than a million copies and there were other versions by Roy Hamilton and June Valli. Liberace recorded it in 1955 too, though his version was more popular in Britain than in the U.S. The most successful British recording was by Jimmy Young—it topped the charts, the only version to do so on either side of the Atlantic in 1955.

"Unchained Melody" has been a hit for every generation since its first release in 1955. In 1963, Vito and the Salutations recorded an up-tempo version but it was the Righteous Brothers 1965 revival of the song that is best remembered—it was an enormous hit in the U.S. and the U.K. simultaneously, without getting to the top position in either chart. Their version was a hit all over again when it was used on the soundtrack of the 1990 film *Ghost* to accompany the erotic pottery scene. It sold more than a million copies and it topped the charts in Britain. Then in 1995, actors Robson Green and Jerome Flynn sang it the British TV series *Soldier, Soldier* and their recording was the number one hit for seven successive weeks. In 2002, another British singer, Gareth Gates, took "Unchained Melody" to the top of the U.K. charts all over again. To date, more than 500 artists have recorded the song including Elvis Presley, LeAnn Rimes, Sarah McLachlan, John Lennon and James Galway.

And the Winner Is...

Love Is a Many-Splendored Thing

from *Love Is a Many-Splendored Thing*
Music: Sammy Fain
Lyrics: Paul Francis Webster

Han Suyin's book *A Many Splendored Thing* uses for its title a phrase from Francis Thompson's poem "The Kingdom of God," though the "many splendored thing" there is the love of God. The filmmakers intended to use Suyin's

Jennifer Jones in *Love Is a Many Splendored Thing* **(Fox, 1955).**

title for their movie and Fain and Webster were contracted to supply a song with the same title. This they did, only to find that the film's title had been changed to *Love is a Many-Splendored Thing*. The songwriters started again and produced a song so successful in the charts before the film's release that huge ticket sales were almost guaranteed. But fans who went to see it on the strength of the hit song had a long wait before they heard it—it is sung only during the final scene and over the closing credits, by the studio chorus.

The film is set in Hong Kong just before and during the Korean War and involves a love affair between William Holden as Mark Elliott, a newspaper's war correspondent, and Jennifer Jones (as Dr. Han Suyin), who is supposed to be Eurasian. Hollywood wasn't quite brave enough to cast the genuine article.

The background score is by Alfred Newman and he makes extensive use of the hit song's melody. In fact, his score consists mostly of variations on the theme; we also hear it on a radio in one scene and played by Macao hotel dance band in another. Then at the end of the film, when Jennifer Jones has received the news that her lover has been killed in Korea, she goes to "the high and windy hill," their special place. As she grieves, the studio chorus sings "Love Is a Many-Splendored Thing."

There is an introductory verse to the Oscar-winning song that was not used in the movie, or in any of the recorded versions. In it the singer describes meeting a girl in the streets of Hong Kong; he asks her, "What is love?," and her reply is "Love Is a Many-Splendored Thing."

It is a lushly romantic song with a lyric that teeters on the brink of sheer corn. It is closely associated with the Four Aces and it was their version that topped the American charts for five weeks, giving them their fifth-million seller. In Britain it sold almost as well, reaching number two in the charts. They sing as usual with the accent very much on the upper register and their version is monotonously over-dramatic. But their record was so successful that many still believe that the all-male quartet sings the song over the closing credits of the film. The normally reliable Stanley Green in his *Encyclopedia of the Musical Film* perpetuates the error.

Love Is a Many-Splendored Thing collected eight Oscar nominations, winning for three: the title song, Alfred Newman's score and Charles LeMaire's costume design. A CBS-TV soap opera based on the film and sharing its title and theme song ran in the U.S. from 1967 until 1973.

1956

Jerry Lewis was again the Hollywood host of the awards ceremony held in the RKO Pantages Theater while Celeste Holm hosted from the NBC Century Theatre in New York. Carroll Baker presented the Best Song award. Bing Crosby sang "True Love" but on film, the other nominated songs coming from Tommy Sands ("Friendly Persuasion"), Dorothy Dandridge ("Julie"), The Four Aces ("Written on the Wind") and Gogi Grant ("Que Sera, Sera").

The Nominations

Dimitri Tiomkin and Paul Francis Webster for "Friendly Persuasion (Thee I Love)" from *Friendly Persuasion* (Allied Artists)

Leith Stevens and Tom Adair for "Julie" from *Julie* (MGM)

Jay Livingston and Ray Evans for "Whatever Will Be, Will Be (Que Sera, Sera)" from *The Man Who Knew Too Much* (Paramount)

Cole Porter for "True Love" from *High Society* (MGM)

Victor Young and Sammy Cahn for "Written on the Wind" from *Written on the Wind* (Universal)

Friendly Persuasion (Thee I Love)

from *Friendly Persuasion*
Music: Dimitri Tiomkin
Lyrics: Paul Francis Webster

Friendly Persuasion concerns a family of Quakers, properly named the Society of Friends, hence the film's mildly punning title. The film collected six Oscar nominations, including one for Best Picture. It is set in Indiana during the American Civil War and stars Gary Cooper and Dorothy McGuire as the parents, Jess and Eliza Birdwell, and Anthony Perkins as Josh, one of their sons. For the most part the film depicts an idyllic life but the shadow of the Civil War is always present. There is much discussion about the Quaker attitude to war and violence and eventually the story hinges on Cooper's pacifism conflicting with his desire to kill the murderer of his friend. He confronts the killer, gun in hand, but is unable to pull the trigger. In Cooper's superb portrayal it is quite clear that he refrains because of the inner strength stemming from his convictions as a Quaker.

The Quakers in the film address each other as "thee" and "thou," and these words occur frequently in the song's lyric. Pat Boone sings it over the opening and closing credits and variations on the melody are frequently heard as mood music. The song, like the film, expresses something of the innocence and beauty of the Quaker family's life and it also conveys Cooper's screen character very effectively. He is a Quaker and therefore committed to pacifism; he is also a loving and loved husband and father. The song describes his feelings of love through images taken from rural life. The meadows are green, the hills covered with mulberries and the apple trees are budding but the singer loves his lady more than these. He claims to be too inarticulate to list all the many ways she gives him pleasure but his arms are strong like an oak and he will kiss her in "friendly persuasion."

"Friendly Persuasion" was Pat Boone's fourth million-seller and it was on the U.S. charts for 24 weeks, reaching number eight. In the U.K. it remained in the charts for 21 weeks, reaching number three. The Four Aces also recorded the song but had only moderate success with it.

Julie

from *Julie*
Music: Leith Stevens
Lyrics: Tom Adair

The film *Julie* has a highly unlikely and overwrought story involving the insanely jealous Lyle Benton (Louis Jourdan) and his attempts to kill his wife Julie (Doris Day). The climactic moments occur on an airliner: Doris is the stewardess and Jourdan has followed her on board. He shoots the pilot and co-pilot, but is shot himself. He dies convinced that Doris and all the passengers will also perish when the plane crashes. But he reckons without the plucky stewardess, who, with the help of radar and radio instruction from air traffic control, brings everyone home safely. Unbelievably, Andrew L. Stone, who also directed the film, was Oscar-nominated for his screenplay.

The song is sung over the opening credits in fervid style by Doris Day, with a studio chorus interjecting the name "Julie" at the beginning of every verse and at the end of the last one. The rather clumsy lyric has all the clichés of an inferior romantic novel and those overworked and almost meaningless words used so often in them—"ecstasy," "destiny" and "eternity"—get a full airing. The song's burning atmospherics set the melodramatic tone for the rest of the film, and hint heavily at Jourdan's murderous intentions, with lines about the danger in his eyes.

Only two recordings of "Julie" exist, one by Doris and another by Harry James and His Orchestra—an instrumental version.

True Love

from *High Society*
Music and Lyrics: Cole Porter

When MGM cast three of the best and most influential popular singers of the twentieth century in *High Society*, it was highly unlikely that Grace Kelly—who had never sung on screen before—would be required to stand comparison with them by doing her own singing in the film. Musical director Johnny Green listened to her voice and even had her sing to him in his office; he decided that he would have to find a voice double for her. But Grace thought otherwise and she was determined that she would sing in the film, alongside Bing Crosby, Frank Sinatra and Louis Armstrong.

Six months earlier, when she was first offered the part, she had started singing lessons. The character she was to play would have to sing twice in the film—a deliberately off-key version of "You're Sensational," the song that Frank Sinatra sings to her, and then the big romantic number, "True Love," with Bing Crosby. When Johnny Green told her that she would be dubbed, she went straight to MGM's head of production Dore Schary and pleaded her case. Schary was convinced, overruled Green, Grace did her own singing— and made a great success of it. Though the song is rather sugary and sentimental, it comes over well, not just because of Bing's fine singing, but because Grace's artlessly simple performance, her calm poise and serenity, give the scene a warm and appealing sincerity. Johnny Green was forced to admit that his first judgment was wrong and he was especially impressed by the fact that she managed to sing in harmony with Bing. Saul Chaplin was associate musical director with Green and he devised an arrangement for "True Love" which meant that she never had to carry the tune by herself.

High Society is a musical remake of *The Philadelphia Story* (1940), with Grace Kelly, Bing Crosby and Frank Sinatra in the roles originated by Katharine Hepburn, Cary Grant and James Stewart. The song "True Love" occurs when C.K. Dexter Haven III (Bing Crosby) is trying to prevent the remarriage of his ex-wife, Tracy Samantha Lord (Grace Kelly). She is a blue-blooded member of Newport's "high society" and her husband-to-be is a stuffed shirt played by John Lund.

On the eve of the wedding, Bing gives Grace a none-too subtle reminder

Bing Crosby and Grace Kelly aboard the *True Love* in *High Society* (MGM, 1956).

of their honeymoon. They had spent it idyllically—"sun-tanned" and "wind-blown"—on a yacht called *True Love*, so Bing's wedding present is a large-scale model of the boat. As Grace sails it on the swimming pool, she is overtaken by fond memories and a flashback reveals her with Bing on the real yacht. As dusk falls, Bing picks up a concertina and begins to sing "True Love." Grace joins with him when he repeats the last five lines.

The scene—and the song—makes it clear that Grace's marriage to Lund will not go ahead and that she and Bing will be reconciled. The sweet song has conveyed their love for each other far more effectively than pages of dialogue.

"True Love" is very simple and quite unlike the witty and sophisticated songs for which Cole Porter is generally known. But the first song he wrote for this scene in *High Society* was apparently very beautiful though Saul Chaplin felt that it was too sophisticated. He suggested to Porter that a simpler, old-fashioned sounding song would be more appropriate. Porter agreed, scrapped his original effort and went off to try again. Three days later, he came back with "True Love."

Bing and Grace recorded "True Love" with the superb MGM Studio Orchestra conducted by Johnny Green. When Bing appeared on *The Ed Sullivan Show* to promote *High Society* and sing "True Love," Sullivan opined that the song would be second only to "White Christmas" in sales. Certainly it was hugely popular, selling more than a million copies—and Sullivan's prediction came true. When Grace Kelly became Princess Grace of Monaco, she also became the only royal personage to have earned a gold disc. *High Society* was the last film she made.

"True Love" was the twenty second million-seller for Bing Crosby and it was also the first Cole Porter song to achieve a gold record. It lasted for 22 weeks on *Your Hit Parade*, reaching as high as number two, remarkable at a time when rock 'n' roll was dominating the charts. It had enormous success in the British charts too, reaching number four and selling well for 27 weeks. Jane Powell also had a U.S. hit with the song.

With "True Love" such a hit, MGM decided it had a good chance of winning the Oscar. To help its chances, Cole Porter hired a publicity man, Stanley Musgrove, an old friend who had a good track record in promoting nominated songs. He managed to plant a number of stories about "True Love" in the trade papers but the fastidious Porter restrained him from anything that might be regarded as vulgar. Porter also refused to attend the Academy Awards but as soon as he heard that "Que Sera, Sera" had won he sent Musgrove a telegram with the message "Whatever will be, will be, dear Stanley."

In 1998, a stage version of *High Society* opened on Broadway; Melissa Errico and Daniel McDonald took the roles originally played by Kelly and Crosby.

Written on the Wind

from *Written on the Wind*
Music: Victor Young
Lyrics: Sammy Cahn

Victor Young's Oscar nomination for "Written on the Wind" was posthumous—he died in late 1956, five months before the Award Ceremony. The film *Written on the Wind* is an everyday story of Texan oil millionaires, the Hadleys, with Dorothy Malone as Marylee, the nymphomaniac of the family, and Robert Stack as the psychotic Kyle. Rock Hudson and Lauren Bacall, as an alcoholic, are also heavily involved. Malone won an Oscar as Best Supporting Actress and Stack was nominated as Best Supporting Actor. All the elements of the TV soap opera are there—the film set the mold for melodramas such as *Dallas* and *Dynasty*.

The Four Aces sing the title song over the lengthy opening credit sequence: Robert Stack is driving wildly through the night, drinking from a bottle as he speeds along. As the credits roll, he drives up to a grand mansion and Hudson is observing his approach from an upstairs window. In another room, Bacall awakes as she hears the car, and falls drunkenly out of bed. Malone also watches Stack from her bedroom window. All the while there are shots of trees bending in the wind and leaves blowing wildly about. This is a unsubtle reference to the song's lyric that mentions the "dying leaves" of autumn. As Stack enters the house, the leaves blow in behind him, scattering everywhere. Soon a gunshot sounds and a male figure staggers from the house, gun in hand, and falls down the steps. Bacall reaches her bedroom window but falls over again....

And so the atmosphere is set for the overblown drama to come; the sequence is so full of action that the song is hardly noticed, despite the appropriately overwrought performance of it by The Four Aces. Perhaps this is just as well as the words are barely worth hearing. They seem to be referring to a love affair that is now over because of unfaithfulness—the promises the lovers made to each other are broken, just "written on the wind." The singer confesses to having a faithless lover's heart and, certainly, most of the film's characters are self-indulgent dysfunctionals, disloyal to their partners. The music seems to swell in ecstasy and there is a passionate solemnity about the song that brings it close to the edge of parody. The Four Aces made the only American recording and it reached number 14 in the charts. In the U.K., Lorrae Desmond recorded it. This talented Australian singer spent quite a period in the U.K. in the 1950s and became a popular actress and singer there before returning Down Under. Her recording of "Written on the Wind" was unsuccessful.

And the Winner Is...

Whatever Will Be, Will Be (Que Sera, Sera)

from *The Man Who Knew Too Much*
Music and Lyrics: Jay Livingston and Ray Evans

When Alfred Hitchcock was planning *The Man Who Knew Too Much,* he decided that James Stewart would be ideal in the main role. He approached Stewart's agency and he was told that he could have him only if he took Doris Day as well. They also suggested that a pair of songwriters on their books, Jay Livingston and Ray Evans, should write a song for Doris to sing in the proposed film. Hitchcock reluctantly accepted the package. Since a crucial element of the plot involves a statesman from an overseas country, and since the movie opens with a North African setting, he suggested to the songwriters that the song should have some words in a foreign language in the title.

As it happened, Livingston had recently seen the 1954 film *The Barefoot Contessa,* set in Italy. In one scene, Rossano Brazzi takes Ava Gardner to his magnificent old family home and there, carved in stone over the entrance, was the family motto: "Che Sera Sera." Brazzi says that this is Italian for "What will be, will be." Livingston suggested to Evans that this should be their song's title but they should change the "che" to the Spanish "que" because of all the Spanish speakers in America. They completed the song and Hitchcock was very pleased with their efforts. But Doris Day was not.

In her biography, Day relates that when Livingston and Evans first played "Que Sera, Sera" for her she was disappointed with it. She felt that, while it was highly suitable in the context of the film, it was just a children's song and would have no appeal to the record-buying public. There was another song called "We'll Love Again" written for the film that she much preferred. She admits to making a huge error of judgment—"Que Sera, Sera" became the most popular of all her recordings, her sixth million-seller, and it topped the charts for six weeks. It was on the U.S. charts for 27 weeks and reached number two. "Que Sera, Sera" soon became her trademark song and eventually the signature tune of her CBS-TV series.

Doris Day went on to write about "Que Sera, Sera":

> Whether because of its utter simplicity, which made it so easy to remember and easy to sing, or because its philosophy hit a universally responsive chord, after the film's release it was sung by everyone, everywhere I went. [From *Doris Day: Her Own Story* by AE Hotchner]

The song is a series of questions—a young child asking about the future. The mother answers each one with a variation on the phrase *wait and see*, frequently used by parents: "Whatever will be, will be."

"Que Sera, Sera" becomes a crucial element in the plot: This simple, unaffected lullaby is the vehicle by which she finds her kidnapped son. Doris plays the role of Jo McKenna and her doctor husband, Ben, is played by James Stewart. They are on holiday in North Africa when we first hear "Que Sera, Sera" as she is getting their son Hank (Christopher Olsen) ready for bed. The song is clearly part of their bedtime ritual. At one stage the boy puts his fingers in his mouth and whistles along, ear-splittingly, and his whistling becomes significant later.

Soon after, Stewart becomes "The Man Who Knew Too Much" when he inadvertently learns of a conspiracy to assassinate a statesman who will soon be visiting London. The conspirators abduct the son to force his father's silence. Near the end of the film, when Stewart and Day have thwarted the assassination attempt in the Albert Hall, they track down their son to a foreign embassy. Doris is asked to a sing for the assembled guests and the song she chooses is of course "Que Sera, Sera." She sings it unnaturally loudly, hoping that her son, imprisoned somewhere in the building, will hear it. Naturally he does and his ear-splitting whistle leads Stewart to him. The family is reunited for a happy ending.

Doris Day sings "Que Sera, Sera" at the embassy in *The Man Who Knew Too Much* **(Paramount, 1956).**

"Que Sera, Sera" has had more screen outings: In 1960, Doris sang it in *Please Don't Eat the Daisies*, then in 1966 she sang part of it in *The Glass Bottom Boat*. In 1965, Australian singer Normie Rowe released a rock'n'roll version, with the lyrics considerably changed. It was an enormous hit and stayed in the Australian charts for more than six months.

The title is subject to a great deal of variation: Livingston and Evans originally called it "Que Sera, Sera" but as songs nominated for the Academy Award have to be in English, the title had to be in English too; therefore it appears in the film's credits as "Whatever Will Be." This is often extended to "Whatever Will Be, Will Be," with the original title in brackets.

1957

RKO Pantages Theatre was the sole venue for the 1957 awards and there were six hosts: Bob Hope, James Stewart, Rosalind Russell, David Niven, Jack Lemmon and—on film—Donald Duck. Among the highlights of the evening's entertainment was a medley of previous Oscar-winning songs, performed by Bob Hope and Rhonda Fleming, Betty Grable and Harry James, Marge and Gower Champion, Mae West and Rock Hudson, Shirley MacLaine and others. Maurice Chevalier presented the Oscar for the year's Best Song. When the nominated songs were performed, it took six singers to do full justice to "April Love." On stage for it were Ann Blyth, Shirley Jones, Anna Maria Alberghetti, Jimmie Rodgers, Tab Hunter and Tommy Sands. The other songs needed only one performer each—Johnny Mathis for "Wild Is the Wind," Dean Martin for "All the Way," Vic Damone for "An Affair to Remember" and Debbie Reynolds for "Tammy."

The Nominations

Harry Warren, Harold Adamson and Leo McCarey for "An Affair to Remember (Our Love Affair)" from *An Affair to Remember* (Fox)

Jimmy Van Heusen and Sammy Cahn for "All the Way" from *The Joker Is Wild* (Paramount)

Sammy Fain and Paul Francis Webster for "April Love" from *April Love* (Fox)

Jay Livingston and Ray Evans for "Tammy" from *Tammy and the Bachelor* (Universal)

Dimitri Tiomkin and Ned Washington for "Wild Is the Wind" from *Wild Is the Wind* (Paramount)

An Affair to Remember (Our Love Affair)

from *An Affair to Remember*
Music: Harry Warren
Lyrics: Harold Adamson and Leo McCarey

Leo McCarey directed and co-scripted the 1939 success *Love Affair*, starring Irene Dunne and Charles Boyer. Nineteen years later he decided to make it again, this time with Deborah Kerr and Cary Grant as the stars, playing Terry McKay and Nickie Ferrante, the couple who fall in love on an ocean liner. And, as in the earlier film, because they are engaged to other people they agree to test their relationship by staying apart for six months and then meeting at the top of the Empire State Building. An accident to Deborah Kerr prevents her from keeping the rendezvous.

Having seen what a hit song can do to promote a film, McCarey wanted a title song that would have a life of its own and firmly register in the minds of the moviegoing public. Veteran songwriter Harry Warren wrote a lovely melody and McCarey, having co-written both the story and script, wanted to ensure the dramatic relevance of all four songs in the film by writing the lyrics himself. It was on Harry Warren's advice that he called on Harold Adamson for assistance.

The title, *Love Affair*, was there immediately in the opening line—the first three words are "Our love affair...." But at this stage McCarey discovered that RKO would not part with the rights to the original title—what to do about the song? The last line supplied the answer: "A love affair to remember." The new film and its title song were renamed *An Affair to Remember*, leaving a title song which does not quite contain the name of the film in its lyric.

Harry Warren's melody is so beautifully written with exactly the right semi-classical feel that the film's musical director, Hugo Friedhofer, was able to incorporate it into his musical score; he received an Oscar nomination for it. But Warren had found great difficulty in writing just the right kind of melody and has said that he must have written about 25 tunes before he found one he was satisfied with. The lyric does not have the same quality as the melody and it makes great use of overblown words and phrases such as "wondrous," "eternity" and "fervent pray'r."

The song is used extensively in the film, Vic Damone singing it first over the opening credits. Later, Grant takes Kerr to meet his elderly grandmother—a former concert pianist, played by Cathleen Nesbitt—and she plays them the melody. Kerr stands next to her at the piano and picks up the song sheet to sing along. The words are in French, written for the film by Tanis Chandler.

Now the song is firmly established as the couple's love theme. Kerr later has a job as a singer in a smart Boston nightclub and there she performs "An

Affair to Remember" again, this time in the English version. Marni Nixon dubbed for Deborah Kerr, so skillfully imitating her voice that many moviegoers were convinced that Kerr was doing her own singing. (It was Nixon who had dubbed for Deborah Kerr so well in *The King and I* the previous year.)

Philips Records planned an LP album of songs and music from the film and announced that Grant and Kerr would be duetting on it. When the album was released, the duet was not included though the stars' glamourous photograph was on the sleeve's cover. Vic Damone sings the title song on the album and other tracks feature the singing of Marni Nixon with another version of "An Affair to Remember" and other songs from the film.

Cary Grant and Deborah Kerr in *An Affair to Remember* **(Fox, 1957).**

The 1993 film *Sleepless in Seattle* makes many references to *An Affair to Remember*, including actual film clips and phrases from the title song sung by Marni Nixon. It also concludes at the top of the Empire State Building. And in 1994 a rather characterless version of *Love Affair* appeared, starring Warren Beatty and Annette Bening as the lovers, with Katharine Hepburn as the aunt.

April Love

from *April Love*
Music: Sammy Fain
Lyrics: Paul Francis Webster

April Love was aimed squarely at the youth market, cashing in on the huge popularity of clean-cut teen idol Pat Boone. He plays the part of Nick Conover, a young man who has stolen a car in Chicago and is sent on probation to his uncle's farm. There he meets the Templeton sisters, Liz and Fran, played by Shirley Jones and Dolores Michaels. At first he seems to be more attracted to Dolores, the older sister, and a small amount of inconsequential drama ensues before he ends up with Shirley.

The song occurs when they are all at a local dance. Boone has won a $15 door prize in a lottery but must sing a song before he can claim his winnings. The song he chooses is "April Love"; he sings with velvety charm and all the girls look on, entranced.

When he finishes the song, to ecstatic applause, the impressed emcee hands him his money and remarks that as Pat's performance was so well-received it "just doesn't seem enough." Back with the girls, he dashes Shirley Jones' hopes by asking her sister for a dance. Later, as Pat and the sisters drive home, Shirley begins to sing the song again. Pat joins in but in spite of this it still seems as though Dolores is the one he is hankering for. But soon afterwards he turns his attentions to Shirley and the melody of "April Love" accompanies scenes between them as their romance gathers pace.

The song has a pleasing melody and the workmanlike words describe the highs and lows of young love. Boone's record topped the U.S. charts for a fortnight and remained on the bestseller lists for 26 weeks. It was in the British charts for 23 weeks but its highest position there was seventh.

Tammy

from *Tammy and the Bachelor*
Music and Lyrics: Ray Evans and Jay Livingston

The four films about Tammy were intended as wholesome family entertainment. The first of them was *Tammy and the Bachelor* (1957), starring Debbie Reynolds as Tammy. And though she is strongly associated with the song "Tammy," it is the Ames Brothers who sing it first in the film, over the opening credits.

Debbie plays the part of a 17-year-old from the bayou who has a heavy crush on a rich young man named Pete, (Leslie Nielsen). Pining for Pete, she sits at her window on a moonbright night and pours out her heart in song: All of nature knows that Tammy is in love but does the object of her affection know?

Debbie does sing "Tammy" in a very appealing, wistful style but there is not a spark of originality in words or music. The bucolic folksiness, with the song's references to hooty owls and whippoorwills, is contrived and artificial. The rhymes are the obvious ones—"charms" with "arms"—and often weak, as with "of" and "love."

Immediately after finishing the song, Debbie's homespun innocence is emphasized when she remarks, "Just think—that same moon shinin' on me this very minute is shinin' down on Pete's tomatoes."

But had it not been for this banal song, we might never have heard any more of Tammy. *Tammy and the Bachelor* was doing such poor business that Universal withdrew it from release. No one at the film studio saw much commercial potential in the song either and the Debbie Reynolds' version was taken directly from the soundtrack rather than being rerecorded in the studio.

But when the Ames Brothers released their recording, it was an instant hit, eventually reaching number five. Reynolds' version was even more successful: It shot to the top spot and stayed there for five weeks. In Britain, "Tammy" was Reynolds' most successful recording—it was in the charts there for 17 weeks, reaching the number two spot. Universal rushed to rerelease the film and—while it was not a huge success—it more than repaid its initial investment and the studio was encouraged to nominate the song for the Oscar. But any chance of Livingston and Evans winning the Award may have been scotched when Universal sent a letter to Academy members, asking for their votes. The letter was written in a girl's handwriting and signed "Tammy." In 1957, this was resented as blatant advertising although such practices are commonplace today.

"Tammy" was not the first million-seller for Debbie Reynolds—that was her 1951 recording with Carleton Carpenter of "Aba Daba Honeymoon," taken from the soundtrack of the film *Two Weeks With Love*. But "Tammy" was enormously successful and when Debbie developed a popular cabaret act in later life, it was her most requested song.

Wild Is the Wind

from *Wild Is the Wind*
Music: Dimitri Tiomkin
Lyrics: Ned Washington

In this melodramatic film, Anthony Quinn plays Gino, a widowed sheep farmer who goes back to Italy to marry Gioia, his dead wife's sister, played by Anna Magnani. (Both actors were nominated for Oscars). Back on the Nevada ranch and ill-treated by Quinn, she finds herself unable to resist the charms of Bene, his adopted son, played by Tony Franciosa. All the main performances are stridently overblown and the lyrics of the title song give a clear indication of the preposterous drama to come.

The singer sings to his lady and tells her that his love is as wild as the wind and his wild hunger for love must be satisfied. Her touch brings the sound of music; her kiss makes his world begin. She must cling to him tightly because they are both creatures of the said wild wind.

Johnny Mathis sings the song over the opening credits and his recording was on the singles charts for 18 weeks, reaching as high as number 22. Nina Simone recorded the song in 1959 and David Bowie recorded his rather hysterical version in the 1970s.

And the Winner Is...

All the Way

from *The Joker Is Wild*
Music: James Van Heusen
Lyrics: Sammy Cahn

Sammy Cahn is reputed to have written more songs for Frank Sinatra than for anyone else so it is understandable that Sinatra would take for granted the quality of the songs brought to him by the lyricist. In his autobiography *I Should Care*, Cahn illustrates this by telling what happened when he and Jimmy Van Heusen wrote "All the Way" and, with Cahn's agent Lilian Schary, took it to Sinatra:

> Came 4 P.M., we were in the living room and he emerged from the bedroom looking like *all* of the Dorian Grays. He looked at me,

Frank Sinatra as Joe E. Lewis sings to an inattentive member of his audience in *The Joker Is Wild* (Paramount, 1957).

grimaced and said, "You before breakfast—yechh." I looked back.
"Hey, from where I'm standing, I'm not sure who's being punished
more." Van Heusen gave me an intro and we went into "All the
Way." When I'd sung the last immortal word and note, Frank
turned and said, "Let's eat." We had a marvelous meal—lunch for
us, breakfast for him—and left. Outside, Lillian had tears in her
eyes. "How could he not like that song?" she said. I said, "Oh, he
loved it." "How do you know?" she said. "Because he loves them
all."

Sinatra's reaction might have been offhand, but there is no doubt that
he thought highly of the song. Soon after his meeting with the songwriters,
he went to Walter Scharf, the musical director of *The Joker Is Wild*, telling
him that the song was a potential Oscar winner and should have a great deal
of emphasis in the film. Scharf agreed and "All the Way" was used in one
form or another in eight key scenes.

The film tells the story of Joe E. Lewis and how, as a speakeasy singer
in the days of Prohibition, he defied Chicago gangsters and had his vocal
chords severed as a result. When we first hear "All the Way," Sinatra, as Lewis,
has just opened in a smart club against the wishes of the mob. As he begins
the song, the big boss enters and takes a prominent seat. Sinatra is uneasily
aware of him and shoots glances his way as he sings.

A few weeks of film time after this first performance of "All the Way,"
the singer's career has advanced and he is in his hotel room listening to his
own recording of the song. It is at this point that the gangsters burst in, beat
him almost to death and slash his vocal chords, ending his career as a singer.

Recovered, he gets works as part of a knockabout burlesque team, dressed
as a clown, complete with fright wig and false nose. At a benefit night, Sophie
Tucker reveals his true identity to the audience and asks him to sing. The
audience calls out for "All the Way." Hesitantly he begins, his voice crack-
ing, and we know he will never reach that big note on "All" in the third line.
He covers his embarrassment with a few wisecracks, suggesting that the
Chicago gangsters were really music critics. His jokes work well and so Joe
E. Lewis' new career as a comedian is signalled.

After the show, he meets Letty Page, a wealthy society girl, played by
Jeanne Crain; they dance together to the melody of "All the Way" and the
next few times it is heard, it is used as their romantic theme. Later, tired of
his lack of commitment, Jeanne marries another man; Sinatra, on the rebound,
marries Martha Stewart, a chorus girl played by Mitzi Gaynor. His career
deteriorates, his gambling and drinking worsen, and during a drunken appearance at a nightclub, he notices Crain and her husband in the audience. He
sings a version of "All the Way" with new lyrics that reflect his obsession with
gambling and the sporting life ... but he stops singing as he sees Crain leaving the club, and all the way out of his life.

The final airing of the song occurs at the end of the film when he has reached rock bottom. Mitzi Gaynor has walked out on him, and so has his long-suffering friend and accompanist Austin Mack, played by Eddie Albert. Wandering the city streets alone at night, he fancies he hears himself singing "All the Way" as he passes a boarded-up nightclub. Reflecting bitterly on what might have been, he decides to reform his life and the film ends on this hopeful note.

So the song punctuates every important turn of the film's plot and with this emphasis it is no wonder that the film is often called "All the Way." In fact, Paramount later reissued the film under that title.

"All the Way" expresses the need for total commitment in a relationship, for fidelity and devotion in good times and bad, all of which is ironic given the lack of these qualities shown by the character Sinatra plays. The lyric is simple and unelaborated, with the sound of everyday speech, and its imagery of love being taller than a tree or deeper than the sea is straightforward, even conventional. Yet when sung by a singer as great as Sinatra, it comes over with real power, and it is the very simplicity and directness which helps to give it that potency.

Sinatra's recording was an enormous hit around the world. Backed by "Chicago," it was his sixth million-seller and spent 30 weeks in the American charts as well as 20 in the list of British bestsellers. Sinatra used the song for years afterwards in his concert appearances. On his ill-advised *Duets* album of 1993 he performs "All the Way" with the vapid Kenny G. This track is the low point of the album.

1958

Bob Hope, Tony Randall, Mort Sahl, Laurence Olivier, David Niven and Jerry Lewis were the hosts for the 1958 Awards, held at the RKO Pantages Theater. Sophia Loren and Dean Martin presented the Best Song Oscar. They introduced the singers and dancers of the nominated songs who performed them as a medley: Anna Maria Alberghetti, Tuesday Weld, Connie Stevens, Nick Adams, Dean Jones and James Darren joined forces to sing "Almost in Your Arms"; John Raitt sang "A Certain Smile," with a dance routine from Marge and Gower Champion; Taina Elg danced to "Gigi" while Tony Martin sang the song; Eddie Fisher sang "To Love and Be Loved"; Howard Keel and Rhonda Fleming duetted on "A Very Precious Love."

The Nominations

Sammy Fain and Paul Francis Webster for "A Certain Smile" from *A Certain Smile* (Fox)

Alan Jay Lerner and Frederick Loewe for "Gigi" from *Gigi* (MGM)

Jay Livingston and Ray Evans for "Love Song from *Houseboat* (Almost in Your Arms)" from *Houseboat* (Paramount)

Jimmy Van Heusen and Sammy Cahn for "To Love and Be Loved" from *Some Came Running* (MGM)

Sammy Fain and Paul Francis Webster for "A Very Precious Love" from *Marjorie Morningstar* (Warner)

A Certain Smile

from *A Certain Smile*
Music: Sammy Fain
Lyrics: Paul Francis Webster

Johnny Mathis made a rare on-screen appearance as a cabaret performer in *A Certain Smile*. He had a string of hit songs starting in the late 1950s and he was an obvious choice to sing the title song. Mathis' light baritone voice, with its trembling vibrato, brings a wistful, bittersweet quality to the tender love ballad. His smooth singing sets the tone for this tale of Dominique, a girl student (Christine Carere), who falls in love with Luc, a philandering older man, played by Rossano Brazzi. Joan Fontaine plays Francoise, Brazzi's wife. "A Certain Smile" is short, but effective. It describes how a smile can bring the joy of love at first sight, but when that love has run its course and you seem to have gotten over the heartbreak, the recollection of that first smile brings back the pain.

Mathis' recording was on the U.S. charts for more than three months but reached no higher than the number 14 position. It fared better in the U.K. where it got to number four and stayed on the charts for 16 weeks.

Love Song from Houseboat (Almost in Your Arms)

Music and Lyrics: Jay Livingston and Ray Evans

In *Houseboat*, Sophia Loren plays Cinzia Zaccardi, a housekeeper employed by the widowed Tom Winters (Cary Grant) to do the housework and to look after his three precocious children. She is actually an Italian socialite who is trying to get away from her overprotective father. This ménage sets up residence on the houseboat of the title and it is here that we first hear the Oscar nominee. Cary Grant's eldest son David, played by Paul Petersen, is giving Sophia an English lesson. They hear the sound of a band playing in a country club on the shore and Sophia recognizes the tune as an Italian one. Young Paul says he knows it too—and comments that it's a bit "cornball." But Sophia says that she thinks it's "very pretty" and starts to sing along in Italian, with young Paul giving an English translation.

Had this been the song's only airing, it could not have been nominated. Because of protests when the same songwriters' "Mona Lisa" won the Oscar in 1950, the rules were changed to make sure that any nominated song must be presented in English. Therefore, in a later scene, Sam Cooke sings the song in full in English. We don't see him—his voice is just heard in the background as Cary Grant and Sophia dance at a country club. The romance that has been threatening through most of the film finally breaks out.

The lyric of the song can barely be heard above the dialogue. But this is no hardship as young Paul's earlier "cornball" judgment is accurate: It has little originality and there is a certain mechanical facileness in the many internal rhymes throughout the song ("near/here," "look/book," etc). The inverted English in the phrase "with all my heart to your arms I'll fly" is an awkward way to ensure a rhyme with "sigh."

Sam Cooke recorded the song but a version by Johnny Nash was marginally more successful, reaching only number 78 on the charts.

To Love and Be Loved

from *Some Came Running*
Music: James Van Heusen
Lyrics: Sammy Cahn

Directed by Vincente Minnelli, *Some Came Running* is not a musical though it has a few songs used in the background. The film stars Frank Sinatra but he does not sing, not even the Oscar-nominated "To Love and Be Loved." An uncredited vocal trio in a bar performs it during a scene between Frank and Shirley MacLaine. Clearly Minnelli didn't consider the song strong enough to be given any particular emphasis and it can barely be heard as Sinatra and Maclaine dance and talk together.

Some Came Running is based on a novel by James Jones who described it (his novel) as being about "the separation between human beings—the fact that no two people ever totally get together; that everyone wants to be loved *more* than they want to love." Minnelli asked the screenwriters and the songwriters to retain this theme. Certainly the characters played by Sinatra and MacLaine are in keeping with it: Sinatra plays Dave Hirsch, a writer with writer's block returning to his hometown after World War II. He finds that he no longer fits in. Ginny Moorhead, MacLaine's rootless character, has low self-esteem and drinks heavily. She has fallen for Sinatra but he doesn't return her feelings. Sinatra marries her on the rebound from a failed relationship with Martha Hyer, who plays Gwen French, a prim teacher. His gloomy indifference to the wedding ceremony makes the words of the song an ironic counterpoint to their situation. The lyric stresses that love gives life its meaning and paints a picture of love as a shelter from the vicissitudes of life.

The melody flows loosely and the verses follow an irregular pattern so that the second verse is shorter than the first. Its imagery is mostly conventional though it must be one of the first popular songs to refer to the space race with the line: "Let others race to the moon."

The vocal trio's version of the song was never released as a single but is included on the soundtrack album. Sinatra himself seems to have liked the song—he recorded it as a single with the Nelson Riddle Orchestra twice in 1958, but neither version made any impression on the hit parade.

A Very Precious Love

from *Marjorie Morningstar*
Music: Sammy Fain
Lyrics: Paul Francis Webster

"A Very Precious Love" was given every chance to make a huge impact as the theme song from *Marjorie Morningstar*. Its over-lush melody is heard many times on the soundtrack and the song itself is sung three times. But director Irving Rapper never lets us hear the full lyric—each time it is performed, it is interrupted by dialogue.

Gene Kelly sings it first. Surrounded by adoring young people at the summer camp where he is the director of drama, he sings "A Very Precious Love" as he accompanies himself on the piano. He tells his admirers that it is a song from his soon-to-be produced Broadway musical. Natalie Wood, as Marjorie Morgenstern, is one of them and she falls heavily for this suave older man as he sings the tender love song.

A chorus later sings it on a balmy evening by the "summer lake" mentioned in the lyric. The romance between the virginal Natalie and world-

Natalie Wood and Gene Kelly in *Marjorie Morningstar* (Warner, 1958).

weary Kelly has not progressed well. Much to Kelly's chagrin, she has hung onto her virtue, her "very precious love," looking for marriage, not a summer fling. He has rejected her. Now, at the lakeside, she sees loving couples all around, emphasizing her loneliness as she stands wistfully beneath the lanterns mentioned in the second verse.

Kelly sings the song again near the end of the film. As Natalie watches, she sees more adoring young things gazing at Kelly and falling for his charms. She realizes that her feelings were the romantic yearnings of a naïve girl and leaves the room without making her presence known. In case the audience fails to appreciate her new maturity, the owner of the camp speaks to her as she goes, remarking that she seems to have "grown up." "I have," says Natalie with heavy irony.

In the song, the singer urges his girl to enjoy the moment, to realize the transitory nature of romance, that lanterns lose their light and "hearts can break." He wants her to give him her "very precious love" now and enjoy at least one ecstatic night. The melody is pretty enough, though rather overblown, and the lyric never really rises above the clichéd phrases of the conventional love song.

There were a number of recordings of the song with the most successful in the U.S.A. being by the deep-voiced close harmony group, The Ames Brothers. In Britain, Doris Day had the most popular version. The song turned up again on film in 1987 when director Clint Eastwood used it on the soundtrack of his *Heartbreak Ridge,* sung there by Jill Hollier.

And the Winner Is...

Gigi

from *Gigi*
Music: Frederick Loewe
Lyrics: Alan Jay Lerner

The title song from *Gigi* is a soliloquy, the puzzled thoughts and musings of Gaston Lachaille, played by Louis Jourdan. During the course of the song, he comes to realize that Gigi is not an adolescent girl whom he adores like a doting uncle but a full-grown woman he loves. In terms of Gaston's character, the plot and the underlying theme of the film, the song is very important.

When they first meet, it seems to Gaston that Gigi is just a naïve child and there is nothing in her behavior towards him that could change his mind. He treats her in a condescending if avuncular manner, and when he takes her to the Palais de Glace he has champagne but for her he orders a childish concoction. Later in the film comes the momentous shift in his feelings when he sings "Gigi." During the course of singing the song, he journeys from

worldly-wise cynicism to romantic idealism and becomes a man whole heart-
edly in love.

The theme of the story—the transformation of Gigi from child to
woman—is signalled at the beginning of the film when Maurice Chevalier,
as Gaston's uncle Honore Lachaille, sings "Thank Heaven for Little Girls";
his gratitude is for the fact that they grow up "in the most delightful way."
As he sings a group, of girls are playing ball and Chevalier draws special
attention to one of them—Gigi.

Gigi, played by Leslie Caron, is being prepared for life as a rich man's
mistress, trained in all the arts of pleasing a man by her grandmother, Madame
Alvarez (Hermione Gingold), and her Aunt Alicia (Isabel Jeans). However,
Gigi is a wilful pupil who cares little for fine clothes or ladylike behavior.
When Madame Alvarez realizes that Gaston is falling in love with Gigi, she
suggests to him that he should support her financially, as he would a mistress. He is shocked by the suggestion, still seeing Gigi as a "funny, awkward
little girl." He rushes angrily from the apartment, slamming the door behind
him. He strides down the street, shouting the first lines of the song, declaring that Gigi is still a baby.

Soon he is in the park and he stops to rest on a bench near a fountain.
It is the same part of the park where Gigi earlier sang her song "The
Parisians," expressing her irritated puzzlement about their artificiality, their
incessant pursuit of love. Like Gaston at the beginning of his song, she was
annoyed and frustrated, and she insisted that she could not understand
Parisian lovers. Now Gaston expresses similar puzzlement, but it is his own
feelings about Gigi that he does not comprehend.

Suddenly he is thoughtful and the melody of the song becomes gentle
as he recalls an occasion when he found Gigi delightful and far from boring.
He stands and seems to want to brush aside this recollection but his exclamations are not quite as positive as they were. As he walks along, he tells
himself again that Gigi is just a child, then almost reluctantly he begins a
proper realization of Gigi's charms, now recalling how her dress clung to her
figure. He makes one more unconvincing attempt to persuade himself that
she is still a child but as he sings he is walking onto a park bridge, an image
that suggests that he is also making a psychological crossing-over.

He sits again to rest on the same bench near the fountain; behind him
on a pond, white swans glide across the water. Though she was never an ugly
duckling, Gigi is now transformed in his mind like the swan in the fairy story
and he realizes that he is in love with a real woman.

Gaston now returns to the apartment of Madame Alvarez and as he
rings the bell, the last part of the melody of his song plays on the soundtrack.
He greets Gigi's grandmother and tells her that he has business to discuss
with her. He intends at this point to make Gigi his mistress. He asks Gigi
to be nice to him, and he will be nice to her. At first Gigi is appalled by the
idea and she sums up the situation precisely: "To be nice to you means that

Gaston (Louis Jourdan) sings the title song in *Gigi* (MGM, 1958).

I should have to sleep in your bed. Then when you get tired of me, I would have to go to some other gentleman's bed." But later, because she loves him, she reluctantly agrees: "I'd rather be miserable with you than without you," she says.

Gaston takes his new mistress to Maxim's to show her off. She is dressed for the evening in a long, elegant white dress, her hair upswept, emphasising her swan-like neck. The feathers at her shoulders reinforce the swan motif.

But this poised and proper Gigi, though stunning to behold, is now just like all the other women that Gaston wearied of. It was the wilful, playful Gigi with whom he fell in love, and he is horrified at what he has done to her. He rushes her back to her grandmother and next the day returns with a proposal of marriage. Goodness prevails and it is Gaston, just as much as Gigi, who has been transformed.

Superbly performed by Louis Jourdan, and directed by Vincente Minnelli with great skill and imagination, "Gigi" is one of the best of all film songs and it provides one of *Gigi*'s most memorable sequences. It expresses the character's shifting emotions far more effectively than pages of dialogue, and also perfectly sums up the theme of the film. It is very similar in its dramatic function to "I've Grown Accustomed to Her Face," sung by Prof. Higgins about Eliza in *My Fair Lady*—also written by Lerner and Loewe.

Great song though it is, Lerner and Loewe had a great deal of difficulty in writing "Gigi" and struggled for three months without success. Eventually Loewe came up with the melody which Lerner describes in his autobiography as "one of the most rapturous he ever composed." He goes on to describes its birth:

> I was sitting on the john. Fritz [Frederick Loewe] was at the piano in the living room, dressed in the Byronesque costume in which he always works—his baggy underwear. Suddenly an exquisite melody came wafting down the hall, causing me to drop my newspaper. "My God!" I yelled. "That's beautiful." Leaping from my perch with my trousers still clinging to my ankles, I made my way to the living room like a man on tiny stilts. "Play that again," I said. He did. I started to walk up and down with excitement and almost broke my jaw on the coffee table. Assuming that having fallen down I would get up, Fritz paid no attention and continued playing. Within an hour he had finished it—except for the last two lines. For once, the last two lines took the composer three days to write. [From *The Street Where I Live* by Alan Jay Lerner]

At the Academy Awards, *Gigi* won nine Oscars, the most ever up to that time. And with the inclusion of Maurice Chevalier's Honorary Award "for his contributions to the world of entertainment over more than half a century," the total is ten. Tony Martin, who sang "Gigi" at the Awards, managed to forget the words of the Oscar-winning song and had to "la-la" his way through the second half of it.

A number of singers recorded "Gigi" but Vic Damone's was the best-selling version in the U.S. Billy Eckstine had the most popular version of the song in the U.K. where it was in the charts for 14 weeks and reached as high as number eight.

When *Gigi* was presented in a stage version on Broadway in 1973, Daniel Massey, son of Raymond, took Louis Jourdan's role. Karin Wolfe played Gigi and Alfred Drake had the role played by Chevalier. The notices were disastrous and it closed early in 1974, leaving behind only an original cast recording.

Appendix 1:
The Songwriters

Tom **ADAIR**, lyricist, was born on June 15, 1913. His Oscar-nominated song is "Julie" but he is best known for his collaboration with composer Matt Dennis, with whom he wrote such songs as "Everything Happens to Me" and "Violets for Your Furs." He also he wrote scripts for a number of TV comedy hits including *F Troop, I Dream of Jeannie* and *Gomer Pyle U.S.M.C.* He died in 1988.

Harold **ADAMSON**, lyricist, was born on December 10, 1906. He had his first hit in 1930 with "Time on My Hands," written for the show *Smiles.* His collaborator on the lyrics was Mack **GORDON**, and Vincent **YOUMANS** composed the music. He moved to Hollywood in 1933. In addition to his five Oscar-nominated songs ("Did I Remember?," "My Own," "Change of Heart," "I Couldn't Sleep a Wink Last Night" and "An Affair to Remember"), he wrote the lyrics for "A Lovely Way to Spend an Evening," "Comin' in on a Wing and a Prayer" and "My Resistance Is Low." He also wrote the theme song for the *I Love Lucy* TV series, with composer Eliot **DANIEL**. He died on August 17, 1980.

Louis **ALTER**, composer, was born on June 18, 1902, and died on November 3, 1980. His first songs were written for Broadway, beginning with *Earl Carroll's Vanities* in 1925. In Hollywood two of his songs were Oscar-nominated ("A Melody from the Sky" and "Dolores"). His other film songs include "You Turned the Tables on Me" and "Rainbow on the River."

Harold **ARLEN** was born Hyman Arluck on February 15, 1905. Early in his career he teamed with lyricist Ted **KOEHLER** to write songs for the Cotton Club, including "Stormy Weather" and "I've Got the World on a String." *The Wizard of Oz* is his best-known film score but he had a total of nine songs nominated for the Oscar, winning once for "Over the Rainbow." He was also a celebrated composer on Broadway, and his shows include *Bloomer Girl*, written with Yip **HARBURG**. He died on April 23, 1986.

Gene **AUTRY**, the first of the singing cowboys of the movies, was born on September 29, 1907, and died in October 1998. His first solo role was in the serial *Phantom Empire*; he subsequently made over 100 movies with Monogram,

255

Republic and Columbia. He wrote or co-wrote many songs, the most success-ful being "That Silver-Haired Daddy of Mine" and "Have I Told You Lately That I Love You?" He recorded extensively and "Rudolf the Red-Nosed Rein-deer" is one of the biggest-selling Christmas songs of all time. "Be Honest with Me" was his only Oscar-nominated song.

Ary **BARROSO** was born on November 7, 1903, and he died on February 9, 1964. The Brazilian composer is best remembered for his song "Aquarela do Brasil" which became "Brazil" in its English version. It was featured in the Disney film *Saludos Amigos* and after its success and the Oscar nomination for the title song, Walt Disney invited him to work in Hollywood. He refused and lived out his life in Brazil.

Irving **BERLIN**'s career is well-documented and he is perhaps the best known of all American songwriters. Jerome **KERN** once said of him, "He *is* Ameri-can music." He was born Israel Baline in Siberia on May 11, 1888, and died on September 22, 1989, at age 101. Hollywood made 18 films that featured his songs but he also wrote some of the most successful Broadway shows of all time (including *Annie Get Your Gun* and *Call Me Madam*) as well as many songs for Tin Pan Alley. He received seven nominations for the Best Song Oscar but won the Award only once—for 1942's "White Christmas."

Ralph **BLANE** was born Ralph Hunsecker on July 26, 1914, and died on Novem-ber 13, 1995. He was a composer and lyricist and worked most often with HUGH MARTIN (born August 11, 1914). Their partnership began when they comprised half of a vocal quartet in Broadway musicals. They are best known for their songs written for *Meet Me in St. Louis;* other songs for that musical include "The Boy Next Door" and "Have Yourself a Merry Little Christmas." Their only other Oscar-nominated song is "Pass That Peace Pipe." Blane also wrote lyrics—only with other composers including Harold ARLEN and Harry WARREN; he wrote "The Stanley Steamer" with the latter.

Nicholas **BRODSZKY** was born in Russia on April 20, 1905, and died in Hol-lywood on December 24, 1958. His first music was written for European operettas and then for British films, including *The Way to the Stars* (1945). In Hollywood he was on staff at MGM and four of his songs were Oscar-nomi-nated: "Be My Love," "Because of You," "My Flaming Heart" and "I'll Never Stop Loving You."

Jack **BROOKS** was born February 14, 1912, in Liverpool, England, and died on November 8, 1971. In Hollywood he wrote lyrics for a number of composers and three of his songs were Oscar-nominated: "Ole Buttermilk Sky," "That's Amore" and "Am I in Love"; he wrote both words and music for the latter.

Lew **BROWN** was born Louis Brownstein in Russia on December 10, 1893, and died on February 5, 1958. With partners Buddy DESYLVA and Ray Hender-son, he wrote lyrics for many successful songs for the Broadway stage includ-ing "The Best Things in Life Are Free" and "Button Up Your Overcoat." In Hollywood the trio wrote "Sonny Boy" for Al Jolson before Brown went on to work with other composers, including Harold ARLEN. "That Old Feeling" was his only Oscar-nominated song.

Walter **BULLOCK** was born on May 6, 1907, and died on August 19, 1953. "When

Did You Leave Heaven" is his best known song though he received one more Oscar nomination in 1940, for "Who Am I?" He penned the lyrics for these two songs and he also wrote screenplays. Among his best-known are *Springtime in the Rockies* and *The Farmer Takes a Wife*.

Johnny **BURKE** was born on October 3, 1908, and died on February 25, 1964. Five of his songs were nominated for the Oscar: "Sleighride in July" and four introduced by Bing Crosby: "Pennies from Heaven," "Only Forever," "Aren't You Glad You're You" and "Swinging on a Star." In all, he wrote the lyrics for 23 Crosby films, most of them with Arthur JOHNSTON or James VAN HEUSEN. In the 1990s, the Broadway show *Swinging on a Star* was based on his songs.

Sammy **CAHN**, lyricist, was born on June 18, 1913, and died on January 15, 1993. He received more Oscar nominations than any other songwriter. From 1943 to 1975, 26 of his songs were nominated and four of them were winners: "Three Coins in the Fountain," "All the Way," "The Best of Everything" (1959) and "Call Me Irresponsible" (1963). His first hit came in 1937 when he and composer Saul Chaplin adapted a Yiddish song "Bei Mir Bist Du Schon," a huge hit for the Andrews Sisters. In addition to his Oscars, he also won an Emmy for "Love and Marriage," written with Jimmy VAN HEUSEN for a TV musical version of Thornton Wilder's play *Our Town*. He wrote songs for four Broadway shows, the most successful being *High Button Shoes*, the longest-running show of 1947. The music was by Jule STYNE.

Hoagy **CARMICHAEL**, composer and lyricist, was born on November 22, 1899, and died on December 27, 1981. His best-known song is "Stardust" (words by Mitchell Parish). He wrote many successful songs for Hollywood movies and also acted in a number of them, including *To Have and Have Not* and *Canyon Passage*. He performs his own Oscar-nominated song "Ole Buttermilk Sky" in the latter. His other nominated song is "In the Cool, Cool, Cool of the Evening," which won in 1951.

Phil **CHARIG** was born on August 31, 1902, and died on July 21, 1960. He composed the music for Broadway and Hollywood, as well as for two London stage shows, both starring Jack Buchanan. In *That's a Good Girl* (1928), Buchanan introduced "Fancy Our Meeting," perhaps Charig's best-known song. Charig's most successful stage show was *Follow the Girls*—it ran on Broadway for more than two years, 1944-46. "Merrily We Live" was his only Oscar-nominated song.

Frank **CHURCHILL** was born on October 20, 1901, and died on May 14, 1942. He composed the music for most his songs for the Disney studios and amongst his best-known are "Who's Afraid of the Big Bad Wolf?," written for *The Three Little Pigs*, and the songs from *Snow White and the Seven Dwarfs* such as "Whistle While You Work." His Oscar-nominated songs were "Baby Mine" and "Love Is a Song." He won an Oscar for the score of *Dumbo* and was also nominated for scoring *Bambi* and *Snow White*.

Con **CONRAD**, born Conrad K. Dober in New York on June 18, 1891, was the first composer to win the Best Song Oscar, for "The Continental." He had his first big hit in 1920 with "Margie," lyric by Benny Davis. He also wrote "Ma,

He's Making Eyes at Me," lyric by Sidney Clare. He died on September 28, 1938.

Eliot **DANIEL** was born in 1908 and died on December 6, 1997. He wrote the lyrics for two Oscar-nominated songs, "Lavender Blue" and "Never." His best-known song is one for which he was not able to take credit for quite some time—the theme song for TV's *I Love Lucy*. Because he was under contract to 20th Century–Fox, his name was removed from the show's credits for the first two series.

Mack **DAVID**, lyricist, was born July 5, 1912, and received eight Oscar nominations including "Bibbidi-Bobbidi-Boo" in 1950 and the title song for *The Hanging Tree* in 1959. His other nominations occurred in the 1960s and include "The Ballad of Cat Ballou" (1965). In 1950 he wrote the English lyrics for "La Vie en Rose." He died on December 30, 1993.

Gene **DE PAUL** was born on June 17, 1919, and died on February 27, 1988. His most highly regarded music was written for *Seven Brides for Seven Brothers*; he also collaborated with Johnny **MERCER** on the Broadway show *Li'l Abner*. His only Oscar-nominated song is "Pigfoot Pete"; his best-known movie song is "I'll Remember April."

Buddy **DE SYLVA**, born on January 27, 1895, had a huge hit in 1920 with "April Showers." He teamed with co-lyricist Lew **BROWN** and composer Ray Henderson to write some highly successful shows in the 1920s and '30s, including *Good News*. In Hollywood they wrote "Sonny Boy" for the Al Jolson film *The Singing Fool* and when the partnership ended in 1930, De Sylva turned to screenwriting and film production, working on four films for Shirley Temple at Fox before becoming executive producer at Paramount from 1939 to 1944. He co-founded Capitol Records in 1942. "Wishing" (1939) was his only Oscar-nominated song. He died on July 11, 1950. The life stories of De Sylva and his songwriting partners were told, Hollywood style, in the 1956 movie *The Best Things in Life Are Free*. It starred Gordon MacRae as De Sylva, with Ernest Borgnine and Dan Dailey as his partners.

Walter **DONALDSON**, composer and lyricist, was born in Brooklyn on July 15, 1893. He is best known for his Broadway musical *Whoopee* which included the songs "Makin' Whoopee" and "Love Me or Leave Me." He also wrote "My Mammy" for Al Jolson. His Hollywood songs include "My Baby Just Cares for Me," written with Gus **KAHN**. His only Oscar nomination was for "Did I Remember?" He died on July 15, 1947.

Al **DUBIN** was born in Zurich, Switzerland, on June 10, 1891, and was two years old when his family migrated to the U.S. With composer Joseph Burke he wrote "Tip Toe Through the Tulips" and "Painting the Clouds with Sunshine" but he is best known for his collaboration with Harry **WARREN**, writing the song lyrics for such seminal Warner Bros.' musicals as *42nd Street* and the *Gold Diggers* series. With Warren he won the 1935 Oscar for "Lullaby of Broadway"; he was also nominated for "Remember Me?" and "We Mustn't Say Goodbye." He died on February 11, 1945.

Roger **EDENS** was born on November 9, 1905, and died on July 13, 1970. From 1945 to 1954 he was a close associate of Arthur Freed in the famous unit producing musicals at MGM. He had two Oscar-nominated songs, writing the music for "Our Love Affair," and working with Hugh MARTIN and Ralph BLANE on both words and music for "Pass That Peace Pipe." He won three Oscars for his scoring of *Easter Parade*, *On the Town* and *Annie Get Your Gun*.

Edward ELISCU was born on April 26, 1901, in New York. He was a playwright, producer and actor as well as a lyricist and he wrote songs with Vincent YOUMANS and Billy Rose for the Broadway show *Great Day!* These included "More Than You Know" and "Without a Song." His Oscar-nominated song was "The Carioca." In the 1950s his liberal views offended Senator McCarthy and he was blacklisted in Hollywood. He died in June 18, 1988.

Ray EVANS *see* Jay LIVINGSTON

Sammy FAIN was born Samuel Feinberg in New York on June 17, 1902. Early hits include "Let a Smile Be Your Umbrella" and "When I Take My Sugar to Tea." Ten of his film songs were Oscar-nominated and he won the award twice, for "Love Is a Many-Splendored Thing" and "Secret Love." On Broadway, he contributed songs to the highly successful Olsen and Johnson shows *Hellza-poppin'* and *Sons o' Fun*. Amongst his other shows is *Flahooley*, written with Yip Harburg. He died on December 6, 1989.

Dorothy FIELDS is the most successful female lyricist in the history of popular music in the USA and she was the first to win a Best Song Oscar, for "The Way You Look Tonight." She was also nominated for "Lovely to Look At." She was born in New Jersey on July 15, 1904, and wrote her first songs for the Cotton Club in the 1920s. Her first successes came with composer Jimmy McHUGH with whom she wrote "On the Sunny Side of the Street" and "I Can't Give You Anything but Love." She wrote the libretto with her brother Herbert for eight Broadway shows including *Annie Get Your Gun*. She was still active into the 1960s, writing the lyrics for *Sweet Charity* (1966) and for *Seesaw* (1973). She died on March 28, 1974.

Sylvia FINE, composer and lyricist, was born on August 29, 1913, and died on October 28, 1991. She was married to Danny Kaye and was a powerful influence on his career. She wrote for him many of the tongue-twisting novelty songs for which he was noted. Kaye was the star of Cole Porter's Broadway show of 1941, *Let's Face It*, and Porter allowed the interpolation of two songs by Sylvia and Max Liebman for Kaye to perform. These were "Melody in 4-F" and "Fairy Talk"; the theater critic of *Newsweek* thought them superior to Porter's songs. Kaye performed "Melody in 4-F" again in his first movie, *Up in Arms*. Sylvia was nominated for "The Moon Is Blue" and her second Oscar nomination came in 1959 for the song "The Five Pennies." She wrote the words and music and Kaye sang it in the movie of the same name, a biopic of Red Nichols.

George FORREST *see* Robert WRIGHT

Ralph FREED was born on May 1, 1907, and died on February 13, 1973. He was the younger brother of MGM producer Arthur Freed. His best-known songs are the Oscar-nominated "How About You?" and "Sandman" (music by Bonnie Lake), the theme song of the Dorsey Brothers Orchestra.

Kim GANNON was born on November 18, 1900, and died on April 29, 1974. He had three songs nominated for the Oscar: "Always in My Heart," "Too

Much in Love" and "Endlessly." He also wrote the lyrics for "I'll Be Home for Christmas."

George **GERSHWIN** was born Jacob Gershvin in New York on September 26, 1898. One of the greatest American composers, he wrote for the concert hall as well as for the stage and screen. His tragic death at the age of 38 was a huge loss to the world of music. "They Can't Take That Away from Me" is his only Oscar-nominated song. His other film songs include "A Foggy Day" and "Love Is Here to Stay." He died on July 11, 1937.

Ira **GERSHWIN** was born Israel Gershvin in New York on December 6, 1896, and died on August 15, 1983. He worked extensively with younger brother George and also with Jerome KERN, Vernon Duke, Kurt Weill and others. He wrote the lyrics for three Oscar-nominated songs: "They Can't Take That Away from Me," "Long Ago (and Far Away)" and "The Man That Got Away." He also worked on two other films with his brother: *A Damsel in Distress* and *The Goldwyn Follies.*

Herschel Burke **GILBERT** wrote the score for *The Moon Is Blue* and the music for the Oscar-nominated title song. He was the first composer to receive three successive Academy Award nominations in each of three music categories: In 1952 he was nominated for Best Score for *The Thief*, in 1953 for Best Song for "The Moon Is Blue" and in 1954 for Best Music Director for his work on *Carmen Jones.* A pioneer of background music scoring for television, Gilbert's theme and music for *The Rifleman* led to his being hired as executive music director for Four Star Television. From 1959 to 1964, he composed music for numerous Four Star series, including *The Dick Powell Theatre* (for which he received two Emmy nominations), *The Detectives, Starring Robert Taylor, The Rogues, The DuPont Show, Burke's Law* and *The Loretta Young Show.* In 1964 he became executive music director for CBS-TV where he conducted the music for *Gilligan's Island* and other shows. His score for an episode of *Rawhide* won the Western Heritage Award of the Cowboy Hall of Fame. He was born on April 20, 1918, and died on June 8, 2003.

Ray **GILBERT**, lyricist, was born on September 15, 1912, and died on March 3, 1976. His only Oscar-nominated song is "Zip-a-Dee-Doo-Dah," which won in 1947. He also wrote the English lyrics for "Baia" (music by Ary Barroso) and "The Three Caballeros" (music by Manuel Esperon). In 1950 he added lyrics to Kid Ory's jazz classic "Muskrat Ramble."

Fred **GLICKMAN** (1949-2001) shared music and lyric writing duties with Hy HEATH and Johnny LANGE for the Oscar-nominated "Mule Train." He was a staff songwriter at Republic Studios, producing songs mainly for Westerns and crime movies. Among his other songs are "The Saga of Jesse James" and "Machine Gun Momma."

Mack **GORDON** was born Morris Gittler in Warsaw on June 21, 1904, and died on March 1, 1959. One of the most successful lyricists in Hollywood, nine of his songs were Oscar-nominated, including "Chattanooga Choo Choo." He won the Oscar with "You'll Never Know." He worked mainly with composers Harry WARREN and Harry REVEL and with the latter he wrote "Did You Ever See a Dream Walking?," "Once in a Blue Moon" and many other hit songs. With Warren he had even more hits, including "Serenade in Blue" and "The More I See You," in addition to four Oscar-nominated songs.

Mort **GREENE**, Oscar-nominated for his lyrics for "When There's Breeze on Lake Louise," was born on October 3, 1912. Among his best-known songs are "Stars in Your Eyes," "Weary Blues" and the theme song for the TV series *Leave It to Beaver*. He died on December 28, 1992.

Oscar **HAMMERSTEIN** II was born on July 12, 1895, and died on August 23, 1960. His glittering 18-year partnership with composer Richard RODGERS is well-documented but he worked with many others: He wrote the book and lyrics for *Rose-Marie* (music by Rudolf Friml) and *The Desert Song* (music by Sigmund Romberg), and with Jerome KERN wrote book and lyrics for one of the most influential of all American musicals, *Show Boat*. His film songs include "The Folks Who Live on the Hill" (music by Jerome Kern) and "When I Grow Too Old to Dream" (music by Romberg). Five of his songs were nominated for the Oscar, winning with "The Last Time I Saw Paris" and "It Might As Well Be Spring."

E. Y. **HARBURG**, known as "Yip," was born Isidore Hochberg on April 8, 1896. He is best-known as the lyricist of *The Wizard of Oz* and for his Broadway shows including *Finian's Rainbow* (with Burton LANE) and *Bloomer Girl* (with Harold ARLEN). He wrote the words for the famous song that became the anthem of the Depression, "Brother, Can You Spare a Dime?," and he teamed with composer Vernon Duke to write "April in Paris." He won the 1939 Best Song Oscar for "Over the Rainbow" and had two other songs nominated: "Happiness Is a Thing Called Joe" (1943) and "More and More" (1945). He died on March 5, 1981.

Leigh **HARLINE** was born on March 26, 1907, and died on December 10, 1969. For nine years he worked in the Disney studio's music department; then in 1942 he began working as a freelancer scoring many films, including most of the Blondie series. Seven of his music scores were nominated for Oscars and he won for *Pinocchio*. His best-known song is that film's Oscar-winning "When You Wish Upon a Star."

Hy **HEATH** was born Walter Heath on July 9, 1890, and he died on April 3, 1965. Best-known for co-writing music and lyrics for the Oscar-nominated "Mule Train," he also wrote "Take These Chains from My Heart" with Fred ROSE.

Ray **HEINDORF** was born on August 25, 1908, and died on February 1980. He was a staff composer with Warner Bros. for many years, writing cue music for a number of films, including ones starring Doris Day. He received 17 Oscar nominations for his film scores, winning three times (*Yankee Doodle Dandy*, *This Is the Army* and *The Music Man*). He was co-composer of the Oscar-nominated song "Some Sunday Morning."

Edward **HEYMAN**, lyricist, was born on March 14, 1907, and died on March 30, 1981. He wrote or co-wrote the lyrics for a number of well-known songs including "Body and Soul," "Blame It on My Youth" and "I Cover the Waterfront." His Oscar-nominated song is "Love Letters."

Al **HOFFMAN**, composer, was born in Russia on September 25, 1902, and died on July 21, 1960. He wrote songs for 18 British musical films including "Everything's in Rhythm with My Heart," introduced by Jessie Matthews in *First a Girl*. In Hollywood he worked at the Disney studios and co-wrote the Oscar-nominated "Bibbidi-Bobbidi-Boo." His other songs include "Mairzy Doats" and "If I Knew You Were Comin' I'd Have Baked a Cake."

Frederick **HOLLANDER**, composer, was born of German parents in London on October 18, 1896, and died in Munich on January 18, 1976. He began work in Hollywood after the success of the German film *The Blue Angel* in which Marlene Dietrich sang "Falling in Love Again," his best-known song. He also wrote "The Boys in the Back Room" for Dietrich to sing in *Destry Rides Again*. "Whispers in the Dark" was the first of two Oscar-nominated songs for which he wrote the music; the other is "This Is the Moment."

Ramez **IDRISS**, composer and lyricist, sometimes known as Ramey, was born on September 11, 1911, and died on February 5, 1971. He wrote film songs with George TIBBLES and they were Oscar-nominated for "The Woody Woodpecker Song," their best-known song. Idriss wrote special material for the Ritz Brothers, Eddie Cantor, Jimmy Durante and Marion Hutton, later working in TV. He worked in that medium with Tibbles and wrote scripts for some episodes of *My Three Sons*, as well as some of the music.

M. K. **JEROME**, composer, was born July 18, 1893, and died on May 24, 1981. He is best-known for his Oscar-nominated songs "Some Sunday Morning" and "Sweet Dreams, Sweetheart." His other songs include "Just a Baby's Prayer at Twilight (For Her Daddy Over There)" and "Jose O'Neill (The Cuban Heel)."

Arthur **JOHNSTON**, composer, was born on January 10, 1898, and died on May 1, 1954. Early in his career he was copy secretary for Irving Berlin. Many of his film songs were written for Bing Crosby; they include "Learn to Croon" and "The Moon Got in My Eyes," as well as the Oscar-nominated "Pennies from Heaven." This and "Cocktails for Two," introduced by Danish singer Carl Brisson in *Murder at the Vanities*, are probably his best-known songs.

Gus **KAHN** was born in Coblenz, Germany, on November 6, 1886, and his family emigrated to America when he was five. His first songs were published in 1906 and among his most successful, written for Broadway with Walter Donaldson, are "Makin' Whoopee" and "Love Me or Leave Me." "The Carioca" and "Waltzing in the Clouds" are his Oscar-nominated songs. He also wrote (with Johnny MERCER) the lyrics for "It Had to Be You," once described as the best popular song ever. He died on July 2, 1941; and his film biography *I'll See You in My Dreams* (1951), starred Danny Thomas.

Bert **KALMAR**, lyricist and screenwriter, was born on February 16, 1884, and died on September 18, 1947. From 1917 until his death he wrote exclusively with composer Harry RUBY (January 27, 1895–February 23, 1974) and their partnership was celebrated in the film *Three Little Words*, where Fred Astaire played Kalmar and Red Skelton played Ruby. They worked first on Broadway, their shows including *Animal Crackers* starring the Marx Brothers. For that show, they wrote "Hooray for Captain Spaulding," the song that Groucho Marx used as his theme song. In Hollywood they wrote two Marx Brothers movies, *Horse Feathers* and *Duck Soup*. "Three Little Words" is their best-known song but they also wrote "Who's Sorry Now?" and "Nevertheless." Their only Oscar nomination was for "A Kiss to Build a Dream On."

Walter **KENT**, composer, was born on November 29, 1911, and died on March 1, 1994. He wrote the music for "The White Cliffs of Dover" and "I'll Be Home for Christmas." His two Oscar nominations were for "Too Much in Love" and "Endlessly."

Jerome **KERN** was born in New York on January 27, 1885. He was one of the most influential of American composers and is recognized as the father of the modern Broadway musical. He enjoyed many successes but *Show Boat* is his acknowledged masterpiece. Seven of his songs were nominated for the Academy Award, and he won with "The Way You Look Tonight" and "The Last Time I Saw Paris." His other movie songs include "The Folks Who Live on the Hill," "A Fine Romance" and "I'm Old-Fashioned." He died in New York on November 11, 1945.

Ted **KOEHLER**, lyricist, was born on July 14, 1894, and began his famous collaboration with composer Harold **ARLEN** in 1930; "Get Happy" was one of their first hits. They wrote many of their songs of the early 1930s for Cotton Club revues; these included "Stormy Weather" and "I've Got the World on a String." They moved to Hollywood in 1934 and wrote the title song for *Let's Fall in Love*. Subsequently, Koehler worked with other composers including Jimmy McHUGH and Burton LANE. Koehler and Arlen teamed up again to write the Oscar-nominated "Now I Know." The composer of his other two nominated songs, "Sweet Dreams, Sweetheart" and "Some Sunday Morning," was M. K. JEROME. Koehler died on January 17, 1973.

Burton **LANE**, composer, was born Burton Levy on February 2, 1912, and died on January 5, 1997. In Hollywood, he collaborated with various lyricists, writing "Everything I Have Is Yours" with Harold ADAMSON and "The Lady's in Love with You" with Frank LOESSER. He also wrote music for Broadway shows, partnering Yip HARBURG for *Finian's Rainbow* and Alan Jay LERNER for *On a Clear Day You Can See Forever*. He also wrote the Oscar-nominated "Too Late Now" with Lerner; his other nomination was for "How About You?"

JOHNNY **LANGE** was born on August 15, 1909. He is best known for combining with Hy HEATH and Fred GLICKMAN to write words and music for the Oscar-nominated "Mule Train." He also partnered with Hy Heath to write "Uncle Remus Said" for Walt Disney's *Song of the South*.

Jack **LAWRENCE**, lyricist and composer, was born on April 7, 1912. A prolific songwriter, his hit songs include "Tenderly," "Yes, My Darling Daughter" and "All or Nothing at All." He also wrote the English lyric for "La Mer," which became "Beyond the Sea." He was Oscar-nominated for "Hold My Hand."

Ernest **LECUONA**, pianist and bandleader, is probably the most successful composer to come from Cuba, where he was born on August 7, 1896. Best-known for the melody that became "The Breeze and I," he also wrote very popular tunes such as "The Peanut Vendor," "Malaguena" and "Say Si Si." His only

Oscar nomination was for the title song from *Always in My Heart*. He died on November 29, 1963.

Lester **LEE** was born on November 7, 1905, and died on June 19, 1956. He wrote the music for one Oscar-nominated song: "Sadie Thompson's Song (Blue Pacific Blues)." Most of his other work was for the movies, including the title songs for *The Blue Gardenia* and *Fire Down Below*. His biggest hit was the title song he wrote with lyricist Ned Washington for *The Man from Laramie*.

Alan Jay **LERNER**, lyricist, librettist and screenwriter, was born on August 31, 1918, and died on June 14, 1986. He wrote book and lyrics for some of Broadway's finest shows, including *My Fair Lady, Brigadoon, Paint Your Wagon* and *Camelot*, all collaborations with composer Frederick LOEWE. They also combined to write one of the greatest of screen musicals in *Gigi*. Three of Lerner's movie songs were nominated for the Oscar: "Too Late Now" (music by Burton Lane), "Gigi" (the winning song in 1958) and "Little Prince" (1974).

Jay **LIVINGSTON** and Ray **EVANS**, composers and lyricists, wrote words and music for many memorable songs and won the Oscar three times, for "Buttons and Bows," "Mona Lisa" and "Que Sera, Sera." They were nominated for four others, including "Dear Heart" in 1954 (music by Henry Mancini). They also wrote for television, including the songs for the first TV musical in color, *Satins and Spurs* (1954), as well as theme songs for such shows as *Bonanza* and *Mr Ed*. Jay Livingston was born Jacob Levison on March 28, 1915, and died on October 19, 2001. Ray Evans was born on February 4, 1915.

Jerry **LIVINGSTON** wrote the music for three Oscar-nominated songs: "Bib-bidi-Bobbidi-Boo," "The Hanging Tree" (1959) and "The Ballad of Cat Bal-lou" (1965). He was born Jerome Levinson on March 25, 1909, and died on July 1, 1987.

Frank **LOESSER** was born on June 29, 1910, and died on July 26, 1969. He is best-remembered for his great Broadway musicals such as *Guys and Dolls* and *How to Succeed in Business Without Really Trying*, for which he wrote both music and lyrics. He began his songwriting career in Hollywood as lyricist only, working with a variety of composers. Early successes include "Small Fry" and "Two Sleepy People." Five of his film songs were nominated for the Oscar: He wrote the lyrics for "Dolores" and "They're Either Too Young or Too Old," and music and lyrics for "I Wish I Didn't Love You So," "Baby, It's Cold Outside" (the winner in 1949) and "Thumbelina."

Frederick **LOEWE**, composer, was born in Berlin on June 10, 1904. With Alan Jay LERNER he wrote seven Broadway shows, including *Brigadoon, Paint Your Wagon, My Fair Lady* and *Camelot*. Also with Lerner he wrote the songs for *Gigi*, including the Oscar-winning title song. They were also nominated for "Little Prince" (1974). He died on February 14, 1988.

Herb **MAGIDSON** was born on January 7, 1906. Early in his career he wrote material for Sophie Tucker; he later wrote the lyrics for four Broadway shows, though he is best-known for his movie songs. One of his biggest hits was "Music, Maestro, Please." Three of his songs were nominated for the Academy Award and he won the very first one for "The Continental." His other nominations were for "Say a Pray'r for the Boys Over There" and "I'll Buy That Dream." He died on January 2, 1986.

Hugh **MARTIN** *see* Ralph **BLANE**

Johnny **MARVIN** wrote more than 80 songs for Gene AUTRY films and many of them, like "Dust," his only Oscar-nominated song, show a real familiarity with life in the old West. Marvin was born on July 11, 1887, in Butler, Oklahoma, on a covered wagon—his parents were pioneers on their way to buy a ranch in Curtis County (or so his publicity says). Marvin grew up on the ranch, learning all the skills of the cowboy before running away to join a circus as a stunt rider. Eventually he found his way into vaudeville as a singing cowboy, billed as Honey Duke and His Uke. In the mid–1920s he lived in New York, had a network radio show and made a series of popular recordings. Around this time he met and befriended the young Gene Autry. When Autry became a big star, Johnny moved out to Hollywood and soon became a resident songwriter with the Gene Autry entourage. Among his epics of the West are such songs as "The Bowlegged Cowboy" and "Keep Rollin', Lazy Longhorns." During the Second World War he toured the Pacific bases with comedian Joe E. Brown, singing for the troops. Contracting dengue fever in Papua, he returned to Hollywood where he died of a heart attack on December 20, 1944.

Jimmy **McHUGH** was born on July 10, 1892, and he died on May 23, 1969. He is best known for his collaboration with lyricist Dorothy FIELDS, with whom he wrote many popular songs including "I'm in the Mood for Love" and "On the Sunny Side of the Street." He shared an Oscar nomination with her for "Lovely to Look At" but worked with other lyricists for his other nominated songs: "My Own," "I'd Know You Anywhere," "Say a Pray'r for the Boys Over There" and "I Couldn't Sleep a Wink Last Night."

Johnny **MERCER** was born on November 18, 1909, and died on June 25, 1976. Though mainly a lyricist, he was also a composer, writing words and music for such songs as "Something's Gotta Give" and "I'm an Old Cowhand." Between 1936 and 1971, 18 of his songs were nominated for the Best Song Oscar and four of them were winners: "On the Atchison, Topeka and the Santa Fe," "In the Cool, Cool, Cool of the Evening," "Moon River" and "Days of Wine and Roses." He also wrote songs for Broadway musicals, including *Li'l Abner*, was a successful singer with many hit records, and co-founded Capitol Records.

Sidney **MITCHELL** was born in Baltimore on June 15, 1888. His first hit song, written for the 1918 *Ziegfeld Follies*, glories in the title of "Would You Rather Be a Colonel with an Eagle on Your Shoulder or a Private with a Chicken on Your Knee?". He was one of the first lyricists to work in Hollywood and he wrote songs for *Pigskin Parade*, Judy Garland's feature debut. His Oscar nomination was for "A Melody from the Sky." He died on February 25, 1942.

James **MONACO**, composer, was born on January 13, 1885, and he died on October 16, 1945. He wrote the music for many film songs and seven for Bing Crosby, including *Road to Singapore*, the first of the famous *Road* series. "You Made Me Love You," written in 1912 with Joseph McCarthy, was one of his first big hits. He also wrote "Crazy People" which Burns and Allen adopted as their theme song. He was nominated for the Best Song Oscar four times, for "Only Forever," "We Mustn't Say Goodbye," "I'm Making Believe" and "I Can't Begin to Tell You."

Larry **MOREY**, lyricist, was born on March 26, 1905, and died on May 8, 1971. He worked in the main for the Disney Studios and wrote the songs for *Snow White and the Seven Dwarfs* with Frank CHURCHILL. These two also wrote the Oscar-nominated "Love Is a Song" from *Bambi*; Morey's other nomination was for "Lavender Blue."

Richard **MYERS**, composer and lyricist, was born on March 25, 1901, and died on March 21, 1977. He wrote the music for a number of Broadway shows, mainly in the 1920s and '30s, then turned to production for the remainder of his career. He wrote the music for the song that became "Hold My Hand" some years before Jack LAWRENCE added the lyrics. This song was nominated for the 1954 Oscar.

Josef **MYROW** was born in Russia on February 28, 1910, and died on December 24, 1987. He was a staff composer at 20th Century–Fox and worked mainly with lyricist Mack GORDON, with whom he wrote the Oscar-nominated "You Do" and "Wilhelmina," both for Betty Grable movies. Their other well-known songs include "You Make Me Feel So Young."

Alfred **NEWMAN**, composer, was born on March 17, 1901, and died on February 17, 1970. He wrote the scores for more than 200 movies, most of them at 20th Century–Fox. Most of the songs he wrote were for non-musicals and include the Love Theme from *Airport* ("The Winds of Chance") and the title songs for *Anastasia* and *How the West Was Won*. His Oscar-nominated songs were "Through a Long and Sleepless Night" and the title song for the 1959 movie *The Best of Everything*. He was nominated many times for his film scores and won on nine occasions; his winning films include *Alexander's Ragtime Band, Mother Wore Tights* and *Love Is a Many-Splendored Thing*.

Charles **NEWMAN** was born on February 22, 1901, and died on January 9, 1978. In the 1930s he wrote lyrics for a number of songs composed by bandleader Isham Jones, including "You've Got Me Crying Again." His Oscar-nominated song is "Silver Shadows and Golden Dreams."

Lionel **NEWMAN** was born on January 4, 1916, and died on February 2, 1981. He was one of the famous Newman family, brother of Alfred, and worked in Hollywood mostly as a music director. He received nine Oscar nominations for his film scores, winning with *Hello, Dolly!* His best-known song is "Again" which gave Vic Damone his first million-seller. He composed the music for two Oscar-nominated songs, "The Cowboy and the Lady" and "Never." Randy Newman, himself nominated eight times for the Best Song Oscar and winning in 2001 for "If I Didn't Have You" from *Monsters, Inc.*, is his nephew.

Lloyd B. **NORLIN** was born on March 23, 1918. He wrote words and music for the Oscar-nominated song "Out of the Silence." There are different spellings of his surname—most references give it as "Norlind" but ASCAP, the credits of *All-American Co-Ed* and his alma mater, Northwestern University, spell it "Norlin." ASCAP lists him as writing only eight songs, one of them being the Northwestern University Shout. He died on May 11, 2000.

Alex **NORTH**, composer, was born on December 4, 1910, and died on September 8, 1991. His film music earned him 15 Oscar nominations, 14 for his scores and one for the song "Unchained Melody." He was awarded a Lifetime Achievement Oscar in 1986. His first nomination came in 1951 for *A Streetcar Named Desire*, a score regarded as groundbreaking as the first to use jazz as an integral part of the action. Other film scores include *Spartacus* and *Viva Zapata!*, both Oscar-nominated.

Ben **OAKLAND**, composer, was born on September 24, 1907, and died on August 26, 1979. He was a self-taught pianist and made his concert debut at the age of nine in Carnegie Hall. Later he was accompanist to stage stars Helen Morgan and George JESSEL. His best-known songs are "I'll Take Romance" (lyrics by Oscar HAMMERSTEIN) and "I'll Dance at Your Wedding" (lyrics by Herb MAGIDSON). He wrote music for most of the 28 *Blondie* films made between 1938 and 1950. He seems to have specialized in series—he also wrote music for Jungle Jim and Charlie Chan movies. Perhaps the most notable films he worked on are *Mr. Smith Goes to Washington* (1939) and *His Girl Friday* (1940).

Harry **OWENS** was born on April 18, 1902, and died on December 12, 1986. He first went to Hawaii in 1934 to lead the orchestra at the Royal Hawaiian Hotel. After the success of "Sweet Leilani," he moved to America where he and his new band popularized Hawaiian music. He played regularly at the Cocoanut Grove nightclub and had his own TV series in the 1950s. He wrote more than 300 songs and made over 150 records.

Lew **POLLACK**, composer, was born on June 16, 1895, and died on January 18, 1946. His Oscar-nominated song is "Silver Shadows and Golden Dreams" but he is best-known for "My Yiddishe Mama," the song he wrote with Jack Yellen for Sophie Tucker in 1925. He also wrote 1926's "Charmaine," the tune that was such an enormous hit for Mantovani in 1951. On the other side of this record was another Pollack song, "Diane," written in 1927. Originally, both songs had lyrics by Erno Rapee.

Cole **PORTER**, composer and lyricist, was born on June 9, 1891. He wrote words and music for 23 Broadway musicals and many of his songs have become standards, if not classics. He is noted especially for his witty and sophisticated lyrics but he also wrote superb love ballads such as "Ev'ry Time We Say Goodbye" and "I Concentrate on You." Four of his songs were nominated for the Oscar and among his other film songs were "Easy to Love," "In the Still of the Night" and "Don't Fence Me In." He died on October 15, 1964.

Hugh **PRINCE**, composer, was born on August 6, 1906, and died on January 15, 1960. He was Oscar-nominated for "Boogie Woogie Bugle Boy" and with the same lyricist, Don RAYE, he also wrote "Beat Me Daddy, Eight to the Bar" and "She Had to Go and Lose It at the Astor."

Arthur **QUENZER** was born on October 20, 1905. Writing song lyrics as a freelancer was a sideline to his career as a reeds and violin player with various orchestras from the 1920s to the '50s. He was radio and recording musician with Gordon Jenkins, Victor YOUNG and David ROSE. Two of his 1938 songs were nominated for the Oscar: "The Cowboy and the Lady" and "Merrily

We Live"; among his other songs is "Yo Ho Dee O Lay Hee," written for the Laurel and Hardy movie *Swiss Miss*.

Ralph **RAINGER** was born Ralph Reichenthal on October 7, 1901. He worked almost exclusively in Hollywood with Leo ROBIN though he did write "I Wished on the Moon" with Dorothy Parker and "Moanin' Low" with Edgar Fairchild. With Leo Robin, apart from his four Oscar-nominated songs, he also wrote the music for "Blue Hawaii," "Ebb Tide" and "Easy Living." His career was cut short on October 23, 1942, when he was killed in an air crash.

Don **RAYE** was born Donald Wilhoite, Jr., on March 16, 1909, and died on January 29, 1985. He wrote the lyrics for songs in many films for Universal and was Oscar-nominated for "Boogie Woogie Bugle Boy" and "Pigfoot Pete." His other film songs include "I'll Remember April."

Harry **REVEL** was born in London, England, on December 21, 1905, and died on November 3, 1958. He composed music for stage musicals in Berlin, London and New York and five of his Broadway shows had lyrics by Mack GORDON, with whom he moved to Hollywood in 1929. This pair wrote many popular film songs including "Did You Ever See a Dream Walking" and "Love Thy Neighbor." But Mort GREENE wrote the lyrics for Revel's first Oscar-nominated song, "When There's Breeze on Lake Louise." His other nomination was for "Remember Me to Carolina," written with Paul Francis WEBSTER.

Leo **ROBIN** was born on April 6, 1895. He was one of Hollywood's most successful lyricists—ten of his songs were nominated for the Academy Award and he won in 1928 for "Thanks for the Memory." His first success came in 1927 when he collaborated on the lyrics for Vincent YOUMANS' Broadway show *Hit the Deck*. In Hollywood he wrote the words for many well-known songs including "Louise," "Beyond the Blue Horizon" and "Love Is Just Around the Corner." In 1949 he worked with composer Jule STYNE to write the songs for one of Broadway's most successful shows, *Gentlemen Prefer Blondes*, in which Carol Channing introduced "Diamonds Are a Girl's Best Friend." He died on December 29, 1984.

Richard **RODGERS** was born on June 28, 1902, and died on December 30, 1979. One of Broadway's finest composers, from 1919 to 1943 he worked with lyricist Lorenz Hart, writing the scores for 29 stage musicals. They wrote their first original film songs in 1931 for *The Hot Heiress*. Many of their stage successes were also filmed. Rodgers' partnership with Oscar HAMMERSTEIN began with *Oklahoma!* in 1943, and in 1945 they wrote their only original film songs for *State Fair*, a score that included the Oscar-winning "It Might as Well Be Spring."

Ann **RONELL** is best known for her song "Willow Weep for Me," a great favorite with jazz singers and musicians for its appealing chord changes and bluesy qualities. She was the first woman to write and conduct the music for a major film soundtrack, *Tomorrow the World* (1944), and she was the second woman after Dorothy Fields to receive a Best Song Oscar nomination. In addition to her song "Linda," she was also nominated for the music score she wrote for *The Story of G. I. Joe*. She was born Ann Rosenblatt on December 25, 1905, and died on her birthday in 1993. She studied composition at Radcliff and met George GERSHWIN at this time. He helped her later to become a rehearsal pianist for his show *Rosalie* (1928). He also encouraged her to change her name to Ronell and when she wrote "Willow Weep for Me" in 1932 she dedicated it to him.

In 1933 she moved to Hollywood and worked first at the Disney Studios where, with Frank E. CHURCHILL, she wrote new words and music for "Who's Afraid of the Big Bad Wolf?" She also wrote "Mickey Mouse and Minnie's in Town" which the studios accepted as the official Mickey Mouse birthday song. She became music director for Paramount and United Artists and in 1942 she was the first woman to write both music and lyrics for a Broadway show, *Count Me In*.

David **ROSE** was born in London, England, on June 15, 1910, and died on August 23, 1990. After starting as an arranger for NBC Radio in Chicago, he moved to Hollywood in 1928 and led the orchestra for the Mutual Broadcasting network. In 1944 he composed the huge hit tune "Holiday for Strings." In 1958, he wrote "The Stripper" for a television show called *Burlesque*, starring Dan Dailey. His work in television included being musical director for the series *Little House on the Prairie*. David Rose won four Emmys.

Fred **ROSE** was born on August 24, 1897, and died on December 1, 1954. With Gene AUTRY, he wrote words and music for the Oscar-nominated song "Be Honest with Me." He wrote songs mostly for Western films but his biggest hit was "Take These Chains from My Heart," written with Hy HEATH.

Harry **RUBY** *see* Bert KALMAR

Arthur **SCHWARTZ**, composer, was born on November 25, 1900, and died on September 4, 1984. With longtime partner and lyricist Howard Dietz he wrote many fine stage musicals, the most successful being *The Band Wagon* (1931), a score that includes "Dancing in the Dark." When this was filmed in 1953, they added the show business anthem "That's Entertainment." His Oscar-nominated songs were "They're Either Too Young or Too Old" and "A Gal in Calico."

Artie **SHAW** was born Abraham Arshawsky on May 23, 1910. One of the leading bandleaders of the swing era, he was also a prolific composer, writing instrumentals in the main. He received an Oscar nomination for "Love of My Life."

Leith **STEVENS** was born on September 13, 1909, and died on July 23, 1970. He composed the music for one Oscar-nominated song, the title song for the Doris Day movie *Julie*. He wrote film music for a number of studios—for Paramount he scored *When Worlds Collide* and *The War of the Worlds*. He also received Oscar nominations for his scores for *The Five Pennies* and *A New Kind of Love*.

Georgie **STOLL**, sometimes credited as George Stoll or George E. Stoll, was born on May 7, 1905, and died on January 18, 1985. A leading Hollywood composer, he was nominated eight times for his scoring of films, winning once for *Anchors Aweigh*. He is credited as lyric writer for the nominated song "Our Love Affair."

Robert **STOLZ** was born in Austria on August 25, 1880. He was greatly honored as a composer and conductor in Europe. He wrote the music for many

Viennese operettas and 40 film scores but was forced to flee to the U.S. in 1940 to escape the Nazi regime. His song "Waltzing in the Clouds" was nominated for an Oscar, as was his music for the film *It Happened Tomorrow*. He returned to Vienna in 1946 and died on June 27, 1975.

Jule **STYNE** was born Jules Stein in London, England, on December 31, 1905. He composed the music for many film songs, mainly with Sammy CAHN, with whom he received seven of his ten Oscar nominations. They won once with "Three Coins in the Fountain." Among his other nominations is "Funny Girl," written in 1968 as the title song for the film version of his Broadway show. His other famous Broadway shows include *Gentlemen Prefer Blondes* and *Bells Are Ringing*. He died on September 20, 1994.

George **TIBBLES**, composer and lyricist, was born on June 7, 1923, and died on February 14, 1987. He wrote film songs with Ramey IDRISS including the Oscar-nominated "Woody Woodpecker Song." He was also a writer and producer for television, working on various shows including *Leave It to Beaver*, *My Three Sons*, *The Addams Family* and *The Brady Bunch*.

Dmitri **TIOMKIN** was born in the Ukraine on May 10, 1894. He studied music at the St. Petersburg Conservatory, became a concert pianist and left Russia for the U.S. in 1925. He began writing film scores in 1933 and is acknowledged as one of Hollywood's most influential composers. He won seven Golden Globes and was nominated for 22 Oscars, eight of them for songs. He won the Award four times: for the title song from *High Noon*, and for his film scores for *High Noon*, *The High and the Mighty* and *The Old Man and the Sea*. He died on November 11, 1979.

James **VAN HEUSEN** was born Edward Chester Babcock on January 26, 1913, and died on February 7, 1990. He wrote music for songs in 23 Bing Crosby films and also wrote 76 songs for Frank Sinatra. One of his first hits was "Darn That Dream," written for a 1939 Broadway show. His first songwriting partner in Hollywood was Johnny BURKE with whom he wrote three Oscar-nominated songs, winning in 1944 for "Swinging on a Star." In 1964 he teamed up with Sammy CAHN and 11 of their songs were nominated; they won three times, with "All the Way," "High Hopes" and "Call Me Irresponsible." They also wrote two Broadway shows together, *Skyscraper* and *Walking Happy*, and won an Emmy for "Love and Marriage." In 1962 they wrote the songs for *Road to Hong Kong* in which Bob Hope played a character named Chester Babcock.

Edward **WARD** was born in St. Louis on April 2, 1896, and worked in Hollywood mainly as a composer of film scores. He received Oscar nominations for five of them, including *Phantom of the Opera* in 1943. "Always and Always" and "Pennies for Peppino" were his two Oscar-nominated songs; his other songs include "Dreaming of Castles in the Air" and "Who Takes Care of the Caretaker's Daughter." He died on September 26, 1971.

Harry **WARREN** was the most successful of all Hollywood composers with 131 of his movie songs becoming hits. Eleven were nominated for the Academy Award and he won on three occasions, with "Lullaby of Broadway," "You'll Never Know" and "On the Atchison, Topeka and the Santa Fe." He was born

Salvatore Guaragna in Brooklyn on December 24, 1893, and died in Los Angeles on September 22, 1981.

Ned WASHINGTON, lyricist, was born on August 15, 1901, and died on December 20, 1976. His first hit film song was "The Nearness of You" in 1938, and shortly afterwards he began writing for the Disney studios. He won the 1940 Oscar for "When You Wish Upon a Star" from *Pinocchio* and was nominated for "Baby Mine" from *Dumbo* and the title song for *Saludos Amigos*. Eight more of his songs were nominated and he won again in 1952 for "High Noon."

Paul Francis WEBSTER was born on December 20, 1907. He wrote his first hit song, "I Got It Bad and That Ain't Good," in 1941 with Duke Ellington and later had 16 Oscar nominations for his songs, writing lyrics for a wide range of composers. He won the Award three times, for "Secret Love," "Love Is a Many-Splendored Thing" and "The Shadow of Your Smile." He died on March 23, 1984.

Richard WHITING was born on November 12, 1891, and died on February 10, 1938. His Hollywood career began in 1929 but he returned to Broadway in 1933 to write songs for *Take a Chance* in which Ethel Merman introduced "Eadie Was a Lady." His other well-known film songs include "Too Marvelous for Words," "Louise" and "On the Good Ship Lollipop." His Oscar-nominated song was "When Did You Leave Heaven?" His daughter is the singer Margaret Whiting.

Charles WOLCOTT was born on September 29, 1906, and is best known as a composer of film music for the Disney studios, 1938–48. He received Oscar nominations for his scores for *Saludos Amigos*, *The Three Caballeros* and *Song of the South*. His title song for *Saludos Amigos* was also nominated. Wolcott was a pianist-arranger with Glen Gray and the Casa Loma Orchestra in the 1920s and with the Paul Whiteman Orchestra in the early 1930s. In the 1950s, he was music director at MGM, where he composed the scores for a number of films including *Blackboard Jungle*. He died on January 26, 1987.

Robert WRIGHT (1914–) and George FORREST (1915–1999) wrote music and lyrics together for more than 70 years, frequently basing their work on melodies by classical composers. Their first Hollywood successes came with the score for *Maytime* and *The Firefly*, writing "Donkey Serenade" for the latter. On Broadway their most successful shows were *Song of Norway*, based on works by Greig, and *Kismet*, based on melodies by Borodin. Three of their film songs were nominated for the Oscar: "Always and Always," "It's a Blue World" and " Pennies for Peppino."

Allie WRUBEL, composer, was born on January 15, 1905, and died on December 13, 1973. He was a woodwind player with Paul Whiteman's orchestra and wrote his first song in 1931. In 1934 he went to Hollywood and wrote songs for many films. His 1938 song "Music, Maestro, Please" was his first number one hit. "I'll Buy That Dream" also made number one and was nominated for the Oscar. He won the award in 1947 for "Zip-a-Dee-Doo-Dah."

Vincent YOUMANS was born on September 27, 1898. He was one of the major composers of the 1920s and two of his stage musicals—*No, No, Nanette* and *Hit the Deck*—were among the most successful Broadway shows of the decade.

Songs from these shows include "Tea for Two," "I Want to Be Happy" and "Hallelujah!" To celebrate the huge success of *Flying Down to Rio*, Youmans purchased a new boat that he christened *The Carioca* after his Oscar-nominated song. Shortly afterwards, he contracted tuberculosis and retired from show business. Ill health dogged the last years of his life and he died on April 5, 1946.

Victor **YOUNG** was born on August 8, 1900, and studied music in Warsaw, later becoming a concert violinist. He began his career as a Hollywood composer in 1936 and wrote more than 300 film scores in the next 20 years. Young received 22 Oscar nominations, but won only once, in 1957, for *Around the World in 80 Days*—but the award was announced after his death, which occurred on November 10, 1956. Three of his nominations were for the songs "Love Letters," "My Foolish Heart" and "Written on the Wind."

Appendix 2:
The Nominated Songs,
1959–2004

The winning song for each year appears in **bold**.

1959

High Hopes (Van Heusen-Cahn) *A Hole in the Head*
The Best of Everything (Newman-Cahn) *The Best of Everything*
The Five Pennies (Fine) *The Five Pennies*
The Hanging Tree (Livingston-David) *The Hanging Tree*
Strange Are the Ways of Love (Tiomkin-Washington) *The Young Land*

1960

Never on Sunday (Hadjidakis) *Never on Sunday*
The Facts of Life (Mercer) *The Facts of Life*
The Faraway Part of Town (Previn-Langdon) *Pepe*
The Green Leaves of Summer (Tiomkin-Webster) *The Alamo*
The Second Time Around (Van Heusen-Cahn) *High Time*

1961

Moon River (Mancini-Mercer) *Breakfast at Tiffany's*
Bachelor in Paradise (Mancini-David) *Bachelor in Paradise*
The Falcon and the Dove (Rozsa-Webster) *El Cid*
Pocketful of Miracles (Van Heusen-Cahn*) Pocketful of Miracles*
Town Without Pity (Tiomkin-Washington) *Town Without Pity*

1962

Days of Wine and Roses (Mancini-Mercer) *Days of Wine and Roses*
Follow Me (Kaper-Webster) *Mutiny on the Bounty*
Second Chance (Previn-Langdon) *Two for the Seesaw*
Tender Is the Night (Fain-Webster) *Tender Is the Night*
Walk on the Wild Side (Bernstein-David) *Walk on the Wild Side*

1963

Call Me Irresponsible (Van Heusen-Cahn) *Papa's Delicate Condition*
Charade (Mancini-Mercer) *Charade*
It's a Mad Mad Mad Mad World (Gold-David) *It's a Mad Mad Mad Mad World*
More (Ortolani, Oliviero-Newell) *Mondo Cane*
So Little Time (Tiomkin-Webster) *55 Days at Peking*

1964

Chim Chim Cheree (Sherman, Sherman) *Mary Poppins*
Dear Heart (Mancini-Livingston, Evans) *Dear Heart*
Hush ... Hush, Sweet Charlotte (De Vol–David) *Hush ... Hush, Sweet Charlotte*
My Kind of Town (Van Heusen-Cahn) *Robin and the Seven Hoods*
Where Love Has Gone (Van Heusen-Cahn) *Where Love Has Gone*

1965

The Shadow of Your Smile (Mandel-Webster) *The Sandpiper*
The Ballad of Cat Ballou (Livingston-David) *Cat Ballou*
I Will Wait for You (Legrand-Demy) *The Umbrellas of Cherbourg*
The Sweetheart Tree (Mancini-Mercer) *The Great Race*
What's New, Pussycat? (Bacharach-David) *What's New, Pussycat?*

1966

Born Free (Barry-Black) *Born Free*
Alfie (Bacharach-David) *Alfie*
Georgy Girl (Springfield-Dale) *Georgy Girl*
My Wishing Doll (Bernstein-David) *Hawaii*
A Time to Love (Mandel-Webster) *An American Dream*

1967

Talk to the Animals (Bricusse) *Doctor Dolittle*
The Bare Necessities (Gilkyson) *The Jungle Book*
The Eyes of Love (Jones-Russell) *Banning*
The Look of Love (Bacharach-David) *Casino Royale*
Thoroughly Modern Millie (Van Heusen-Cahn) *Thoroughly Modern Millie*

1968

The Windmills of Your Mind (Legrand-Bergman, Bergman) *The Thomas Crown Affair*
Chitty Chitty Bang Bang (Sherman Sherman) *Chitty Chitty Bang Bang*
For Love of Ivy (Jones-Russell) *For Love of Ivy*
Funny Girl (Styne-Merrill) *Funny Girl*
Star (Van Heusen-Cahn) *Star*

1969

Raindrops Keep Fallin' on My Head (Bacharach-David) *Butch Cassidy and the Sundance Kid*
Come Saturday Morning (Karlin-Langdon) *The Sterile Cuckoo*
Jean (McKuen) *The Prime of Miss Jean Brodie*
True Grit (Bernstein-Black) *True Grit*
What Are You Doing the Rest of Your Life? (Legrand-Bergman, Bergman) *The Happy Ending*

1970

For All We Know (Karlin-Wilson, James) *Lovers and Other Strangers*
Pieces of Dreams (Legrand-Bergman, Bergman) *Pieces of Dreams*
Thank You Very Much (Bricusse) *Scrooge*
Till Love Touches Your Life (Ortolani-Hamilton) *Madron*
Whistling Away the Dark (Mancini-Mercer) *Darling Lili*

1971

Theme from *Shaft* (Hayes) *Shaft*
The Age of Not Believing (Sherman, Sherman) *Bedknobs and Broomsticks*
All His Children (Mancini-Bergman, Bergman) *Sometimes a Great Notion*
Bless the Beasts and Children (Devorzon-Botkin) *Bless the Beasts and Children*
Life Is What You Make It (Hamlisch-Mercer) *Kotch*

1972

The Morning After (Kasha-Hirschhorn) *The Poseidon Adventure*
Ben (Scharf-Black) *Ben*
Come Follow, Follow Me (Karlin-Karlin) *The Little Ark*
Marmalade, Molasses and Honey (Jarre-Bergman, Bergman) *The Life and Times of Judge Roy Bean*
Strange Are the Ways of Love (Fain-Webster) *The Stepmother*

1973

The Way We Were (Hamlisch-Bergman, Bergman) *The Way We Were*
All That Love Went to Waste (Barrie-Cahn) *A Touch of Class*

Live and Let Die (McCartney-McCartney) *Live and Let Die*
Love (Bruns-Huddleston) *Robin Hood*
You're So Nice to Be Around (Williams-Williams) *Cinderella Liberty*

1974

We May Never Love Like This Again (Kasha-Hirschhorn) *The Towering Inferno*
Blazing Saddles (Morris-Brooks) *Blazing Saddles*
I Feel Love (Box-Box) *Benji*
Little Prince (Loewe-Lerner) *The Little Prince*
Wherever Love Takes Me (Bernstein-Black) *Gold*

1975

I'm Easy (Carradine) *Nashville*
Do You Know Where You're Going To? (Masser-Goffin) *Mahogany*
How Lucky Can You Get? (Kander-Ebb) *Funny Lady*
Now That We're in Love (Barrie-Cahn) *Whiffs*
Richard's Window (Fox-Gimbel) *The Other Side of the Mountain*

1976

Evergreen (Streisand-Williams) *A Star Is Born*
Ava Satani (Goldsmith) *The Omen*
Come to Me (Mancini-Black) *The Pink Panther Strikes Again*
Gonna Fly Now (Conti-Connors) *Rocky*
A World That Never Was (Fain-Webster) *Half a House*

1977

You Light Up My Life (Brooks) *You Light Up My Life*
Candle on the Water (Kasha-Hirschhorn) *Pete's Dragon*
He Danced with Me/She Danced with Me (Sherman, Sherman) *The Slipper and the Rose*
Nobody Does It Better (Hamlisch-Sager) *The Spy Who Loved Me*
Someone's Waiting for You (Fain-Connors) *The Rescuers*

1978

Last Dance (Jabara) *Thank God It's Friday*
Hopelessly Devoted to You (Farrar) *Grease*
Last Time I Felt Like This (Jabara) *Same Time Next Year*
Ready to Take a Chance Again (Fox-Gimbel) *Foul Play*
When You're Loved (Sherman, Sherman) *The Magic of Lassie*

1979

It Goes Like It Goes (Shire-Gimbel) *Norma Rae*
I'll Never Say Goodbye (Shire-Bergman, Bergman) *The Promise*
It's Easy to Say (Mancini-Wells) *10*
The Rainbow Connection (Williams, Ascher) *The Muppet Movie*
Through the Eyes of Love (Hamlisch-Sager) *Ice Castles*

1980

Fame (Gore-Pitchford) *Fame*
9 to 5 (Parton) *9 to 5*
On the Road Again (Nelson) *Honeysuckle Rose*
Out Here on My Own (Gore-Gore) *Fame*
People Alone (Schifrin-Jennings) *The Competition*

1981

Arthur's Theme (Best That You Can Do) (Bacharach-Sager, Cross, Allen) *Arthur*
Endless Love (Richie) *Endless Love*
The First Time It Happens (Raposo) *The Great Muppet Caper*
For Your Eyes Only (Conti-Leeson) *For Your Eyes Only*
One More Hour (Newman) *Ragtime*

1982

Up Where We Belong (Nitzsche, Sainte-Marie—Jennings) *An Officer and a Gentleman*
Eye of the Tiger (Peterik, Sullivan) *Rocky III*
How Do You Keep the Music Playing? (Legrand-Bergman, Bergman) *Best Friends*
If We Were In Love (Williams-Bergman, Bergman) *Yes, Giorgio*
It Might Be You (Grusin-Bergman, Bergman) *Tootsie*

1983

Flashdance ... What a Feeling (Moroder-Forsey, Cara) *Flashdance*
Maniac (Sembello, Matkosky) *Flashdance*
Over You (Roberts, Hart) *Tender Mercies*
Papa, Can You Hear Me (Legrand-Bergman, Bergman) *Yentl*
The Way He Makes Me Feel (Legrand-Bergman, Bergman) *Yentl*

1984

I Just Called to Say I Love You (Wonder) *The Woman in Red*
Against All Odds (Take a Look at Me Now) (Collins) *Against All Odds*

Footloose (Loggins, Pitchford) *Footloose*
Ghostbusters (Parker) *Ghostbusters*
Let's Hear It for the Boy (Pitchford, Snow) *Footloose*

1985

Say You, Say Me (Richie) *White Nights*
Miss Celie's Blues (Sister) (Jones, Temperson, Richie) *The Color Purple*
The Power of Love (Hayes, Colla, Lewis) *Back to the Future*
Separate Lives (Bishop) *White Nights*
Surprise, Surprise (Hamlisch, Kleban) *A Chorus Line*

1986

Take My Breath Away (Moroder, Whitlock) *Top Gun*
Glory of Love (Cetera, Foster, Nini) *The Karate Kid II*
Life in a Looking Glass (Mancini, Bricusse) *That's Life!*
Mean Green Mother from Outer Space (Menken, Ashman) *Little Shop of Horrors*
Somewhere Out There (Horner, Mann, Weil) *An American Tail*

1987

(I've Had) The Time of My Life (Previte, DeNicola, Markowitz) *Dirty Dancing*
Cry Freedom (Fenton, Gwangwa) *Cry Freedom*
Nothing's Gonna Stop Us Now (Hammond, Warren) *Mannequin*
Shakedown (Faltermeyer, Forsey, Seger) *Beverly Hills Cop II*
Storybook Love (DeVille) *The Princess Bride*

1988

Let the River Run (Simon) *Working Girl*
Calling You (Telson) *Bagdad Café*
Two Hearts (Dozier, Collins) *Buster*

1989

Under the Sea (Menken, Ashman) *The Little Mermaid*
After All (Snow, Pitchford) *Chances Are*
The Girl Who Used to Be Me (Hamlisch, Bergman, Bergman) *Shirley Valentine*
I Love to See You Smile (Newman) *Parenthood*
Kiss the Girl (Menken, Ashman) *The Little Mermaid*

1990

Sooner or Later (I Always Get My Man) (Sondheim) *Dick Tracy*
Blaze of Glory (Jovi) *Young Guns II*

I'm Checkin' Out (Silverstein) *Postcards from the Edge*
Promise Me You'll Remember (Coppola, Bettis) *The Godfather, Part III*
Somewhere in My Memory (Williams, Bricusse) *Home Alone*

1991

Beauty and the Beast (Menken, Ashman) *Beauty and the Beast*
Belle (Menken, Ashman) *Beauty and the Beast*
Be Our Guest (Menken, Ashman) *Beauty and the Beast*
(Everything I Do) I Do It for You (Kamen, Adams, Lange) *Robin Hood: Prince of Thieves*
When You're Alone (Williams, Bricusse) *Hook*

1992

A Whole New World (Menken, Rice) *Aladdin*
Beautiful Maria of My Soul (Kraft, Glimcher) *The Mambo Kings*
Friend Like Me (Menken, Ashman) *Aladdin*
I Have Nothing (Foster, Thomson) *The Bodyguard*
Run to You (Friedman, Rich) *The Bodyguard*

1993

Streets of Philadelphia (Springsteen) *Philadelphia*
Again (Jackson, Harris, Lewis) *Poetic Justice*
The Day I Fall in Love (Sager, Ingram, Magness) *Beethoven's 2nd*
Philadelphia (Young) *Philadelphia*
A Wink and a Smile (Shaiman, McLean) *Sleepless in Seattle*

1994

Can You Feel the Love Tonight? (John, Rice) *The Lion King*
Circle of Life (John, Rice) *The Lion King*
Hakuna Matata (John, Rice) *The Lion King*
Junior (Howard, Ingram, Sager, Smyth) *Junior*
Make Up Your Mind (Newman) *The Paper*

1995

Colors of the Wind (Menken, Schwartz) *Pocahontas*
Dead Man Walkin' (Springsteen) *Dead Man Walking*
Have You Ever Really Loved a Woman (Adams, Kamen, Lange) *Don Juan DeMarco*
Moonlight (Williams, Bergman, Bergman) *Sabrina*
You've Got a Friend in Me (Newman) *Toy Story*

1996

You Must Love Me (Webber, Rice) Evita
Because You Loved Me (Warren) *Up Close and Personal*
For the First Time (Friedman, Howard, Rich) *One Fine Day*
I Finally Found Someone (Adams, Hamlisch, Lange, Streisand) *The Mirror Has Two Faces*
That Thing You Do! (Schlesinger) *That Thing You Do!*

1997

My Heart Will Go On (Horner, Jennings) *Titanic*
Go the Distance (Menken, Zippel) *Hercules*
How Do I Live? (Warren) *Con Air*
Journey to the Past (Flaherty, Ahrens) *Anastasia*
Miss Misery (Smith) *Good Will Hunting*

1998

When You Believe (Schwartz) *The Prince of Egypt*
I Don't Want to Miss a Thing (Warren) *Armageddon*
The Prayer (Foster, Sager, Renis, Testa) *Quest for Camelot*
A Soft Place to Fall (Moorer, Owen) *The Horse Whisperer*
That'll Do (Newman) *Babe: Pig in the City*

1999

You'll Be in My Heart (Collins) *Tarzan*
Blame Canada (Parker, Shaiman) *South Park: Bigger, Longer and Uncut*
Music of My Heart (Warren) *Music of the Heart*
Save Me (Mann) *Magnolia*
When She Loved Me (Newman) *Toy Story 2*

2000

Things Have Changed (Dylan) *Wonder Boys*
A Fool in Love (Newman) *Meet the Parents*
I've Seen It All (Bjork, Sigurdsson, von Trier) *Dancer in the Dark*
A Love Before Time (Calandrelli, Dun, Schamus) *Crouching Tiger, Hidden Dragon*
My Funny Friend and Me (Sting, Hartley) *The Emperor's New Groove*

2001

If I Didn't Have You (Newman) *Monsters, Inc*
May It Be (Enya, Ryan, Ryan) *Lord of the Rings: The Fellowship of the Rings*
There You'll Be (Warren) *Pearl Harbor*

Until (Sting) *Kate and Leopold*
Vanilla Sky (McCartney) *Vanilla Sky*

2002

Lose Yourself (Eminem, Bass, Resto) *8 Mile*
Burn It Blue (Goldenthal, Taymor) *Frida*
Father and Daughter (Simon) *The Wild Thornberrys Movie*
The Hands That Built America (The Edge, Bono, Clayton, Mullen) *Gangs of New York*
I Move On (Kander, Ebb) *Chicago*

2003

Into the West (Walsh, Shore, Lennox) *The Lord of the Rings: The Return of the King*
Belleville Rendez-vous (Charest-Chomet) *The Triplets of Belleville*
A Kiss at the End of the Rainbow (McKean, O'Toole) *A Mighty Wind*
Scarlet Tide (Burnett, Costello) *Cold Mountain*
You Will Be My Ain True Love (Sting) *Cold Mountain*

2004

Al Otro Lado del Rio (Drexler) *The Motorcycle Diaries*
Accidentally in Love (Duritz, Vickrey, Immergluck, Malley, Bryson) *Shrek II*
Believe (Ballard, Silvestri) *The Polar Express*
Learn to Be Lonely (Lloyd Webber, Hart) *The Phantom of the Opera*
Look to Your Path (Vois Sur Ton Chemin) *The Chorus*

Bibliography

Aachen, George. *Memorable Films of the Forties*. Sydney: Rastar Press, 1987.

Altman, Rick. *The American Film Musical*. Bloomington: Indiana University Press, 1987.

Benny, Mary Livingstone, and Hilliard Marks, with Marcia Bore. *Jack Benny*. New York: Doubleday, 1978.

Berg, A. Scott. *Goldwyn: A Biography*. London: Hamish Hamilton, 1989.

Bergreen, Laurence. *As Thousands Cheer: The Life of Irving Berlin*. London: Hodder and Stoughton, 1990.

____. *Louis Armstrong: An Extravagant Life*. New York: Broadway Books, 1997.

Bloom, Ken. *Hollywood Song*. New York: Facts on File, 1995.

Bookbinder, Robert. *The Films of Bing Crosby*. Secaucus, NJ: Citadel, 1977.

Bordman, Gerald. *Days to Be Happy, Years to Be Sad: The Life and Music of Vincent Youmans*. New York: Oxford University Press, 1982.

Cahn, Sammy. *I Should Care: The Sammy Cahn Story*. New York: Arbor House, 1974.

Capra, Frank. *The Name Above the Title*. London: W.H. Allen, 1972.

Carmichael, Hoagy. *The Stardust Road and Sometimes I Wonder: The Autobiographies of Hoagy Carmichael*. New York: Da Capo, 1999.

Carrick, Peter. *Thanks for the Memory: A Tribute to Bob Hope*. London: Robert Hale, 1988.

Casper, Joseph Andrew: *Vincente Minnelli and the Film Musical*. Cranbury, NJ: Barnes, 1977.

Chaplin, Saul. *The Golden Age of Movie Musicals and Me*. Norman: University of Oklahoma, 1994.

Clarke, Gerald. *Get Happy: The Life of Judy Garland*. New York: Random House, 2000.

Clooney, Rosemary, with Joan Barthel. *Girl Singer: An Autobiography*. New York: Doubleday, 1999.

Craig, Warren. *The Great Songwriters of Hollywood*. London: Barnes, 1980.

____. *Sweet and Lowdown: America's Popular Song Writers*. Metuchen, NJ: Scarecrow Press, 1978.

Croce, Arlene. *The Fred Astaire and Ginger Rogers Book*. New York: Dutton, 1972.

Epstein, Daniel Mark. *Nat King Cole*. Boston: Northeastern University Press, 1999.

Fehr, Richard, and Frederick G. Vogel. *Lullabies of Hollywood: Movie Music and the Movie Musical, 1915-1992.* Jefferson, NC: McFarland, 1993.

Feinstein, Michael. *Nice Work If You Can Get It: My Life in Rhythm and Rhyme.* New York: Hyperion, 1995.

Fisher, Eddie. *Eddie—My Life, My Loves.* London: W.H. Allen, 1982.

Fordin, Hugh. *Getting to Know Him: A Biography of Oscar Hammerstein II.* New York: Da Capo, 1986.

____. *MGM's Greatest Musicals: The Arthur Freed Unit.* New York: Da Capo, 1996.

Freedland, Michael. *Fred Astaire.* London: W.H. Allen, 1976.

____. *Jerome Kern: A Biography.* New York: Stein and Day, 1981.

Friedwald, Will. *Sinatra! The Song Is You: A Singer's Art.* New York: Scribner, 1995.

Furia, Philip. *Ira Gershwin: The Art of the Lyricist.* New York: Oxford University Press, 1996.

____. *Irving Berlin: A Life in Song.* New York: Schirmer, 1998.

____. *The Poets of Tin Pan Alley.* New York: Oxford University Press, 1990.

____. *Skylark: The Life and Times of Johnny Mercer.* New York: St Martin's, 2003.

Gershwin, Ira. *Lyrics on Several Occasions.* New York: Limelight Editions, 1997.

Giddins, Gary. *Bing Crosby: A Pocketful of Dreams: The Early Years 1903-1940.* Boston: Little, Brown, 2001.

Gourse, Leslie. *Unforgettable.* London: New English Library, 1998.

Grant, John. *Encyclopedia of Walt Disney's Animated Characters.* London: Octopus, 1987.

Green, Benny. *Let's Face the Music: The Golden Age of Popular Song.* London: Pavilion, 1989.

Green, Stanley. *Encyclopedia of the Musical Film.* 2 ed. New York: Oxford University Press, 1987.

Grudens, Richard. *Bing Crosby: Crooner of the Century.* New York: Celebrity Profiles, 2003.

Halliwell, Leslie. *Halliwell's Harvest.* London: Grafton, 1986.

Haskins, James. *Nat King Cole.* London: Robson, 1986.

Haver, Ronald. *A Star Is Born: The Making of the 1954 Movie and Its 1983 Restoration.* New York: Harper and Row, 1988.

Hemming, Roy. *The Melody Lingers On: The Great Songwriters and Their Movie Musicals.* New York: Newmarket, 1986.

Hirschhorn, Clive. *The Hollywood Musical.* 2 ed. London: Pyramid, 1991.

Holden, Anthony. *The Oscars: The Secret History of Hollywood's Academy Awards.* London: Warner, 1994.

Hope, Bob, and Bob Thomas. *The Road to Hollywood: My Love Affair with the Movies.* London: W.H. Allen, 1977.

Hotchner, A.E. *Doris Day: Her Own Story.* London: W.H. Allen, 1976.

Hyland, William G. *The Song Is Ended: Songwriters and American Music, 1900–1950.* New York: Oxford University Press, 1995.

Jablonski, Edward. *Harold Arlen: Happy with the Blues.* New York: Da Capo, 1986.

____, and Lawrence D. Stewart. *The Gershwin Years.* London: Robson, 1974.

Kimball, Robert, ed. *Cole.* New York: Dell, 1992.

Lacey, Robert. *Grace.* London: Sidgwick & Jackson, 1994.

Lees, Gene. *Singers and the Song.* New York: Oxford University Press, 1987.

Lenburg, Jeff. *The Encyclopedia of Animated Cartoons.* New York: Facts on File, 1991.

____. *The Great Cartoon Directors.* New York: Da Capo, 1993.

Lerner, Alan Jay. *The Street Where I Live: The Story of* My Fair Lady, Gigi *and* Camelot. London: Hodder and Stoughton, 1978.

Likeness, George. *The Oscar People: From* Wings *to* My Fair Lady. Mendota, IL: Wayside, 1965.

Lissauer, Robert. *Lissauer's Encyclopedia of Popular Music in America: 1888 to the Present.* New York: Paragon House, 1991.

Loesser, Susan. *A Most Remarkable Fella: Frank Loesser and the Guys and Dolls in His Life: A Portrait by His Daughter.* New York: Donald I. Fine, 1993.

Macfarlane, Malcolm. *Bing Crosby: Day by Day.* Lanham, MD: Scarecrow, 2001.

Maltin, Leonard. *The Disney Films.* 3d ed. New York: Hyperion, 1995.

Martin, Tony, and Cyd Charisse, with Dick Kleiner. *The Two of Us.* New York: Mason Charter, 1976.

McBrien, William. *Cole Porter: The Definitive Biography.* London: HarperCollins, 1998.

Meyerson, Harold, and Ernie Harburg. *Who Put the Rainbow in* The Wizard of Oz*? Yip Harburg, Lyricist.* Ann Arbor: University of Michigan Press, 1995.

Minnelli, Vincente, with Hector Arce. *I Remember It Well.* London: Angus and Robertson, 1975.

Moshier, W. Franklyn. *The Alice Faye Movie Book.* Harrisburg, PA: Stackpole, 1974.

O'Brien, Daniel. *The Frank Sinatra Film Guide.* London: Batsford, 1998.

Osborne, Robert. *70 Years of the Oscar: The Official History of the Academy Awards.* New York: Abbeville, 1999.

Parish, James Robert. *The Fox Girls.* Secaucus, NJ: Castle, 1971.

Peyser, Joan. *The Memory of All That: The Life of George Gershwin.* New York: Simon and Schuster, 1993.

Pickard, Roy. *Frank Sinatra at the Movies.* London: Robert Hale, 1994.

Rodgers, Richard. *Musical Stages: An Autobiography.* London: W.H. Allen, 1976.

Rogers, Ginger. *Ginger: My Story.* New York: HarperCollins, 1991.

Rosen, Jody. *White Christmas: The Story of an American Song.* New York: Scribner, 2002.

Sackett, Susan. *Hollywood Sings! An Inside Look at Sixty Years of Academy Award–Nominated Songs.* New York: Billboard Books, 1995.

Satchell, Tim. *Astaire: The Biography.* London: Hutchinson, 1987.

Schwartz, Charles. *Cole Porter: A Biography.* London: W.H. Allen, 1978.

Sennett, Ted. *Hollywood Musicals.* New York: Harry N. Abrams, 1981.

Sforza, John. *Swing It! The Andrews Sisters Story.* Lexington: University Press of Kentucky, 2000.

Simonet, Thomas. *Oscar: A Pictorial History of the Academy Awards.* Bromley, Kent: Columbus, 1983.

Taylor, Theodore. *Jule: The Story of Composer Jule Styne.* New York: Random House, 1979.

Thomas, Ron. *Bud and Lou: The Abbott and Costello Story.* London: W.H. Allen, 1977.

Thomas, Tony. *Harry Warren and the Hollywood Musical.* Secaucus, NJ: Citadel, 1975.

Thompson, Charles. *Bing: The Authorised Biography.* London: W.H. Allen, 1975.

Whitburn, Joel. *A Century of Popular Music.* Menomonee Springs, WI: Record Research, 1999.

Wilder, Alec. *American Popular Song*. London: Oxford University Press, 1972.

Wiley, Mason, and Damien Bona. *Inside Oscar: The Unofficial History of the Academy Awards* Bromley, Kent: Columbus, 1986.

Wilk, Max. *They're Playing Our Song: Conversations with America's Classic Songwriters*. New York: Da Capo, 1997.

Winer, Deborah Grace. *On the Sunny Side of the Street: The Life and Lyrics of Dorothy Fields*. New York: Schirmer, 1998.

Zinnser, William. *Easy to Remember: The Great American Songwriters and Their Songs*. Jaffrey, NH: David R. Godine, 2001.

Index

Numbers in **bold** refer to photographs.